What they are saying about
Mountain Biking Southern California's Best 100 Trails...

All the classic rides of Southern California under one cover—terrific job!

—BRIAN HEMSWORTH
Editorial Director, *Mountain Biking Magazine*

For anyone who takes mountain biking seriously, the great fat tire rides are all here—from easy to the classic challenges. Hats off to Don and Delaine!

—REX REESE .
Editor, *Southwest Cycling*

...*the* reference book for mountain biking trails—every cyclist needs one!

—BILL McCREADY
Founder/President, *Santana Cycles*

Until now, no one has put together a collection of all the best rides in this area. *Mountain Biking Southern California's Best 100 Trails* offers bicyclists of every level the benefit of local trail expertise, emphasizing safe, low-impact riding and an appreciation for nature that characterizes responsible mountain bike riding.

—PETER HEUMANN
Steering Committee,
Concerned Off-Road Bicyclists Association (CORBA)

I have sampled many aspects of cycling over the years—racing, touring, commuting, ultra-distance events—and have begun to venture off-road lately. Sometimes it's adventurous to strike out on your own, but my experiences have usually been better when I've been guided to the best routes by others. I have enjoyed some of the rides in this book. If the rest are as good, you won't be disappointed.

—PETE PENSEYRES
Race Across AMerica (RAAM) and Ultra-distance Champion

MOUNTAIN BIKING
Southern California's
BEST 100 TRAILS

Edited by

Don Douglass & Delaine Fragnoli

FINE EDGE
Productions
BISHOP, CALIFORNIA

Important Legal Notice and Disclaimer

Mountain biking is a potentially dangerous sport, and the rider or user of this book accepts a number of unavoidable risks. Trails by nature have numerous natural and manmade hazards; they are generally not signed or patrolled and they change with time and conditions.

While substantial effort has been made to provide accurate information, this guidebook may inadvertently contain errors and omissions. The maps in this book are for locator reference only. They are not to be used for navigation and are intended to complement large-scale topo maps. Your mileages will vary from those given in this book. Contact land managers before attempting routes to check for suitability and trail conditions.

The editors, authors, contributors, publishers and distributors accept no liability for any errors or omissions in this book or for any injuries or losses incurred from using this book.

Contributors

Design/layout by Sue Irwin, Eastside Desktop Publishing, Mammoth Lakes, California
Cover design by Marty Hiester, designWorks!, Incline Village, Nevada
Maps by Sue Irwin, Lorraine Schultz, Judy Shephard and Allan Thibault
Printed by a•carlisle and company of nevada, Reno
Front cover photograph: Chris Hatounian
Back cover photograph: Roger O'Malley
Photographers: Ray Ford, pp. 12, 220, 296; Delaine Fragnoli, pp. 26, 29, 30, 41, 283-292; Jim Hasenauer, pp. 169, 171, 178, 180; Brian Hemsworth, pp. 172, 185; Sue Irwin, pp. 44, 294; Mark Langton, pp. 58, 167, 168, 177, 189; Chris Lombardo, pp. 5, 249-279; Paul Maag, pp. 79, 83, 84, 87, 89; Linda McTigue, pp. 65, 191, 203, 205; MIckey McTigue, pp. 53, 198, 208, 212, 223, 225, 228, 232, 233; Robert Rasmussen, pp. 52, 72; Mark Theissen, p. 2; Allen Thibault, pp. 95, 102, 105, 108, 109, 115, 119; Mike Troy, pp. 18, 39, 122-144, 151-159, 165, 193, 235-242; Kevin Woten, pp. 145, 149, 162.

First Printing June 1993
    9 8 7 6 5 4 3 2 1

LIBRARY OF CONGRESS CATALOGING-IN-PUBLICATION DATA

Mountain biking southern California's best 100 trails / edited by Don
    Douglass & Delaine Fragnoli ; maps by Susan Irwin.
        p.   cm.
    Includes index.
    ISBN 0-99938665-20-0 : $14.95
    1. All terrain cycling—California, Southern—Guidebooks.
2. California, Southern—Guidebooks.   I. Douglass, Don, 1932–
II. Fragnoli, Delaine, 1962–   III. Title: Mountain biking
southern California's best one hundred trails.
GV1045.5.C22S685   1993
796.6'4'097949—dc20   93-16038
                                                CIP

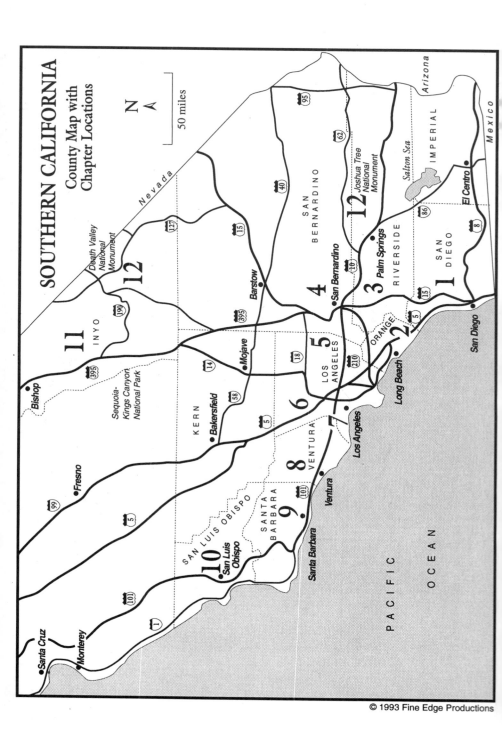

TABLE OF CONTENTS

Acknowledgments

The editors wish to express their gratitude: to the authors involved in this project for their knowledge, insight and perseverence; to the many United States Forest Service, Bureau of Land Management, National Park, State Park and other land management personnel at all levels for their cooperation and encouragement; to Réanne Douglass for her invaluable direction in pulling the many parts of this project together; to book designer, Sue Irwin, for outstanding dedication and skill; to Jim MacIntyre for sagging feats beyong the call of duty; and last, to all those individuals who by responsible riding habits and personal involvement help provide continued access to so many beautiful routes.

Don Douglass and Delaine Fragnoli
Bishop, California
July 1993

This book is dedicated to the Unknown
Trail Builders whose foresight and sweat make
our pleasure possible.

Safety and Precautions

One of the joys of mountain biking on dirt is the freedom to experience nature. However, mountain biking in the backcountry involves unavoidable hazards and risks that each cyclist accepts when leaving the pavement behind. You can increase your safety by being aware of potential dangers, preparing ahead and respecting and remaining alert to the environment in all its variety and changes. Just because a trail is described in this book does not mean it will be safe or suitable for you.

Trails in this book cover an unusually wide range of terrain, elevation, and weather patterns that require different levels of skill and conditioning. A route that is safe for one rider may not be safe for another. It is important that you know and heed your own limitations, that you condition properly both physically and mentally, and that you give thought to your equipment as well as to trail and weather conditions.

En route, take appropriate action, including turning back at any time your judgment and common sense dictates. This book is not a substitute for detailed mountain survival or for cycling texts or courses. We recommend that you consult appropriate resources or take courses before you attempt the more strenuous or remote routes. When you have a question about route suitability or safety, consult local bike shops and land management offices.

This warning and the legal disclaimer herein are not given to discourage your enjoyment, but to remind you to take responsibility for yourself so your feeling of satisfaction comes truly from being independent and self-sufficient.

FOREWORD

Over the last eight years, I have traveled to many domestic and international destinations to race mountain bikes. But my favorite rides are my training rides in Southern California. Here, I can enjoy scenic landscape almost year-round under usually sunny skies. Only in Southern California can I experience desert, sea-kissed coastline, mountains and alpine lakes. With the expert tour guides in this book, you too can discover California's great scenic wild places.

I knew Don Douglass was one of those expert route finders when I first met him in 1986. He was hosting a challenging 50-mile mountain bike race known as the Sierra 7500. Most of the original race course is described in this book, modified and improved as the Coyote-High Sierra Traverse. With an average elevation of 10,000 feet, the outstanding views of the Sierra Crest to the west and Owens Valley to the east make this ride one of the most outstanding in the country.

I personally covered the original Sierra 7500 race course in six hours, one minute, and without a seat for 98% of the time. My seat post broke off a mile into the race, and I was stuck with giving up or trying to finish. The big question was, Could I ride 49 miles without impaling myself on the jagged seatpost?

I decided to go for it and managed to finish first—before the reigning women's national champion—and found that Don's course had changed my life. Certain inner qualities came out in me that day that might still lie dormant had I stayed home or turned back.

In your journeys, too, you will tap your inner strength, determination and fervor as you travel the various routes described in this book. Don't worry, you can take your pick of short, easy rides for families and beginners, as well as challenging backcountry classics. And you can use a seat and not hurry!

Don and Delaine have selected well-known authors from different regions of Southern California to describe in detail their cherished local rides. Accurate descriptions of trail data were meticulously gathered to help you prepare and enjoy your backcountry adventures. Throughout your travels you will experience the best in trails, vegetation, wildlife, views, thrills and spills.

Each time I ride off-road in beautiful backcountry I feel a sense of peacefulness and happiness. I am always amazed at how much terrain my bicycle and I can cover and how quickly the time passes. I appreciate being a fit athlete so I can thoroughly enjoy my mountain bike experiences, and I urge you to discover your own potential so you can feel as thankful and blessed as I do.

Whether you choose to ride in the desert, the mountains, or along the coast, this field guide is a must and will provide you with the information you need to explore Southern California's beauty. *Go for it!*

Cindy Whitehead
Slalom, Downhill, and Cross-Country Mountain Bike Champion
and Inductee in the Mountain Bike Hall of Fame

A Letter from the Bureau of Land Management

United States Department of the Interior

BUREAU OF LAND MANAGEMENT
California State Office
2800 Cottage Way, Room E-2845
Sacramento, California 95825-1889

IN REPLY REFER TO:

Welcome to some of the best mountain biking country in the United States ... the Public Lands of Southern California. From the subtle to the sublime, vivid and exciting riding opportunities await your exploration. Thrill your senses to the variety of environments that include desert mountain ranges and a valley so deep that it seems to disappear below the towering Sierra Nevada.

The Bureau of Land Management administers millions of acres of Public Land. A few of these areas are described in this book. Imagine the remoteness and majesty that these lands have to offer. Imagine yourself and your family exploring the panoramic roads of the Santa Rosa Mountain National Scenic Area. No matter what your experience level is, you will find a myriad of roads and trails that will challenge and enlighten.

During the past several years I have had the pleasure of working with many in the mountain biking community. I have watched the evolution and growth of the industry and activity. I have discovered that mountain bikers care deeply about the environment and have a tremendous volunteer ethic. Don and Reanne Douglass, pioneers of the mountain bike movement, have contributed greatly to raising public awareness of access and other related needs. Most importantly, they have worked tirelessly to codify the International Mountain Bike Association (IMBA) Rules of the Trail for bikers to aspire to. The IMBA Rules have become a well-known standard of courtesies supported by industry, public agencies and mountain bikers.

Apply these courtesies to others you encounter on the trail. It will increase the acceptance of you and your fellow mountain bikers in the community of recreationists that we serve. Through these efforts and your sensitivity to others, I embrace your cause and invite you to some of the best riding in California.

Contact us at any of our many offices throughout the state for information on specific trail restrictions, information on recreation opportunities or on becoming a partner in our programs. Your interest and involvement in your Public Lands is invaluable.

Ed Hastey

Ed Hastey
State Director
State of California

A Letter from the U.S. Forest Service

United States Department of Agriculture	Forest Service	Inyo National Forest	873 N. Main St. Bishop, CA 93514 (619)873-2400

Dear Mt. Bike Enthusiast:

Mountain biking is one of the fastest growing recreational activities on public lands today. It is a recreational use that is generally "light on the land" and considered to be appropriate in most places. We recognize that some of the very best mountain bike riding in California exist within national forests. I encourage you to use and enjoy the routes that have been included in this publication.

I applaud the efforts of the publishers, the editors and the authors of *Mountain Biking California's Best 100 Trails*, in educating the public to a wide range of recreational opportunities, as well as stressing the need for responsible riding habits. During all your rides, please practice good mountain bike ethics by following the **IMBA Rules of the Trail**, particular by staying on existing and open roads and trails, being considerate of other users, leaving gates as you find them, controlling your speed, and packing out your trash. You are generally responsible for your own personal safety, which includes knowing what hazards might exist and using proper safety procedures and equipment to minimize the inherent risks associated with mountain biking.

If you are unfamiliar with an area, we recommend that you study existing guidebooks and topographical maps to plan your trip. Please contact the nearest ranger station for local trail information and/or regulations before you start your ride. Since we care about what you think of management of your national forests, I encourage you to share with us your ideas on how we can improve our services and facilities.

Sincerely,

Bill Bramlette

BILL BRAMLETTE
Recreation Officer
Inyo National Forest

Caring for the Land and Serving People

IMBA RULES OF THE TRAIL

1. **Ride on open trails only.** Respect trail and road closures (ask if not sure), avoid possible trespass on private land, obtain permits and authorization as may be required. Federal and State wilderness areas are closed to cycling.

2. **Leave no trace.** Be sensitive to the dirt beneath you. Even on open trails, you should not ride under conditions where you will leave evidence of your passing, such as on certain soils shortly after a rain. Observe the different types of soils and trail construction; practice low-impact cycling. This also means staying on the trail and not creating any new ones. Be sure to pack out at least as much as you pack in.

3. **Control your bicycle!** Inattention for even a second can cause disaster. Excessive speed maims and threatens people; there is no excuse for it!

4. **Always yield trail.** Make known your approach well in advance. A friendly greeting (or bell) is considerate and works well; startling someone may cause loss of trail access. Show your respect when passing others by slowing to a walk or even stopping. Anticipate that other trail users may be around corners or in blind spots.

5. **Never spook animals.** All animals are startled by an unannounced approach, a sudden movement, or a loud noise. This can be dangerous for you, others, and the animals. Give animals extra room and time to adjust to you. In passing, use special care and follow the directions of horseback riders (ask if uncertain). Running cattle and disturbing wild animals is a serious offense. Leave gates as you found them, or as marked.

6. **Plan ahead.** Know your equipment, your ability, and the area in which you are riding – and prepare accordingly. Be self-sufficient at all times, wear a helmet, keep your machine in good repair, and carry necessary supplies for changes in weather or other conditions. A well-executed trip is satisfying to you and not a burden or offense to others.

WELCOME TO MOUNTAIN BIKING
SOUTHERN CALIFORNIA

Southern California offers mountain bikers year-round opportunities and challenges found nowhere else.......from urban, palm-lined beaches to remote desert canyons and gorges, from thick pine and fir forests to the alpine zones in the High Sierra and White Mountains, from gently rolling oak-covered hills for the family to twisting gnarly singletrack for the technical expert. Ride below sea level in Death Valley National Monument or climb 14,200-foot White Mountain. This is mountain biking at its best!

We assembled the who's who of mountain biking authors in Southern California and asked them for their favorite rides. This book is a result of their collective efforts. You will benefit from their years of experience and know-how as they share with you areas and rides—from the well known to the not-yet-discovered that have helped make mountain biking America's fastest growing sport.

The authors—experts in their own areas—include the founder of the International Mountain Biking Association, its current president, the founders and directors of a number of successful regional mountain biking clubs, numerous federal, state, and local trail advisory group members across Southern California, two editors of mountain biking magazines, and a Mountain Bike Hall of Fame inductee. Their collective experience is a history of the activity they are dedicated to.

How To Use This Book

With so many great trails to choose from, selecting the best was difficult (hence, the 102 rides). Obviously *best* means different things to different people. Some rides were included for their outstanding scenic value, others for their historical significance, others simply for their high fun factor. A few were included because they were quintessentially Californian in some way. We have also attempted to represent a variety of terrain and levels of difficulty.

We have organized all this information in an easy-to-use way. Each chapter is dedicated to a particular area, usually a county or national forest. The chapters are organized in a loop, beginning in San Diego and traveling north to San Luis Obispo County, northeast to Owens Valley and the Eastern Sierra Nevada, and south to the California desert. Within each chapter we have tried to group rides in the same vicinity.

At the beginning of each ride you will find capsule information to let you decide quickly if a ride is for you or not. Ride distance is included as is a rating of difficulty. Mileages shown are approximate and may vary among riders and odometers. We rated the rides for strenuousness (from easy to very strenuous) and for technical difficulty (non-technical to extremely technical). The ratings are a subjective assessment of what the average fit rider (acclimatized to elevation) might consider the route. If you are a racer you may find some of our difficult rides to be moderate. If you are new to the sport you may find our mildly technical rides challenging. Know your limits and be honest in evaluating your skill level. We also recommend that you check with local bike shops and land managers for their evaluation of your fitness for a particular ride. We do not know your skill level and consequently cannot be responsible for any losses you may incur using this information. Please see the important legal notice and disclaimer.

For elevation we include whatever elevation information seems pertinent to that particular ride. Rides with lots of elevation gain and loss will give you that information. Rides at high elevations will include such information. Ride Type lets you know if the ride is a loop, an out-and-back trip, a multiple day tour or if it requires a car shuttle. It also tells you the trail surface; for example, fire road loop with singletrack return. Last, we suggest the best season for riding each route. If after reading the capsule information you are not sure if a ride is for you, the text of each ride description should give you additional information with which to make a decision.

Please note that the routes described in this book are not patrolled and contain natural hazards. Trail conditions and surfaces are constantly changing. Check with local land managers for latest trail and access conditions. Pertinent phone numbers are included in each chapter.

Throughout we have tried to be consistent in presentation. We have tried, however, to retain some of the character and tone of each individual author. Mountain biking is a very individualistic sport, and we think that should be reflected in any writing about the sport. Remember also that each odometer gives different results and yours will vary.

We hope you think of this book as a group of friends getting together to tell you about their favorite bicycling spots. We believe our authors' enthusiasm for their areas will be contagious.

Enough talk! Get on your bike and start riding! You've got over 100 trails to explore and the best trail guides around!

SPECIAL CONSIDERATIONS

To enhance your pleasure and safety we ask that you observe the following Special Considerations:

1. **Courtesy.** Extend courtesy to all other trail users and follow the golden rule. Observe the IMBA Rules of the Trail. The trails and roads in Southern California are popular with many user groups: hikers, equestrians, fishermen, ranchers, 4-wheel drive enthusiasts, hunters, loggers, and miners. Mountain bikers are the newest user group, so set a good example of courtesy and respect.

2. **Preparations.** Plan your trip carefully; develop and use a check list. Know your abilities and your equipment. Prepare to be self-sufficient.

3. **Mountain Conditions.** Be sensitive at all times to the natural environment: the land, beautiful and enjoyable, can also be frightening and unforgiving. The areas covered by this book often provide extremes in elevation, climate and terrain. If you break down, it may take you longer to walk out than it took you to ride in! Check with your local Red Cross, Sierra Club, or mountaineering textbooks for detailed mountain survival information. Know how to deal with dehydration, hypothermia, altitude sickness, sunburn and heatstroke. Always be prepared for:

Intense Sun: Protect your skin against the sun's harmful rays by wearing light colored long-sleeved shirts or jerseys and a hat with a wide brim. Many of the rides in this book are at relatively high altitude, and the higher you go, the more damaging the sun becomes. Use sunscreen with a sufficient rating. Wear sunglasses with adequate protection. Guard against heatstroke by riding in early morning or late afternoon when the sun's rays are less intense.

Low Humidity: East-facing slopes and high elevation usually have low humidity. To avoid headaches or cramps, start each trip with a minimum of two or more large water bottles. (*Gallons* of water may not be sufficient for *really* hot weather or hard rides.) Force yourself to drink before you feel thirsty. Carry water from a known source, or treat water gathered from springs, streams and lakes. Untreated drinking water may cause Giardiasis or other diseases.

Variations in Temperature and Weather Conditions: Carry extra clothing—a windbreaker, gloves, stocking cap—and use the multi-layer system so you can quickly adapt to different weather conditions. Afternoon thundershowers occur frequently in the high country, so keep an eye on changing cloud and wind conditions and prepare accordingly.

Fatigue: Sluggish or cramping muscles and fatigue indicate the need for calories and liquids. Carry high-energy snack foods such as granola bars, dried fruits and nuts to maintain strength and warmth. To conserve energy, add layers of clothing as the temperature drops or the wind increases.

Fire Closures: Many mountain and foothill areas are closed to the public during times of high fire danger. Please check ahead of time with local authorities, and observe such fire closures. Always be extremely careful with fire.

Smog Alerts: Although most of the rides in this book are outside the Los Angeles Basin, if you cycle within the Basin during the summer we recommend that you listen to the smog forecasts over local radio stations. Heavy exercise is unwise at midday or during smog alerts.

4. Maps and Navigation. The maps in this book are not intended for navigation but as guides to the appropriate forest or USGS topographic maps which we recommend you carry and use. Have a plan ready in advance with your cycling group in case you lose your way (it's easy to do!). En route, record your position on the trip map(s); noting the times you arrive at known places. Be sure to look back frequently in the direction from which you came, in case you need to retrace your path. Do not be afraid to turn back when conditions change, or if the going is tougher than you expected. Before you leave on a ride, tell someone where you're going, when you expect to return, and what to do in case you don't return on time. Ask that person to call the proper officials if you are more than six hours overdue, giving full details about your vehicle and your trip plans. (At the end of each chapter you will find the author's local book cited. For more detailed information concerning local conditions and specific safety hazards, please consult the individual book.)

5. Horses and Pack Animals. Some of the trails in Southern California are used by recreational horse riders as well as cyclists and hikers. Horses can be spooked easily, so make them aware of your presence *well in advance of an encounter.* A startled horse can cause serious injuries both to an inexperienced rider and to itself. If you come upon horses moving *toward* you, yield the right-of-way, even when it seems inconvenient. Carry your bike to the downhill side and stand quietly, well off the trail in a spot where the animals can see you clearly. If you come upon horses *moving ahead of you in the same direction,* stop well behind them. Do not attempt to pass until you have alerted the riders and asked for permission. Then, pass on the downhill side of the trail, talking to the horse and rider as you do. It is your responsibility to ensure that such encounters are safe for everyone. Do not disturb grazing sheep or cattle.

6. Respect the Environment. Minimize your impact on the natural environment. *Remember, mountain bikes are not allowed in Wilderness Areas and in certain other restricted areas.* You are a visitor, so ask when in doubt. Leave plants and animals alone, historic and cultural sites untouched. Stay on established roads and trails, and do not enter private property. Follow posted instructions and use good common sense. If you plan to camp, you may need a permit. Contact the nearest land management agency for information.

7. Control and Safety. Crashes usually don't cause serious injury, but they occasionally can and do. Stay under control and slow for the unexpected. Wear protective gear—helmet, gloves, and glasses to protect yourself from scrapes and impacts with rocks, dirt, and brush. Guard against excessive speed. Avoid overheated rims and brakes on long or steep downhill rides. Lower your center of gravity by lowering your seat on downhills. Lower your tire pressure on rough or sandy stretches. In late summer and fall, avoid opening weekend of hunting season, and inquire at local sporting goods stores as to which areas are open to hunting. Carry first aid supplies and bike tools for emergencies. *Avoid solo travel in remote areas.*

8. **Trailside Bike Repair.** Minimum equipment: pump, spare tube, patches, 2 tubes of patch glue, 6" adjustable wrench, Allen wrenches, chain tool and spoke wrench. Tools may be shared with others in your group. Correct inflation, wide tires, and avoiding rocks will prevent most flats. Grease, oil, and proper adjustment prevent most mechanical failures. Frequent stream crossings wash out chain grease; carry extra, or use a banana peel!

9. **First Aid.** Carry first aid for your body as well as your bike. If you have allergies, be sure to bring your medicine, whether it's for pollen or bee stings. Sunscreen saves your skin, and insect repellent increases your comfort in many seasons. Bring bandages and ointment for cuts and scrapes, and aspirin for aches that won't go away. Additional first-aid items you might want to carry in your kit are antiseptic swabs, moleskin, a single-edged razor blade, a needle, an elastic bandage, and waterproof matches. For expedition trips, consult mountaineering texts on survival for additional suggestions.

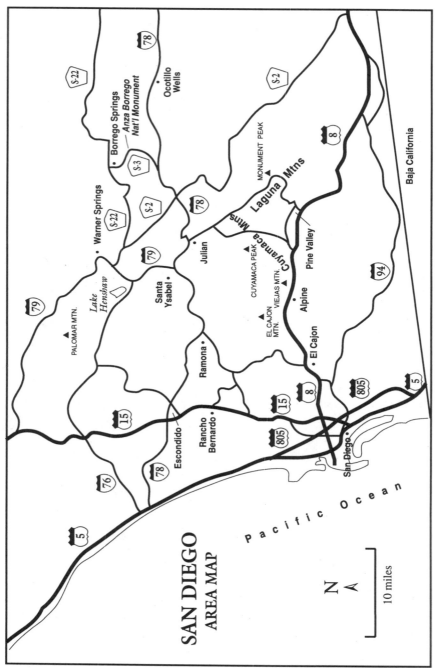

SAN DIEGO
AREA MAP

Pacific Ocean

N

10 miles

CHAPTER 1

San Diego County

By Delaine Fragnoli

Smaller and less famous than Los Angeles to the north, San Diego has many of the virtues of her sister city, but few of the vices. Like L.A., San Diego enjoys a warm and sunny climate most of the year, and thus makes a year-round vacation spot. While she lacks the glitz of Hollywood, she holds her own with cultural attractions: the San Diego Zoo, Balboa Park with its many museums, several missions, and fine examples of Spanish colonial and Victorian architecture. Good restaurants and hotels are easy to find, as are fine shops and coffee houses. In short, San Diego has all the amenities of a large city.

What San Diego doesn't have is L.A.'s smog, bumper-to-bumper traffic or hectic pace. Everything is a little more relaxed in San Diego. Dress is casual, people are mellow and everything moves a half step slower. San Diego is not immune to growth—population is now around 3 million. But she has done a better job of managing growth than L.A. has, having learned from her northern neighbor's uncontrolled urban sprawl. A Stop-Los-Angelezation-Now movement has sprung up to control growth. The city and county have wisely set aside much of their open space, and a full one-third of the land in San Diego county has been dedicated to public use. This includes county parks as well as state parks and recreation areas. In fact, San Diego boasts one of the largest urban parks in the country—Mission Trails Regional Park.

All this land for public recreation makes for many and varied recreational opportunities. What this means for fat-tire fanatics is trails, trails and more trails. Take your pick of beaches, foothills, mountains and desert—all within two hour's drive of the city of San Diego. The county also boasts 2,000 species of wild plants and abundant wildlife.

Near the coast you can enjoy canyon and mesa landscapes, formed by a terraced plain with steep-sided canyons and arroyos. The riding here is pleasant for the beginning/intermediate rider—unless you decide to try those canyons. Then it's decidedly difficult.

To the east, the peninsular ranges rise up to challenge your climbing skills. A series of parallel mountain ranges that run roughly northwest-southeast with high, narrow valleys between them, they cut across the county and constitute the majority of its land. The Laguna and Cuyamaca mountains offer the most challenging and scenic mountain biking in the county. The granny-gear climbs and technical singletrack to be found here make this a mecca for the intermediate/advanced rider. Never fear—beginning riders will still find plenty of scenic, nicely wooded rides. Both areas are a little over an hour's drive from San Diego, and they are among the highest points in San Diego County. Chaparral covers the lower slopes of these mountains but gives way to black oaks and various wild oaks on the higher slopes. Ponderosa pine forest blankets the upper reaches of the area's peaks, while pinyon pine and California juniper thrive on the drier east-facing slopes. By water-starved southern California standards, these mountains are lush.

Farther east is another "hot" spot for San Diego mountain bikers—the Anza-Borrego desert, home to the unusual California fan palm and the endangered desert bighorn sheep. Wildflowers carpet the desert in spring—the best time to ride here. If you miss the flowers, you'll still find the bizarre geologic formations fascinating.

Are you pumping up your tires yet? Come on, grease that chain, let's go!

1 San Clemente/Rose Canyons

Distance: 12 miles
Difficulty: Moderately difficult, technical in spots
Elevation: 400' gain/loss
Ride Type: Loop on a variety of terrain
Season: Year round

This is a great ride for those of you who don't have the time, energy or transportation to get out of the city. It's a good option for intermediate riders, although beginners can have fun on parts of it, too. It also has the virtue of being very scenic. Some say it has the loveliest trees in town: oaks, willows and gnarled sycamores.

The many unmarked roads and trails in the area make this route confusing to follow. Keep your bearings by major landmarks—I-5, I-805, Highway 52, the railroad tracks, the power lines—and you'll be fine.

Getting There: One of the beauties of this ride is its accessibility. Located in San Diego proper, it is easy and convenient to find. San Clemente Canyon is in Marion Bear Memorial Park, where this ride begins. Take Route 52 east from I-5. Exit at Clairemont Mesa Boulevard and follow signs to the park. Parking is available at the lot west of the boulevard. There are restrooms and water here.

To begin your ride, head west from the parking lot and restrooms on a smooth, wide dirt road. You cross a year-round stream several times as you work your way through San Clemente Canyon. A network of singletrack trails runs through here. Explore at will as all of the trails eventually loop back to the main road. Kids should have a blast chasing one

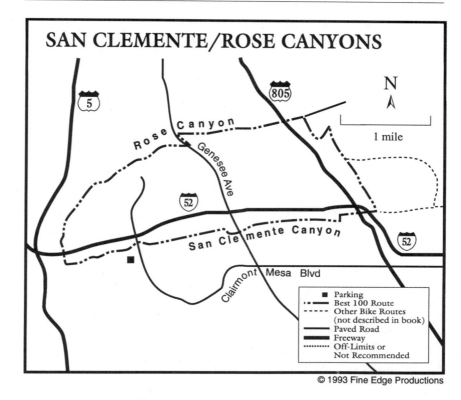

SAN CLEMENTE/ROSE CANYONS

N

1 mile

■ Parking
·—·— Best 100 Route
– – – Other Bike Routes
(not described in book)
——— Paved Road
━━━ Freeway
·········· Off-Limits or
Not Recommended

© 1993 Fine Edge Productions

another along these trails. There are some good side hills, berms and jumps for the budding BMXer as well.

Lovely oaks grace the area, and there are benches under some of them as well as scattered picnic tables if you want a break or if you want to eat after you complete your loop. There are willows and sycamores here, too. Caution: The stream can really flow after a winter storm, so be forewarned!

The main road soon dead-ends at the west end of the canyon. Here you make the first of several unusual twists and turns. Proceed north (right) through the concrete drainage ditch. At the end of the ditch pick up a dirt trail on your right (east) side. Follow this singletrack into Rose Canyon. The downhill-sloping trail will test your sidehill technique, but it is very

manageable overall.

Numerous trails cross the area, so it is easy to get off route. Just keep paralleling the railroad tracks on your left and you won't get lost. You have to detour across Genesee Avenue. The dirt road ends there. Simply head north (that's left) for a couple of blocks on Genesee, then cross diagonally to the northeast corner of the intersection at the traffic light. You can see a yellow gate and a dirt road continuing east toward the I-805.

Soon the trail peters out and you must ride in the streambed. This is very rocky. We're talking deep, fist-sized rocks. How's your balance? And you're going uphill slightly through all of Rose Canyon!

After you cross under I-805, take the road to your right that follows the power lines. Once again, there are several unmarked, criss-crossing roads. Follow the power lines and keep I-805 on your right and you won't get off course. You climb and descend several steep, rocky hills before cresting a plateau (the high point of the ride, 400 feet) out of Rose Canyon and crossing into a nursery. Head to the east (left) end of the nursery where you rejoin a dirt road.

You climb and descend more steep, rocky hills before heading down into San Clemente Canyon. Look for a singletrack on your right. It's a fun, twisty little piece. Cross under I-805 again, this time heading west. Once

again you are up to your hubs in rocks. Keep flailing and eventually there's more dirt and sand than rock. Also keep your eyes peeled for a singletrack on your left that parallels the streambed and will get you out of the rocks. Not that there aren't a few rocks along it as well, but as least you're on firm ground.

Eventually you hook up with the main dirt road that runs through San Clemente Canyon. Continue west to your car. This area is crisscrossed with singletrack, so have fun exploring—the trails all loop away from and then back to the main road.

2 Mission Trails Regional Park

Distance: Depends on options taken
Difficulty: Moderate to strenuous, mildly technical
Elevation: Low point 280', high point 910'
Ride Type: Dirt roads and trails, out and back with loop option
Season: Year round

Like the previous ride, this is a good choice for those of you stuck in the city. Just 8 miles from downtown San Diego, this 5,700-acre tract is one of the largest urban parks in the country. It's excellent for intermediate riders, but advanced riders can challenge themselves by climbing the various peaks in the park. Until last year, Los Penasquitos Reserve was the most popular in-town spot to ride, but officials there have cracked down on mountain bikers, limiting them to the park's main access road and a few other trails. Meanwhile, rangers at Mission Trails encourage bicycling. Except for a few trails that have been deemed "too dangerous," cyclists can use whatever trails they like. To get a map of the park, call 619-533-4051 or 619-463-4015.

Getting There: Take I-8 east from San Diego and exit at Mission Gorge Road. Continue east to Father Junipero Serra Trail (FJST). Note: Father Junipero Serra Trail is closed from sunset to sunrise. Follow it to the Old Mission Dam Historical Area on your left. Park here. There are picnic tables, toilets, and water. You can also park along FJST.

The trail is named for a Spanish priest who was one of the founders of the California mission system. Begun in 1810, the Old Mission Dam, a nationally registered historic site, was the first water supply project in what is now the western United States. Spanish missionaries from Mission San Diego de Alcala used Native American labor to build the adobe tile-lined flume that carried water 5.5 miles to the mission to irrigate crops and provide drinking water. Take time to check out the dam before you begin your ride.

The park has many unnamed, unmarked trails, so it's better to explore than to follow a specific route here. I'm going to suggest different areas for skilled and less skilled riders.

From the dam site, head southwest on FJST. You can also catch a south-running trail across the road from the dam site. The more difficult option, this trail loops around the east side of an unnamed peak (1,194') before reconnecting with FJST. If you choose the FJST, be sure to look to your right to enjoy the San Diego River as it makes its way through the rugged cliffs of Mission Gorge. A lush riparian habitat of willow, cottonwood and sycamore trees thrives along its banks. It's also home to the endangered least Bell's vireo.

Look for a trail on your right that goes down and across the river. If you took the dirt route around the unnamed peak, you cross FJST and join this trail. You climb to the next trail junction, where you have several options. You are now at an area call Suycott Wash, a low lying area be-

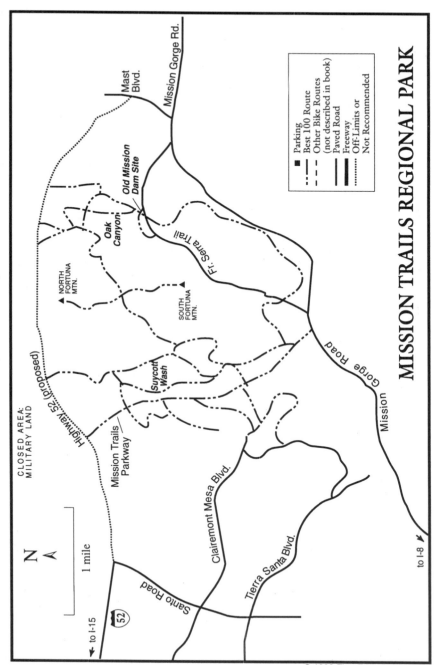

MISSION TRAILS REGIONAL PARK

Parking
Best 100 Route
Other Bike Routes
(not described in book)
Paved Road
Freeway
Off-Limits or
Not Recommended

Mast Blvd.
Mission Gorge Rd.
Old Mission Dam Site
Oak Canyon
Ft. Serra Trail
NORTH FORTUNA MTN.
SOUTH FORTUNA MTN.
Suycott Wash
CLOSED AREA: MILITARY LAND
Highway 52 (proposed)
Mission Trails Parkway
Clairemont Mesa Blvd.
Tierra Santa Blvd.
Santo Road
Mission Gorge Road
to I-8
to I-15
52
N
1 mile

© 1993 Fine Edge Productions

tween the west mesa of the park and the steep hills to the east side. It offers some great rolling trails and winding singletrack. Pick your pleasure. You can spend hours crisscrossing this area—a good place to practice singletrack riding skills. (This area is also accessible from Clairemont Mesa Boulevard, 3 miles east of Interstate 15. Take it to its end. You can enter the park here, or you can hang a right on Rueda Drive, which turns into Calle De Vida, also fine for parking.)

Once you're done playing, the easiest return is the way you came.

Riders who want more of a challenge can head northwest at the trail junction to Suycott Wash. Following the power lines, this route drops into a bowl-shaped valley and then climbs to a saddle (910') between North Fortuna Mountain (1,291') and South Fortuna Mountain (1,094'). You can climb these mountains, but the routes are very technical—some say treacherous. Talked you out of it? Then proceed northwest and descend about 500 feet to cross the creek in Oak Canyon. At the next trail junction, after a small climb, make a right. Another right shortly thereafter takes you down Oak Canyon. When that Ts, a third right takes you back to the dam site. Recrossing the river can be tricky here. If you've left a friend to frolic in Suycott Wash, you can turn around and retrace your tire marks any time.

Two notes of caution here. First, there is much development in and around the park, so conditions could change. State Route 52 is being extended along the north boundary of the park. Mission Trails Parkway, which cuts through Suycott Wash, is due to be built in 1993. A visitor center, near the junction of Mission Gorge Road and FJST, should be open in 1993 as well.

Second, part of the park (on the west side) was used as a weapons training facility during World War II. A young boy was killed last year by an unexploded shell. Some ordnance may remain. If you see any shells or other artillery materials, do not touch them. Mark the spot and call the fire department at 911.

For the latest developments, call park rangers at 619-533-4051.

Laguna Mountain Recreation Area

The Lagunas, farther east and therefore drier than the Cuyamacas, are included within Cleveland National Forest, although the higher regions are part of the Laguna Mountain Recreation Area, which is administered by the Forest Service as a high use, multiple use area. Over 50 miles of hiking trails, numerous picnic areas, campgrounds and nature trails dot the area. The Pacific Crest Trail zigzags through the Lagunas and is strictly off limits to bikes. The other roads and trails are open. With the best singletrack in San Diego County, indeed some of the best in all of Southern California, the Lagunas are an advanced rider's nirvana. The east side of the range is a dramatic meeting of mountain and desert. For more information on camping, contact the Descanso District Office of Cleveland National Forest at 619-445-6235 or 619-473-8824.

Near the top of Sunrise Highway (you can see the sunrise from the highway as it runs along the Lagunas' eastern flank), the small town of Mount Laguna has a store and a restaurant. There's also a Forest Service Information Office—open only on summer weekends. Tom Harrison's Recreation Map of the San Diego Backcountry is a good resource for riding in this area.

The best base for exploring here is the town of Julian, nestled between the Cuyamaca and Volcan mountains at the junction of Highways 78 and 79. A gold rush town, Julian was a rough-and-tumble place 100 years ago. Today it's a rustic retreat for city-weary San Diegoans, and the biggest event of the year is the fall's apple festival.

The George Washington, Julian's first mine, was staked out on Washington's birthday in 1870. When its owners shipped out over a ton of gold ore, a rush was on. Julian was one of several towns that sprung up to service the miners with hotels, saloons, and brothels. The town's founder, Drury Bailey, named it after one of his cousins, Mike Julian, supposedly the handsomest man in town. Julian was the most successful of the boom towns and even rivaled San Diego as the seat of county government. Things settled down when the boom went bust in the 1880s.

Today, antique shops, restaurants and bed and breakfasts beckon to visitors. Main Street is lined with buildings with wooden facades. You can sample Julian's justly famous apple pie, apple cider, apple-you-name-it, and buy any kind of apple knickknack imaginable. (I like Mom's Apple Pie, next to Jack's Market on Main Street.)

The Julian Bicycle Company organizes a Fat Tire Festival every year, usually two consecutive weekends in spring. They are located at 1897 Porter Lane, behind the only gas station in town, or you can call them at 619-765-2200. For information on merchants, lodging, restaurants and events, call the Julian Information Center at 619-765-0707.

3 Noble Canyon

Distance: 19 miles
Difficulty: Strenuous, very technical
Elevation: 2,600' gain/loss
Ride Type: Loop on fire road, paved road and singletrack
Season: Fall and spring best; expect snow in winter; can be crowded on weekends

This tough ride is a local favorite for its scenery and challenge. Control your speed on the 9 miles of singletrack since the Noble Canyon trail is also popular with hikers.

Getting There: From San Diego take I-8 east. Exit at Pine Valley Road and go north. Turn left on Highway 80. Turn right 1 mile later onto Pine Creek Road (a very sharp turn). It's another mile to the Noble Canyon Trail sign on your right. There's a dirt lot right there or you can continue up the road to a developed parking area, complete with restrooms. Bring all the water you will need.

From Julian, go south on Highway 79. Head east on Old Sunrise Highway through Guatay to Pine Creek Road and go left to the Noble Canyon Trail sign on your right.

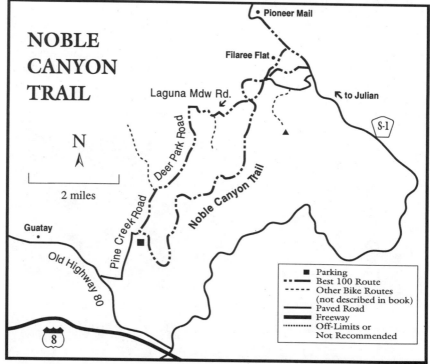

© 1993 Fine Edge Productions

To begin, head north on Pine Creek Road, which turns into Deer Park Road. Often described as a dirt road, it had just been covered by a layer of gravel last time I road it. This is not as ugly as it sounds. The gravel was well packed and caused little to no problems. After some moderate climbing, the road rises more steeply, reaching about a 20 percent grade at one part. After a paved stretch and a cattle guard, turn right onto Laguna Meadow Road. It winds pleasantly around several hills before crossing the Noble Canyon Trail for the first time. If you're whipped you can head down from here.

It's more fun if you continue, turning left toward Filaree Flat. Once you reach Sunrise Highway, head right 1 mile to the Noble Canyon Trailhead and turn right down the trail. At the parking area there you'll probably see mountain bikers being deposited by their friends for the downhill only. Real bicyclists ride up and down. To be fair, some ride the downhill first and finish by coming up the mountain.

Here you're among pines; the trail drops and swerves gently. Don't let the sweet, undulating character of this part of trail lull you into complacency. Before long you hit a tight switchback and cross Laguna Meadow Road. Three more tough switchbacks follow and you're heading into the roughest part of the ride. From here on the trail gets very technical. Call it rock hell. If you don't have suspension, you'll wish you did. There are a few smooth sections for respite and a few stream crossings.

The trail drops into oak shaded canyons in this part before breaking out onto a rocky ledge. Small jagged rocks and a cliff make this potentially the most dangerous section. Once past it, and with all your fillings knocked loose, you have to do a little bit of climbing. There's also some sand at the bottom of the canyon. The very end of the trail becomes unrideable thanks to some boulder fields—unless you're Hans Rey. The trail finally deposits you at your car in the parking area.

4 Indian Creek Trail/ Big Laguna Trail

Distance: 14 miles
Difficulty: Moderate, some technical sections
Elevation: 1,100' gain/loss
Ride Type: Loop with lots of singletrack, some pavement
Season: Fall and spring; in winter expect cold weather and possible snow; can be crowded on weekends.

This route has been one of San Diego's best kept secrets for a while now. In the same area as Noble Canyon, these two trails can be fashioned into a 16-mile loop that is 75 percent singletrack. A little bit of pavement along Sunrise Highway is necessary to complete the loop. The ride offers scenery to die for and miles of smooth, winding singletrack. To complete the picture it has stream crossings and rocky descents, and enough technical sections to keep your bike dancing.

Getting There: From San Diego take I-8 east to Highway 79 north. Follow Highway 79 for 17 miles to the Mt. Laguna turnoff (Sunrise Highway). Take Sunrise Highway 8.5 miles to Pioneer Mail picnic area and park.

From Julian, take Highway 79 for 6 miles south to the Mt. Laguna turnoff (Sunrise Highway). Follow Sunrise Highway 8.5 miles to Pioneer Mail picnic area and park. (You can also park at Kwaaymii Point a mile back up Sunrise Highway. This will add 2 miles to your ride.)

From the Pioneer Mail parking area, head toward the paved entrance to a fire road. At 0.1 mile make a right turn. The pavement soon ends and you pass through a gate. The dirt road forks here and you want to go right. (The left fork leads to another gate.) Stay on the generally rolling main trail as you make a few short, rocky descents.

At 0.3 mile you hit a three-way intersection. Take the trail to the far right. There's another fork soon but this time stay left—it's the obvious route. The trail forks yet again and you want to go left again. There's a downhill at 0.7 mile with a fork. You can take either the easy left side or the more difficult right side. Just 0.5 mile later take the right fork to continue straight down a rocky descent. Your next challenge is crossing Indian Creek. Uphill a tad and you're at the beginning of the singletrack. When you come to the sign post at 1.6 miles, stay on Indian Creek Trail.

Just under 2.5 miles into the ride and you come to a T intersection with a sign post, where you go left on Noble Canyon Trail. You cross Laguna Meadow Road for the first time after another mile. The singletrack resumes across the road. Cross Laguna Meadow Road two more times, jogging right the second time to catch the trail. Watch for a cattle guard there, too. The trail along here is a series of gradual ups and downs—the beginning of the previous ride's singletrack.

Make a right turn onto Big Laguna Trail at 4.5 miles. There is a signpost to guide you. If you continue straight you end up back at Sunrise Highway. This is the prettiest

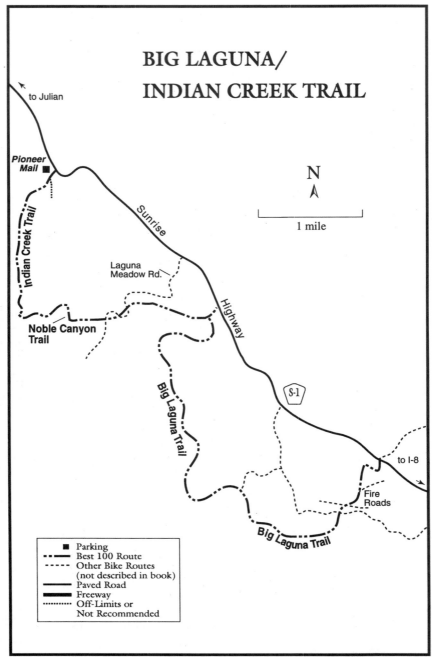

BIG LAGUNA/
INDIAN CREEK TRAIL

to Julian

Pioneer Mail ■

Indian Creek Trail

Sunrise

Laguna Meadow Rd.

Noble Canyon Trail

Highway

N
Λ

|—————————|
1 mile

Big Laguna Trail

S-1

to I-8

Fire Roads

Big Laguna Trail

■ Parking
∙—∙— Best 100 Route
------- Other Bike Routes
(not described in book)
————— Paved Road
▬▬▬ Freeway
·········· Off-Limits or
Not Recommended

© 1993 Fine Edge Productions

part of the ride as you follow smooth, relatively flat singletrack past a meadow on your right. In the spring this mountain meadow is peppered with wildflowers. You also have views of Big Laguna Lake tucked in the meadow, which cradles a few other smaller lakes.

Go right at the trail junction at 7.3 miles to continue on Big Laguna Trail. Pass a sign for Laguna Campground and continue straight towards the Pacific Crest Trail. The trail grows more technical through here, but it is rideable. At 8.9 miles, you cross a dirt road. Another fire road intersects the trail soon after. Continue straight on the trail, which widens into a fire road. At 9.4 miles fork left off the fire road onto a trail—no sign, just a wood post. Less than 0.5 mile later you're back to Sunrise Highway, where a left turn and a 4-mile downhill cruise takes you to your car. Or, if you're up to it, you can go back the way you came.

Cuyamaca Rancho State Park

Cuyamaca Rancho State Park borders Cleveland National Forest and the Laguna Mountain Recreation Area. With about 30,000 acres (13,000 of which are wilderness and closed to bikes), Cuyamaca is one of California's largest state parks. Its beauty and proximity to the city of San Diego make it very popular. West of the Lagunas, the Cuyamacas are wetter and lusher. Numerous springs and creeks trickle through cool, shady forests of willow, sycamore and alder. Three peaks dominate the area—North, Middle and Cuyamaca peaks. Cuyamaca Lake lies to the north. Over 100 miles of trail, about half of which are open to bikes, tantalize bicyclists, hikers and equestrians alike.

The mountains get their name from the Kumeya'ay Indians, who summered in these mountains. The name has been translated as "the place where it rains." Indian artifacts, such as bedrock morteros, can be found throughout the park. The park itself was part of an 1845 Mexican land grant called Rancho Cuyamaca. In 1933 the state acquired the property for use as a park.

There are several campgrounds and picnic areas as well as group campsites, equestrian camps and primitive camps. Paso Picacho is the most centrally located campground for the rides described below. Reservations can be made up to eight weeks in advance through MISTIX at 1-800-444-7275 using a major credit card. Park headquarters can be reached at 619-765-0755. A good map is available there or by mail for a nominal fee. Write 12551 Highway 79, Descanso, CA 92016.

Pick up a free information sheet on mountain bike rides at park headquarters. It gives brief descriptions of seven rides and spells out bicycling regulations in the park. All singletrack in the park is closed to bikes, and there is a 15-mph speed limit. You can also get water at park headquarters.

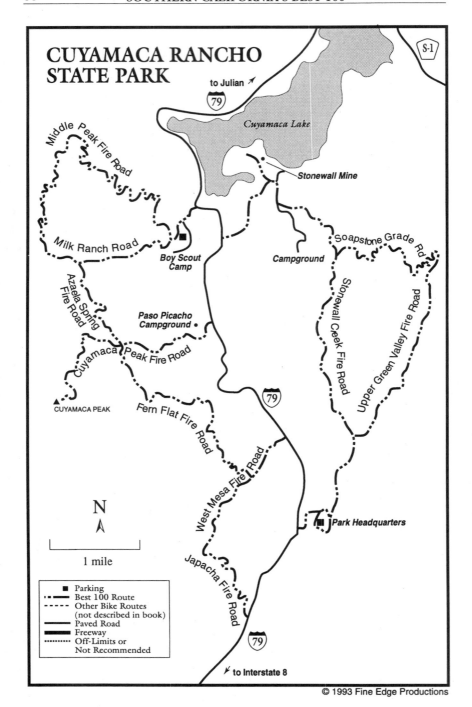

CUYAMACA RANCHO STATE PARK

to Julian ↗
79

Cuyamaca Lake

S-1

Middle Peak Fire Road

Milk Ranch Road

Stonewall Mine

Soapstone Grade Rd

Boy Scout Camp

Campground

Azalea Spring Fire Road

Paso Picacho Campground •

Cuyamaca Peak Fire Road

Stonewall Creek Fire Road

Upper Green Valley Fire Road

▲ CUYAMACA PEAK

Fern Flat Fire Road

79

West Mesa Fire Road

N
⋀

1 mile

Park Headquarters

Japacha Fire Road

79

Parking ■
Best 100 Route –·–·–
Other Bike Routes – – –
(not described in book)
Paved Road ——
Freeway ▬▬
Off-Limits or ·········
Not Recommended

↙ to Interstate 8

© 1993 Fine Edge Productions

5 Soapstone Grade/ Stonewall Creek Loop

Distance: 12.4 miles
Difficulty: Moderate, nontechnical
Elevation: 900' gain/loss
Ride Type: Fire road loop
Season: Fall and spring best, but rideable most of the year

Riders of various ability levels can enjoy this loop. A variety of trail surfaces and the climb up Stonewall Creek Fire Road are challenges for your legs, while the meadows and Lake Cuyamaca along Soapstone Grade are sights for your eyes.

The route also gives you the option of exploring one of the historic mine sites near Julian, the Stonewall Mine. In the 1860s gold was discovered in the Julian area. By 1872 the town of Cuyamaca had sprung up around the Stonewall Mine, named for Stonewall Jackson. The "Jackson" was eventually dropped to appease anti-Southern sentiments in the area. The most extensively developed mine in the region, it employed 200 men during its peak years, 1886 to 1891. Owned by California governor Robert W. Waterman, the mine yielded over $2 million in gold (gold prices at the time were between $16 and $20 an ounce) before its main shaft was sealed in 1892.

Getting There: From Julian, take Highway 79 south for 10 miles. Park at the dirt parking area (east side of the road) across from the Boy Scout Camp. From I-8, take Highway 79 north 14 miles to the parking area.

From the parking area, head south on Highway 79 for 0.5 mile. Turn left onto a paved road. This is easy going. At 1.4 miles a spur to your left leads to Stonewall Mine. The mine is just south of Lake Cuyamaca, called The Lake That Dries Up by the Spanish because it dries up almost to the point of disappearing in the summer.

Back on the main road there is a gate. At 1.7 miles you make a left and almost immediately pass another gate. At 2.8 miles head left at the road junction. You will be coming back up the right fork to complete the loop.

You are now on Soapstone Grade Road. In the next 1.5 miles you descend a steep, rocky section—keep that bike under control! At 4.4 miles Soapstone Grade intersects Upper Green Valley Fire Road. Go right. You continue to lose elevation as you head for the junction with Stonewall Creek Fire Road at 6.8 miles. Go right. You regain most of the lost elevation in the next 2.4 miles. Keep plugging away and try not to dab. The road parallels Stonewall Creek most of the way.

After 9.2 miles you are back at the junction with Soapstone Grade. A left takes you downhill back to the second gate. A right at the junction after that leads back to the first gate. If you didn't explore Stonewall Mine on the way out, you can do it now. Back at Highway 79, you have 0.5 mile to go to your car.

This loop can also be done from Cuyamaca Rancho State Park headquarters. From there it's only a 7-mile ride. From the headquarters parking lot, either of the roads labeled "Authorized Vehicles Only" takes you past the school buildings where the trail heads northeast. When you reach the junction of Stonewall Creek Fire Road and Upper Green Valley Road, head up Stonewall Creek to make the loop clockwise. A right on Soapstone Grade and a right on Upper Green Valley takes you around.

There are a couple of disadvantages, however, to starting at head-quarters. First, parking is limited to 2 hours in the parking lot. If you plan to be longer or have problems—oops. Second, the lot can be full on holidays and weekends.

Regardless of your starting point, you can do this loop in either direction, although I prefer the first option described here. Doing it counterclockwise is easy except for a short, steep 0.5-mile section up Soapstone Grade.

6 Cuyamaca Park Grand Tour

Distance: 17.1 miles
Difficulty: Strenuous, nontechnical
Elevation: 1,720' gain/loss
Ride Type: Fire road loop
Season: Fall and spring best, but rideable all year

Deer. Springs. A 5-mile down-hill. Some of San Diego's largest trees. A look at Cuyamaca Park's west and east sides. Need I say more? Well, I guess I should point out that there's lots of climbing involved. Hey, sometimes you have to pay to play!

Getting There: Follow the directions for the previous ride and park in the same spot.

From the parking area, cross the highway and take the paved road toward the Boy Scout Camp. When it forks take Milk Ranch Road to the right. (To the left is the camp.) The road turns to dirt and there is a gate. Soon after, Middle Peak Fire Road takes off to your right. If you have legs of steel and want to make a hard ride even harder, take Middle Peak (a 1,000-foot climb in 2.8 miles), loop around the mountain of the same

name and rejoin the route at Azalea Spring Fire Road. This would add 5 miles to your ride total. We mere mortals will stay on Milk Ranch Road and only climb 500 feet before turning left onto Azalea Springs Fire Road at 1.7 miles.

After another 200 feet of gain and 0.7 mile, you reach Azalea Springs. Refresh yourself with the cool water, but don't dawdle—you have miles to go before you sleep. Singletracks crisscross this whole area. Stay off of them, since they are all closed to bikes.

The paved Cuyamaca Peak Fire Road crosses your path at 3 miles. If you don't feel like you're getting a workout, you can hang a right and climb a moderate-to-steep 1,200 feet to the peak—the highest point in San Diego County. The view is worth the work, especially if it's a clear day. Stay in control on the descent—you can work up some serious speed. The detour will add about 3 miles to your ride. If you're gagging, you can turn left and take Cuyamaca Peak Fire Road back to Highway 79, where another left returns you to your car.

Now comes the fun part—nearly 5 miles of sweet downhill bliss along Fern Flat Fire Road. At 5.6 miles you come to a T with West Mesa Fire Road on your left (another bail-out point back to Highway 79) and Japacha Fire Road on your right. This is one of the most heavily wooded and pleasant areas of the park. Continue downhill on Japacha. You come to a gate and then intersect Highway 79 at 7.7 miles. Head north (left) on Highway 79 for a mile to the park headquarters on your right. Pass the school camp. When you reach the junction with Stonewall Creek Fire Road and Upper Green Valley Fire Road at 10.3 miles, bear right up Green Valley. (This is a counterclockwise version of the previous ride, starting from park headquarters.) You could omit this loop by staying on Highway 79 to your car, but that's a pretty long pavement slog. Besides, you don't want to be a party pooper!

When you've gone 12.6 miles, turn left onto Soapstone Grade and make some short, steep climbs before intersecting Stonewall Creek Fire Road at 14.3 miles. It's 1 mile to the next trail junction, where you bear right after crossing a gate. You pass another gate before turning left at the next junction (a right would take you to Stonewall Mine). It's less than a mile now to Highway 79—you're almost done. A right on the highway and 0.5 mile of pavement pedaling takes you back to your waiting vehicle. You've done it!

7 Four Canyon Ride

Distance: 26.4 miles, but can be shortened 10 miles by starting in Banner
Difficulty: Strenuous because of length and hideous climb up Oriflamme Canyon; somewhat technical because of the variety of trail surfaces
Elevation: 3,960' gain/loss
Ride Type: Pavement and dirt road loop
Season: Best in late fall, winter, early spring; summer is gruesome
Map: Tom Harrison's Recreation Map of the San Diego Backcountry

Although technically not in Cuyamaca State Park (much of it is actually in Anza-Borrego Desert State Park), this ride starts in Julian, so it's included in this section. As you traverse Banner, Chariot, Rodriquez and Oriflamme Canyons, you pass from pines to chaparral to desert and back.

Difficult climbs and diverse trail surfaces make this a very challenging ride. Be prepared with plenty of food, water and clothing for the different temperatures you're likely to encounter. Run fat tires and low gears for this one. You can get water in Julian and at the Banner store.

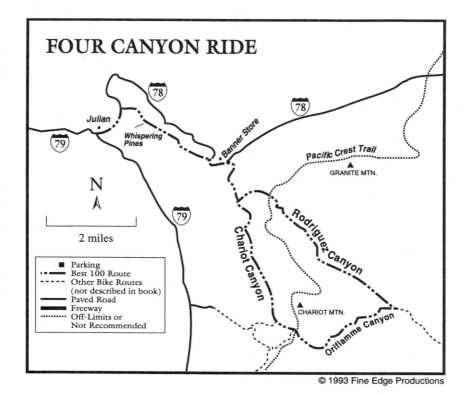

© 1993 Fine Edge Productions

Getting There: Start in Julian. From San Diego, take I-8 to Highway 79 north. Julian is 24 miles north. Park in town. Mileage readings are from Norm's Gas Station near the junction of Highway 79 and Highway 78.

Begin the ride by taking Highway 78 east to Woodland Road in the Whispering Pines housing development. Go right. This first part is on pavement, but at 1.4 miles you reach the trailhead of a dirt road on your left. Enjoy the descent to Banner because you more than make up for it later.

At the junction at 3.0 miles go left. At the gate at 4.6 miles continue straight, taking Highway 78 for 0.4 mile to the Banner Store. You've now descended about 1,400 feet. From the store head south (right) and begin climbing into Chariot Canyon. If you pass Banner Recreation Ranch on Highway 78, you've gone too far.

Turn hard left after 6.4 miles into Rodriquez Canyon. In the next 2 miles you cross a cattle guard and climb 300 feet. At 8.4 miles the Pacific Crest Trail (no bikes allowed) crosses Rodriquez Canyon. Along here you enter Anza-Borrego Desert State Park. As you make your way down the canyon, the grass and scrub-oak vegetation of the upper canyon slowly gives way to desert plants. The 5,633-foot Granite Mountain monolith looms to your left as you travel this canyon. Chariot Mountain is on your right. Much of the area's geography is a result of the several significant faults that run through the area. Rodriquez Canyon parallels the Elsinore Fault, one of the San Andreas Fault's major offshoots.

A fast downhill with loose sand and rocks followed by several stream crossings takes you to the 12-mile

mark. Control your speed because there are possible gate closures along the downhill stretch.

At 12.1 miles you make a fateful right turn into Oriflamme Canyon. Gravity now works against you as you climb from 2,670 feet to 4,160 feet in 3.6 miles. This is where you pay for all the descending you've been

doing. Mason Valley Truck Trail branches off to your left at 15.7 miles. You continue straight. The Pacific Crest Trail crosses your route again and follows the fire road a little ways before resuming on your left. (Remember, no bikes allowed!)

After you pass the Pacific Crest Trail you're back in Chariot Canyon. What sweet relief it is as a quick downhill awaits your throbbing thighs. On the way down you pass the turnoff to Rodriquez Canyon on your right—the one you took earlier in the day. At this point you will have circumnavigated Chariot Mountain, now to your right.

You're back at the Banner Store at 21.3 miles. From this point, simply backtrack the way you came. Remember that downhill you enjoyed on the way out? You guessed it, you have to go up it to finish your beautiful thighbuster ride.

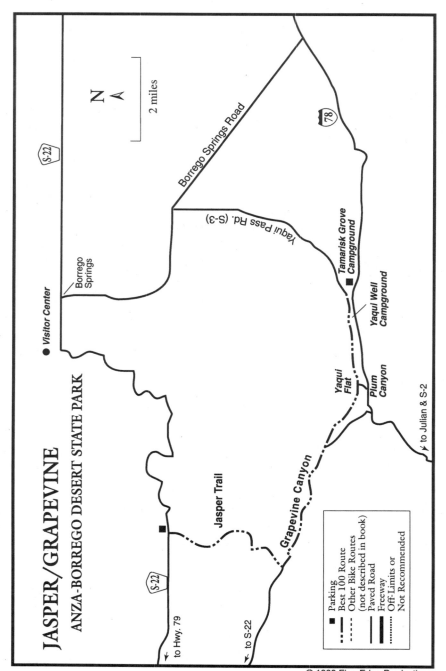

JASPER/GRAPEVINE
ANZA-BORREGO DESERT STATE PARK

N
2 miles

Borrego Springs Road

S-22

78

Yaqui Pass Rd. (S-3)

Borrego Springs

Visitor Center

Tamarisk Grove Campground

Yaqui Well Campground

Yaqui Flat

Plum Canyon

to Julian & S-2

Jasper Trail

Grapevine Canyon

S-22

to Hwy. 79

to S-22

Parking
Best 100 Route
Other Bike Routes (not described in book)
Paved Road
Freeway
Off-Limits or Not Recommended

Anza-Borrego Desert State Park

About 90 miles northeast of San Diego, this rugged desert region is a unique environment. Expect the bizarre and unusual when you ride in Anza-Borrego Desert State Park. Along with the expected rocky washes and sparse vegetation, the park contains one-of-a-kind desert plants such as the California fan palm and other-worldly geological formations: wind caves, fossil shell reefs, rock slots, mudhills, sandstone cliffs and folded rock anticlines. The park is also home to the endangered desert bighorn sheep. Spring, when flowers are in bloom, is a good time to visit. Rainy years are best for spring wildflower shows.

The park is partly named for Spanish explorer Juan Bautista de Anza, who in 1774 created a route across the desert to link Sonora, Mexico, with areas of Northern California. The other half of the park's name comes from the Spanish word for the desert bighorn sheep, *borrego*. The Anza trail was soon replaced by a better route called the Southern Emigrant Trail. Today County Road S2 follows it closely. This route was used extensively during the Mexican War. After the war it was turned into the first wagon route into Southern California, the one that thousands of gold-crazy prospectors traveled during the state's gold rush. Stage routes followed, but soon ended when the Civil War began. After the war, they were rendered obsolete by the transcontinental railroad.

Today's mountain-biking route finders can explore 500 miles of dirt roads, most of which are open to bikes, in this 600,000-acre desert. Most of the trails in the area are soft dirt or sand, so bring your fattest tires and run them with less air pressure than normal for better traction. Many of the roads are open to 4WD vehicles, too, so be on the alert. Bring plenty of water, especially if you plan to camp. Figure on 2 gallons per person per day.

The town of Borrego Springs, located off County Highway S22, is a good jumping off spot for exploring the park, especially the northern end. Travelers will find accommodations and facilities, including the park's Visitor Center, on Palm Canyon Road. Two miles north of the Visitor Center is Borrego Palm Canyon Campground. For more information, call park headquarters at 619-767-5311. The park puts out a good map/brochure of the area. Tom Harrison's Recreation Map of the San Diego Backcountry is also helpful.

8 Jasper Trail/ Grapevine Canyon

Distance: 15 miles
Difficulty: Moderate, mildly technical
Elevation: Net loss of 2,600'
Ride Type: One way downhill on dirt and sand roads
Season: Winter
Comments: You could do this as a round trip of 30 miles if you don't mind slogging uphill through soft sand. It's best done as a one-way trip with a car shuttle. Be aware that this trail is open to motorized travel, so expect 4WDs on the weekends.

Getting There: This ride begins about 10 miles southwest of Borrego Springs near the town of Ranchita. To arrange the car shuttle: Take Highway 78 east from Julian. Park one car at Tamarisk Campground near the junction with S3. Take the other car back down Highway 78 to S2 and go right. Turn right again on Highway S22. After you cross the Anza-Borrego Desert State Park boundary, look off the right hand side of the road for the hard-to-spot Jasper Trailhead. It's between mile markers 6 and 7.

To begin your ride, proceed south on the Jasper trail. The soft trail passes through sparse vegetation, mostly desert bush and cacti, for the first 2 miles. At this point you encounter the ride's only hill, and it's a

steep one, about a 600-foot climb. It's followed by an equally steep downhill. Breathe easy, your work's already done for the day as the rest of the ride is a continuous downhill.

After the steep downhill you turn north and follow a ridge line to avoid a narrow, rocky section of canyon. For a time, you are surrounded by near vertical rock walls. The canyon widens as the road skirts another dropoff. A flat area and a sandy bed lead into Grapevine Canyon.

You have to make a left into Grapevine Canyon when Jasper dead ends. Two springs offer drinkable water just east (that's the direction you're heading) of this junction. Stuart Spring is less than 0.5 mile away, and Angelina Spring is 1.3 miles past that. You might enjoy a break here among the willows.

From here you pedal onto a bluff. Past Angelina Spring about 2.3 miles, the road forks. Go left toward Yaqui Well and follow this road to your waiting pickup vehicle at Tamarisk Campground.

It is possible to shorten the ride by making a right at the fork and heading toward Plum Canyon (if you left your car there instead of at Tamarisk Campground. Parking at Plum Canyon is off of Highway 78 near the 74-mile marker.

If a car shuttle is impossible and you would still like to explore this area, park at Tamarisk Campground and proceed up (west) Grapevine Canyon. Go as far as you wish before turning around and heading back the way you came.

9 Pinyon Mountain/ Split Mountain

Distance: 30 miles
Difficulty: Difficult because of the length; mildly technical
Elevation: Net loss of 1,700'
Ride Type: Dirt and sand roads
Season: Winter
Comments: Requires car shuttle. Carry plenty of water and food.

The Pinyon Mountains, the geographic heart of Anza Borrego, are part of a larger range called the Vallecito Mountains. A herd of big-horn sheep lives in these mountains despite a lack of known year-round water sources. In the past 20 years water tanks have been installed in a couple of spots to help improve the bighorn habitat.

The following ride and two options offer different ways to explore Pinyon and Split Mountains. You can ride west–east from Pinyon Mountain to Split Mountain. You cannot return the same way, however, because the center section of the route is so narrow that two-way traffic has been prohibited. (If and how this is enforced is unclear.) The other two options are to ride from Pinyon Mountain to the one-way section and back, or to ride from Split Mountain to the one-way section and back.

Doing the entire west-to-east ride is more than worth the hassle of arranging a shuttle. Beginning in the high desert at about 4,000 feet near Pinyon Mountain (which receives 15 inches of rain a year), the ride drops to sea level on the Split Mountain end, where the average rainfall is just 3 inches per year. You roll through pinyon pine before dropping down to wind- and water-scarred fossil shell reefs and wind caves. Although there is some climbing, most of the ride is

a cruise. But be alert for sand traps and rocks. Like Grapevine Canyon, this occasionally washboard road is open to motor vehicles.

Getting There: From Julian, take Highway 78 east for 30 miles to Ocotillo Wells. Turn right onto Split Mountain Road. Fish Creek intersection is 10 miles south. Leave one car here. Go back the way you came until you hit Highway S2. Turn left and continue for 5 miles until you cross the Anza-Borrego State Park sign. Immediately on your left (east) is the Pinyon Mountain sign. Park off the trail in this area.

Start your trip by pedaling east on the right fork of the main trail— Pinyon Mountain Road. The left fork climbs North Pinyon Mountain itself. This is a nice side trip, but is best explored when you're not planning to go all the way from Pinyon to Split. Don't be discouraged by the uphill; most of the climbing comes at the beginning. You summit at 3,900 feet, where you find several campsites. Stay on the main trail heading east. Even if you get off it, the side trails eventually lead back. You soon pass Squeeze Rock, so called because it's narrow enough that Jeeps sometimes scrape the rocky slot. Even with your fattest tires you shouldn't have any trouble fitting through the 8- to 9-

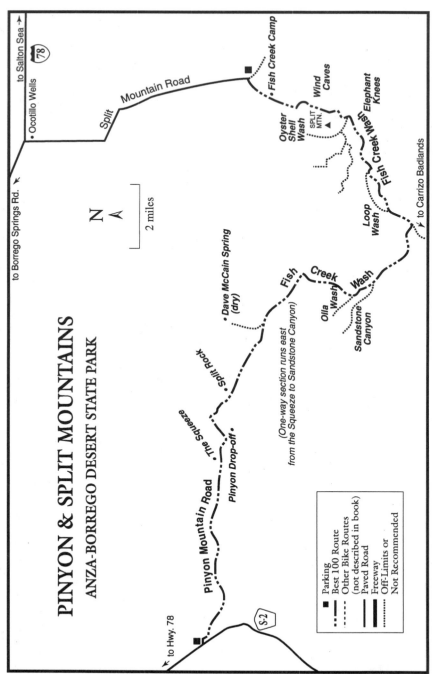

PINYON & SPLIT MOUNTAINS
ANZA-BORREGO DESERT STATE PARK

to Salton Sea →

78

Ocotillo Wells

Split Mountain Road

to Borrego Springs Rd.

N

2 miles

Fish Creek Camp

Wind Caves

Oyster Shell Wash

SPLIT MTN.

Fish Creek Wash

Elephant Knees

to Carrizo Badlands

Loop Wash

Dave McCain Spring (dry)

Fish Creek Wash

Olla Wash

Sandstone Wash

Sandstone Canyon

(One-way section runs east from the Squeeze to Sandstone Canyon)

Split Rock

The Squeeze

Pinyon Drop-off

Pinyon Mountain Road

to Hwy. 78

S-2

Parking
Best 100 Route
Other Bike Routes (not described in book)
Paved Road
Freeway
Off-Limits or Not Recommended

© 1993 Fine Edge Productions

foot-wide trail that passes through solid rock.

At this point you're in the one-way zone. Head downhill for 1 mile before you take a sharp, right turn uphill through some very rocky, rough terrain. You climb hard for a little while, but the trail levels off just before the notorious Drop-Off. Notice the capital letters. This is serious. Vehicles and their occupants have met their demise here. You don't want to be going too fast. Let your brain cells and not your ego rule: walk this section.

This marks the end of Pinyon Mountain Road. You are now in Fish Creek Wash. From this point on it's a cruise to Split Mountain. As you would expect, the wash is pretty sandy. You cross several other washes. Luckily they're clearly marked so you should have no trouble staying on course.

Option 1: Pinyon Mountain Road

This moderate, mildly technical ride takes you 15 miles out and back on dirt road and sand with an 1,800-foot elevation gain and loss. It's best ridden in winter.

Follow the directions for the above ride except you don't need a shuttle. Park at the Pinyon Mountain sign. You can ride Pinyon Mountain Road as far as you like as long as you don't enter the one-way area. A good turn-around point, and the one used for this ride's mileage, is the Pinyon Mountain Valley campground. You could also continue on to see the Squeeze.

A side trip up to North Pinyon Mountain on the way out or the way back will add 2 miles and about 500 feet of climbing. Such a detour makes more sense on this ride than on the through route described above. Once

at the top, don't head downhill even if it does look inviting. The downhill leads to a dead end. This route is less crowded than Pine Mountain Road and is a good choice for those of you who like more solitude.

Option 2: Fish Creek Wash

This 28-mile winter route explores the eastern end of the Pinyon Mountain/Split Mountain area. It is a moderate ride on dirt road and sand and mildly technical, with a 1,000-foot elevation gain and loss. To ride here, park your car at the Fish Creek intersection described in the Pinyon to Split ride.

Near sea level, this area features the most interesting geological formations in the park: folded rock anticlines, Elephant Knees, mudhills and sandstone cliffs. These features demonstrate the recurring battles between sea and land, as one element then the other overwhelmed the area. Faulting has further shaped these tortured landforms. You can't ride to the Wind Caves, but they're worth the hike.

Begin by heading up Fish Creek Wash. The first geologic wonders you encounter are sandstone cliffs. Next is Split Mountain, which does indeed look like a mountain that has been split in two. It actually consists of two stacks of sedimentary rock. Sandstone is prevalent as is fanglomerate—a conglomerate of rock and sand that was once part of an alluvial fan. Remarkable rock contortions here are the result of faulting.

The geology lesson continues as you pass steep cliffs on both sides of your route. The west wall's vertical cracks as well as the debris piles at its bottom are a testament to the 1968 earthquake that rocked the nearby town of Ocotillo Wells.

About 4.2 miles into the ride is

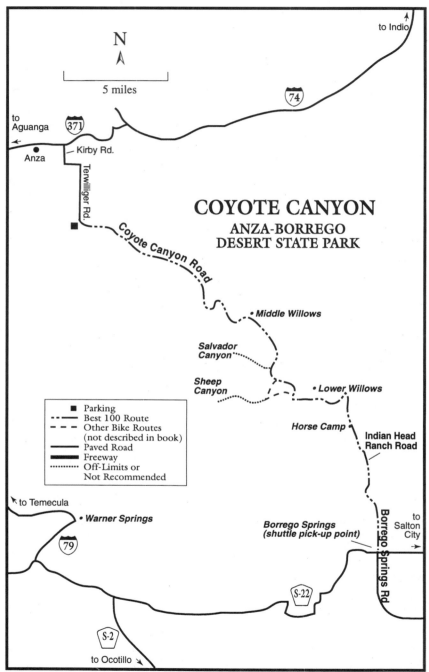

N

5 miles

to Indio

74

to Aguanga

371

Kirby Rd.

Anza

Terwilliger Rd.

COYOTE CANYON

**ANZA-BORREGO
DESERT STATE PARK**

Coyote Canyon Road

• Middle Willows

Salvador
Canyon

Sheep
Canyon

• Lower Willows

Horse Camp

**Indian Head
Ranch Road**

Parking
Best 100 Route
Other Bike Routes
(not described in book)
Paved Road
Freeway
Off-Limits or
Not Recommended

to Temecula

• Warner Springs

79

Borrego Springs
(shuttle pick-up point)

Borrego Springs Rd.

to
Salton
City

S-22

S-2

to Ocotillo

© 1993 Fine Edge Productions

a rock wall with an incredible upside down U (called an anticline). Soon after, when the north fork of Fish Creek Wash veers to the right, stay on the main wash road. Mud Hills Wash appears on your left 0.3 mile later. If you can find a spot to leave your bike, it's worth the hike to see these shimmering hills. The gleam is the result of gypsum chips in the rock.

Continue past Loop Wash and Camels Head Wash on the main road. You keep climbing until you reach Sandstone Canyon, the end of the one-way section, at 12.5 miles. Head up the canyon for another 1.5 miles. At this point you have to abandon your bike if you wish to explore any more. Often called the most spectacular small wash in the whole park, Sandstone Canyon features 200-foot high walls. As the name implies, the walls are beige and brown sandstone. The real marvel is how narrow the canyon is—the walls are about 9 feet apart at their bases. Desert shrubs and catclaw—not a friend to Lycra or tires—are among the few plants that survive here.

To return to your car, simply backtrack through this geologic wonderland. Enjoy the downhill back to your car.

If none of these options appeal to you, you might be interested in the Pinyon Mountain Challenge, over 50 miles of serious riding with 3,500 feet of climbing and 7,500 feet of descending. Sponsored by the R&B Bicycle Club in Julian, the event takes place in early spring and is limited to 100 hardy and experienced riders. Call 619-765-2200 for more information.

10 Coyote Canyon

Distance: 30 miles
Difficulty: Difficult because of length, technical because of road surfaces
Elevation: 250' gain, 3,400' loss; starts in Terwilliger at 3,840' and ends in Borrego Springs at about 200'
Ride Type: One-way downhill on rough, rocky, sandy dirt roads
Season: Winter. The canyon in closed from June 16 to September 15 to protect the watering rights of bighorn sheep. You don't want to be in the area during these hot months anyway.
Comments: It's best to get a friend to drop you off, or arrange a car shuttle. Carry lots of food and water as well as all the tools you will need. You're in the middle of nowhere on this ride.

This point-to-point downhill will test your endurance and bike-handling skills while taking you from the high desert through fragile riparian habitat and to the low desert. You even pass through an orange grove before you're done!

The route is similar to the Coyote Clunker Classic. This organized mountain bike ride is one of Southern California's best known off-road events. It is held each winter, usually the end of January. Contact MGE Racing, 1058 22nd Street, San Diego, CA 92102, (619) 239-4321 for information. Entry fee includes transportation to and from start/end points and a barbecue at the end.

If you do the ride on your own, it's best to convince a friend to drop you off at the start and pick you up at the end. The 90-minute commute between beginning and end makes a car shuttle difficult.

Getting There: This ride actually begins in Riverside County. Take Highway 79 to Aguanga, where you turn north on Highway 371. Fifteen miles later you reach Anza (named for Juan Bautista de Anza). Go 1.5 miles and turn south on Kirby Road. Continue for 4.5 miles to the intersection of Terwilliger Road and Coyote Canyon Road on the left. Park off to the side of the road. If you use a car shuttle, drop the shuttle vehicle in Borrego Springs.

Ride Coyote Canyon Road east. Go right at the T at 1.7 miles. After this the road gets rougher, but the view gets better. You can see Cleveland National Forest off to your right.

After a short, steep hill you reach the entrance to Anza-Borrego Desert State Park at 3.5 miles. The real fun starts here as you begin a steep, rutted and rocky downhill that will challenge intermediate riders. Once you hit Turkey Track, where several canyons converge in a turkey-foot pattern, you are greeted by soft sand. Lower your tires' air pressure and follow the wash southeast.

Those with the energy can take a side trip at 9 miles to Alder Canyon and Baily's Cabin. Others stay on the left fork.

Another 3.5 miles and you reach Middle Willows, an oasis of palm trees and mesquite bushes supported by Coyote Creek. Continue through the wash (you ride through the water

in spots) to the signed junction of Monkey Hill Trail and Main Wash Trail. Go right toward Salvador Canyon. Stay left at Salvador Canyon and again at Sheep Canyon. At 18.6 miles you reach Santa Catarina Springs, where you return to the water.

From here climb south on the auto road. You pass by a historical marker commemorating Anza's trips here. The road bends east, pitches down a slope and comes out below Lower Willows, an environmentally sensitive riparian habitat.

After three more stream crossings and more soft sand you pass an equestrian campground. As you head into Borrego Valley you pass those orange groves mentioned earlier. Borrego Springs Road awaits at 26.5 miles. Turn right. Pedal 3.5 miles to catch Christmas Circle to the center of Borrego Springs. Tah dah! You're done. Or maybe done for. Hopefully your friend is here to pick you up with some cold drinks and victuals.

Those unwilling or unable to ride the entire route may want to park near the first stream crossing on Indian Head Ranch Road outside of Borrego Springs at the bottom of the canyon. For a 12-mile route, head up the canyon toward Lower Willows, then left on the jeep trail to Collins Valley. A loop around the valley is equally pleasant in either direction. Be careful of a horses-only trail off to the right. A longer 20-mile route follows the directions above, but continues on to Middle Willows for an out-and-back route.

Regardless of the route you take, be courteous to other trail users: Lower and Middle Willows are among Anza-Borrego's most popular spots.

CHAPTER 2

Orange County

By Robert Rasmussen

Orange County, located midway between San Diego and Los Angeles, has never been mentioned in the same breath with America's great mountain biking spots. Most people are unaware the area has any good riding. In fact, the county's most well known "peak" is Disneyland's Matterhorn, hardly a boost to the public's perception of Orange County's mountain biking potential.

Many folks think of this area as a resort: four star hotels, elegant restaurants, ocean and miles of beautiful beaches (the Orange Coast). Newport Harbor, in Newport Beach, is the world's largest small boat harbor. Dinghies to million dollar yachts share the harbor's water for most of the year.

The remainder of the county, the place most locals know, is table flat. The land is covered by freeways and housing tracts. It is the last place you'd think would be good mountain biking territory. So where's the mountain biking?

Well, forget the common wisdom. Forget what you thought you knew about Orange County. The fact is there's plenty of good riding here. On your next visit to this area discover the great mountain biking opportunities within thirty minutes to one hour of most Orange County urban centers.

Most of the northern county is a level plain. The south is more mountainous. Inland from the coast, gentle rolling hills rise up from the flatlands. These hills and canyons were the grazing lands of early California's *ranchos*. Soon the hills soar into mountains 3,000 to 5,000 feet in elevation. These high ridges and peaks form the heart of Cleveland National Forest in isolated high country known as the Santa Ana Mountains. The range runs roughly north to south over 30 miles, forming the eastern border of Orange County. You can ride this entire distance atop the Santa Anas. There are also other USFS roads and trails to explore throughout Cleveland National Forest's 50,000-acre Trabuco District.

The valleys of the Santa Ana Mountains are narrow. Small seasonal creeks lined with oak and sycamore trees run through these canyons. Poison oak thrives here too along with the occasional rattlesnake, making cautious off-trail walking a must.

The mountainsides above the valleys are steep and covered with an

impenetrable brush. In full sun (especially from June through October), the areas above tree line can be unbearably hot. Fall and winter are the best times to ride the Santa Anas. Two to three quarts of water per person are needed while riding under these conditions.

The beauty of this backcountry is stunning. The higher elevations offer vistas of the Santa Ana Mountain canyons and foothills. Beyond (depending upon location) you can see several thousand square miles of land over five counties (including several major mountain ranges). The distant snow-capped peaks of winter are a delight to see. West across the sea lies Catalina Island, its rugged contours visible most of the year from the Santa Ana range. In addition to the mountainous terrain of Cleveland National Forest, there are other areas open to mountain biking in Orange County. The State of California and County of Orange maintain several "wilderness" parks that offer a wide variety of mountain biking experiences.

So, forget Disneyland. The best rides in the county are on a bicycle in the hills and valleys of Orange County's outback.

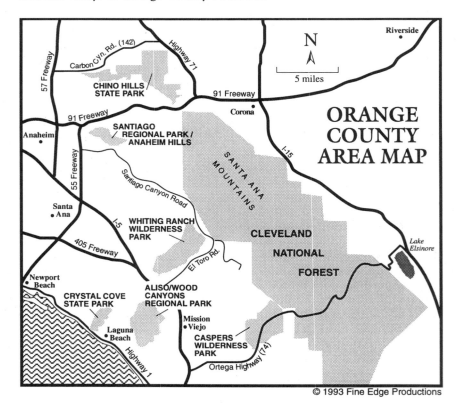

© 1993 Fine Edge Productions

11 *Crystal Cove State Park:* Moro Ridge Route

Distance: 6 miles
Difficulty: Moderate, steep, technical
Elevation: 900' gain
Ride Type: Loop on dirt roads and singletrack
Season: Year round

The very last stretch of open coastal land in Orange County's San Joaquin Hills is a part of Crystal Cove State Park. The area consists of a series of lush valleys and rolling hills high above the Pacific between Laguna Beach and Corona Del Mar. Year after year, the surrounding open areas are transformed piecemeal into suburbia. However, Crystal Cove State Park has saved several priceless coastal areas for public use. Among them is a 3,000-acre paradise called Moro Canyon. In the stillness of the coastal canyons and the shade of the tall trees you can imagine what this land was like not so long ago.

The canyon areas of the park comprise four main ridges and two valleys, running primarily north and south. Abundant plant life and seasonal streams combine to make a lovely place with just about every kind of mountain biking terrain imaginable. The major valley, Moro Canyon, is the main route north and south through the preserve. From Moro Canyon you can intersect with the many connecting trails, going anywhere into the park backcountry.

The early Spanish mapmakers called this place Lomarias de la Costa (ridge of hills on the coast). It was a part of Rancho San Joaquin, one of the many land grant cattle ranches that dominated early California. Jose de Sepulveda, the original grantee, received about 20,000 acres from the California governor in 1836. The land was sold to James Irvine in the 1860s: he purchased nearly half of modern-day Orange County for about 50 cents an acre.

The lands around Moro Canyon were used for farming and grazing from the early Spanish/Mexican days until late into the 20th century. The forested valley and chaparral-covered hills offer beauty and challenge to the mountain cyclist.

You can create many combinations of trails in Moro Canyon. Although small, this area combines both physical and technical challenge with great natural beauty. It also packs in a lot of fun and is probably the most

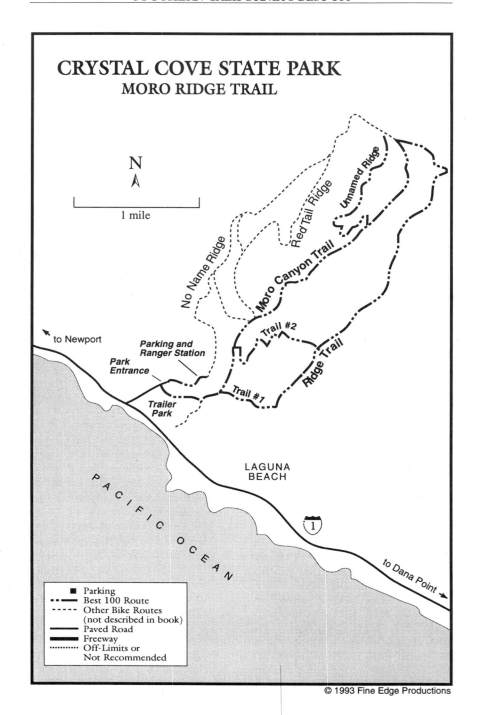

CRYSTAL COVE STATE PARK
MORO RIDGE TRAIL

N

1 mile

No Name Ridge

Red Tail Ridge

Unnamed Ridge

Moro Canyon Trail

Trail #2

Ridge Trail

to Newport

Parking and
Ranger Station

Park
Entrance

Trail #1

Trailer
Park

LAGUNA
BEACH

PACIFIC OCEAN

1

to Dana Point

■ Parking
▬·▬· Best 100 Route
- - - - Other Bike Routes
      (not described in book)
────── Paved Road
▬▬▬ Freeway
·········· Off-Limits or
          Not Recommended

© 1993 Fine Edge Productions

popular mountain bike riding site in Orange County. For more information, park personnel can be reached at 714-494-3539.

Getting There: From the 405 Freeway, take Laguna Canyon Road exit into Laguna Beach. Laguna Canyon dead-ends into Pacific Coast Highway. Turn right, heading north on Pacific Coast Highway 2 miles or so to the El Moro Canyon sign. Turn right. (There's a school on the corner.) Head up the small road and into the park. Park your car here and pay the State Park fee of $5 (there's a vending machine just outside the Ranger Headquarters.) There are restrooms and a nature center here as well as a campground. Rangers' headquarters is your only source of water.

Ride south from the parking lot toward the park entrance. Turn left on the dirt road that parallels the trailer park. The road drops 60 feet over the space of a couple hundred yards. Extreme beginners may wish to dismount and walk their bikes to flatter terrain below. Just a hundred yards or so past the trailer park is the first connector trail heading right to Moro Ridge. Previously closed to the public, Trail #1 was re-opened in September 1992. Once on Moro Ridge, point your bike up (northward), then walk n' ride a gnarly 1/3 mile or so. Farther up the ridge, the elevation becomes more gradual and you begin a long ascent. You travel from the 300 foot range to over 1,000 feet elevation at the far north end of the park. It is a good workout with great views. The trip down is fast and fun, and the track is solid and relatively clean of debris.

You can also reach Moro Ridge on a more gradual route. Ride up Moro Canyon about 1 mile from the trailer park and turn right on the second Moro Ridge connector trail. This gradual trail follows the contours of the land and is "do-able," but strenuous. The trail can make you hot and sweaty and cause you to breathe hard, but the ride down is electrifying.

Atop the ridge, looking to the north end of Moro Canyon, you find one of the park's more distinctive features: a stretch of narrow singletrack for those who enjoy this type of ride.

Approximately 200 to 300 yards before reaching the northern end of Moro Ridge Trail, leave the main road through an entry in a wire fence onto a foot trail. Follow that trail to the top of the hill (elevation 1,000+ feet) and down the other side to a fence line. The trail then continues for about a mile, twisting and turning, climbing and diving along the northern park boundary fence.

This singletrack lies on the high main ridge of the San Joaquin Hills. Among the coastal scrub and cactus there are views west and east along the ridge and down Moro Canyon.

The challenge of this ride is undeniable as the view switches from panoramic to the immediate area around the front wheel of your bike. Sharp turns, steep drops, roots, rocks, spiny cactus and unstable soil combine to demand all your attention and skill. This is first and foremost a technical ride.

Occasionally, you may lose the trail in a small chunk of dirt road. Always bear to the right. Go for the fence line until the end. This 1-mile trail takes you across three of the four major ridge lines and their interconnecting trails.

On these hillsides there used to be a little cactus that grazing cattle ate for brunch, keeping it in check. Now, however, it's spread everywhere and often grows quite close to the trail. Since this is a State Park, all plant species are protected. I urge you to ride cautiously, lest you knock down these cactus plants, damaging their tender spines and ravaging their flesh with your big strong bodies.

About 0.5 mile after entering the singletrack, the path dumps out onto the Moro Canyon Trail. To return to the parking lot you have two options: (1) A left turn takes you down a steep, hard, eroded surface (like riding down a washboard with ball bearings on it). Extreme caution is advised. This trail eventually takes you back to your car.

(2) A right turn from where the singletrack enters the same road will take you uphill a hundred yards or so to a junction of three trails—a much less treacherous route. Turn left and a dirt road gently descends a half mile along an unnamed ridge line. At the southern tip of this ridge, the road drops abruptly, beginning a steep descent to Moro Canyon Trail on the valley floor. This is the route that returns you to the parking lot. The canyon road drops ever so gently through lovely shaded oak groves and grasslands. This portion of the ride is visually pleasant and blessedly downhill!

12 *Aliso/Wood Canyons Regional Park:*
Rock-It/Cholla Loop

Distance: 7.1 miles
Difficulty: Intermediate, technical
Elevation: Begin 1,036'; low point 200'+; end 1,036'
Ride Type: Loop on dirt trails
Season: Year round

One of Orange County's best kept secrets is Aliso/Wood Canyons Regional Park, which is part of Laguna Niguel Regional Park. It lies hidden between Laguna Beach and Laguna Hills, a unique combination of city and county land. Its western portion is part of the Laguna Beach Greenbelt. The high, lush ridges have been secured as a source of open space and recreation. A series of trails and roads crisscross this area above Laguna Canyon Drive. From the ridge four other trails drop down into the park, which is county property. To-gether, these two parcels form an adult playground of over 5,000 acres.

In 1842 Juan Avila received this tract as part of a 13,000-acre land grant (Rancho Niguel). The land was used for farming and cattle grazing through the 1980s. Since then, suburban development has taken over the big California ranches.

For more information about the park, call 714-831-2174.

Getting There: From I-5 in Laguna Hills take La Paz Road south to Aliso Creek Road. Turn right and go 0.5

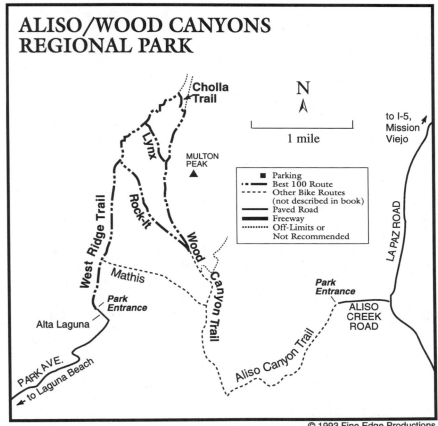

ALISO/WOOD CANYONS REGIONAL PARK

Cholla Trail

Lynx

MULTON PEAK ▲

N
⋏
|———————|
1 mile

to I-5, Mission Viejo

Rock-It

West Ridge Trail

■ Parking
▪·—·— Best 100 Route
----- Other Bike Routes
(not described in book)
——— Paved Road
▬▬▬ Freeway
········· Off-Limits or
Not Recommended

Wood

LA PAZ ROAD

Mathis

Canyon Trail

Park Entrance

Park Entrance

ALISO CREEK ROAD

Alta Laguna

Aliso Canyon Trail

PARK AVE.
← to Laguna Beach

© 1993 Fine Edge Productions

mile to the park entry signs. Cross Aliso Creek and bear to your left to enter the dirt parking lot area.

From Pacific Coast Highway in downtown Laguna Beach, turn onto Laguna Avenue (across from the old Laguna Hotel, one of the city's most famous landmarks). Head inland, and after one block, Laguna Avenue becomes Park Avenue. Park Avenue leads through the city, high into the hills directly to Alta Laguna Boulevard. Turn left and go 200 yards. On your right is a park. The ridge bike path begins at the street's dead-end. The highest point in Laguna Beach

lies within the park: locals call it Top of the World, and the view is fabulous. Water is available only at this entry at Alta Laguna Park.

From the dead end of Alta Laguna, begin your long descent atop the West Ridge Trail. At 1.6 miles you'll see a water tank and facilities to your left. Turn right on a road that intersects nearby. You're now on the Rock-It Trail.

I'm not sure how the trail received its name. But there's a lot of rock everywhere, offering all the excitement of rock n' roll as the steep terrain makes for rocket-like acceleration—more than you will need or want.

This downhill is a thoroughly challenging trail: steep drops, rocky paths and eroded soil. As the trail approaches the lower end of the ridge you see a path to the left and another to the right at the beginning of a large meadow. Take the left path; the right is for hikers only.

Cross through the grassy meadow, which has immense old trees. After about 1/4 mile you enter a steep creek embankment. On the other side turn left onto Wood Can-

yon Trail, the dirt road that runs prominently through the valley.

Continue through the valley another few miles until you see Cholla Trail on your left. It is marked by brown park signs, but there is no mention of the name Cholla. (County Rangers report that new trail signs are on their way.)

After you reach the Laguna Ridge again, turn left from Cholla Trail onto the main trail to return to your car. It's uphill all the way (about 400 feet)—time to pay for all the fun you had!

Cleveland National Forest

A good portion of the Santa Ana Mountains lies within Cleveland National Forest, a rugged area of steep mountainsides and narrow, rocky valleys covered with thick vegetation. Although close to urban areas, Cleveland National Forest is a true backcountry region. The harshness of these mountains will convince you that travel would be impossible without the trails and roads that were so laboriously built here.

The highest peak in the region—Santiago? Saddleback? Modjeska? The answer is all of the above. Saddleback Mountain is actually made up of two separate peaks—Modjeska and Santiago—which are connected by a long ridge.

13 Silverado Canyon to Maple Spring Trail

Distance: 16 miles (or turn back at any point)
Difficulty: Easy, nontechnical
Elevation: Begin/end 900'; high point 2,500'
Ride Type: Out and back on paved and dirt roads
Season: Year round

Silverado Canyon was known by the early Hispanic settlers as Cañada de la Madera (Timber Canyon). The trees in the valley and on the mountain above were cut to form the structural elements of Mission San Juan Capistrano and other early California buildings.

The canyon was renamed Silverado in 1877 after silver was discovered and mined there. More trees were felled to build mine shafts and a thriving city of 1,500 people. The valley boomed. Regular stage transport ran between Los Angeles and Santa Ana. After a few years the silver ore played out and the glory days of Silverado came to a close.

Climbing steadily through Silverado Canyon you pass shady glens, pleasant creeks and pine forests—the latter not immediately associated with this arid coastal region.

Finally, you find panoramic beauty atop the highest ridges of the Santa Ana Mountains.

Getting There: From the City of Orange and the 55 Freeway, take Chapman Avenue east. Chapman becomes Santiago Canyon Road after 5 miles. Continue another 5 miles to Silverado Canyon Road and make a left.

From the I-5 Freeway in the Mission Viejo area take El Toro Road east 7.6 miles to the fork. Go left onto Santiago Canyon Road. Drive north five miles to the Silverado Canyon exit and turn right.

Park at any one of numerous spots near the highway and bordering the Water District facilities. You can get water at the U.S. Forest Service Station at the beginning of Silverado Canyon.

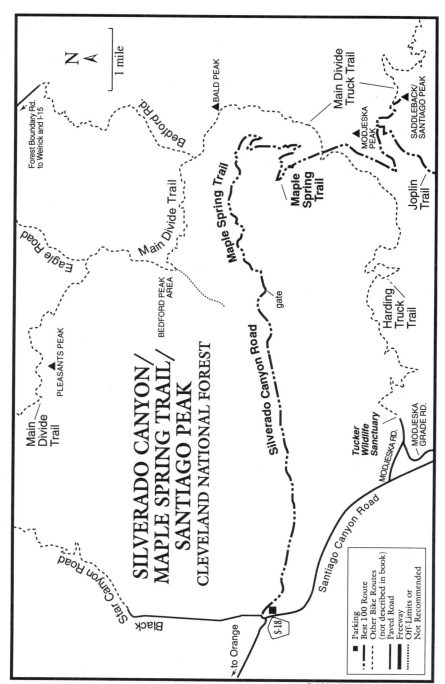

SILVERADO CANYON/
MAPLE SPRING TRAIL/
SANTIAGO PEAK
CLEVELAND NATIONAL FOREST

N
1 mile

Forest Boundary Rd.
to Weirick and I-15

Bedford Rd.

BALD PEAK

Main Divide
Truck Trail

MODJESKA
PEAK

SADDLEBACK/
SANTIAGO PEAK

Eagle Road

Main Divide Trail

Maple Spring Trail

Maple
Spring
Trail

Joplin
Trail

BEDFORD PEAK
AREA

gate

Harding
Truck
Trail

PLEASANTS PEAK

Silverado Canyon Road

Main
Divide
Trail

Tucker
Wildlife
Sanctuary

MODJESKA
GRADE RD.

MODJESKA RD.

Santiago Canyon Road

Star Canyon Road

Black

S·18

to Orange

Parking

Best 100 Route

Other Bike Routes
(not described in book)

Paved Road

Freeway

Off-Limits or
Not Recommended

© 1993 Fine Edge Productions

The first 5.5 miles of the road into Silverado Canyon are on a two-lane blacktop highway. The first 2 or 3 miles are not particularly noteworthy. As you get in farther, however, you'll notice a mixture of old-fashioned and newer homes nestled between the canyon hillsides and Santiago Creek. Many of the old homes look like miniature dollhouses—so tiny, I've often wondered how the occupants were able to stand erect within. Silverado and surrounding canyons are home to many equestrians who prize their livestock, dogs and secluded ranch lifestyle. Please do not trespass on private land.

Moving farther down the canyon, the pavement ends at a metal pipe Forest Service gate. Maple Spring Road (5S04) begins here as a dirt road. Beyond this spot there are no homes, the canyon narrows and the oak trees grow tall and thick along Silverado Creek. The road curves its way gently through the valley, and the sounds of birds and creek predominate. The ride continues in this way for another 2 to 3 miles past the gate. Finally, you cross the creek, make a sharp right turn and begin a steep climb up the hill. I recommend that beginners turn around at this point; more experienced riders will want to continue.

However far you ride, retrace your route back to your vehicle. Grab a cold drink in one of the stores in the canyon or something to eat at the local cafe.

14 Silverado Canyon to Santiago Peak

Distance: 22 miles
Difficulty: Moderate to difficult, nontechnical
Elevation: Begin/end 1,800'; high point 5,687'
Ride Type: Out and back on dirt roads
Season: Year round
Topo Maps: USGS 7.5 minute series (Santiago Peak, Corona South)

Getting There: See the previous ride. Drive up Silverado Canyon to the metal pipe gate.

Begin your trip to Saddleback by heading up Maple Spring Trail to the Main Divide Truck Trail (3S04) and a four-way trail junction. Ascend a slight incline and make a quick right onto the Main Divide Truck Trail. Ride south toward Santiago Peak, the highest part of Saddleback Mountain. Four miles and about 1,000 feet more of elevation gain puts you atop Santiago Peak, up a short spur from the Main Divide Trail.

Depending upon air quality, the views are spectacular. Walk around the peak. Note Catalina Island across the way. Orange County, Los Angeles and Riverside counties lie before you. Drink to replace lost fluids and eat to regain used nutrients. Take a couple "cheesecake" photos for posterity and even some landscape shots—the kind that seem so good in the viewfinder but come back looking like satellite photos of earth.

Return to Silverado Canyon by the same route. Coming down off the peak, be sure to take the left fork of 3S04. (A right turn will drop you off on the wrong side of the mountain and you will have to retrace your route uphill.)

Continue to the four-way trail junction and turn left onto Maple Spring Trail. Go straight downhill toward the stands of pine trees. Avoid road hazards on the descent. Seven miles and seemingly a few moments later you reach your car.

15 Modjeska Canyon's Santiago Truck Trail

Distance: 13 miles
Difficulty: Moderate, nontechnical
Elevation: Begin/end 1,600'; high point 3,400' feet.
Ride Type: Out and back on dirt roads
Season: In dry seasons Santiago Truck Trail may occasionally be closed by the Orange County Fire Marshal. (You can't miss the sign if it is.) Call 714-736-1811 or 714-649-2645 for fire information.
Topo Maps: USGS 7.5 minute series (Santiago Peak)

Modjeska Canyon is another of Orange County's cozy riparian valleys. It is named for Helena Modjeska, a Polish immigrant actress who found success on the American stage. Madame Modjeska purchased several hundred acres in the canyon and built an estate named "Arden," in reference to the forest of Arden in Shakespeare's comedy, *As You Like It.* The home is currently undergoing restoration as a historic monument.

The life of the free-spirited actress is today honored by a group called the Daughters of Helena Modjeska, Orange County women who host stultifying luncheons at which they wear funny hats and consume vast amounts of tea.

Getting There: From the 55 Freeway in Orange, take Chapman Avenue east. Chapman becomes Santiago Canyon Road after 5 miles. Continue 9.1 miles to Modjeska Grade Road, turn left and find a metal gate on your right in about a quarter mile.

From I-5 in Mission Viejo take El Toro Road 7.6 miles east to the fork. Go left onto Santiago Canyon Road, and in 0.9 mile turn right at Modjeska Grade Road. The gate is on the right about a quarter mile up.

Park your car along the black-top. Do not park in the trailhead driveway; your car will be ticketed or towed.

Enter the gate, take the dirt road to your right and ride up into the hills. The road snakes up the contours of the hill. Look above and to your left where you can catch glimpses of the Harding Truck Trail climbing steadily above you towards Saddleback Mountain. The Santiago Truck Trail climbs the high ridge above Mission Viejo. The views below expand with your upward progress, with suburban and canyon views growing to become grand, scenic vistas.

At 6.5 miles you come to the Joplin Road, which drops sharply downhill and dead-ends. Don't make the mistake of taking it. There is no exit.

Santiago Truck Trail forks 1 mile beyond Joplin Road. Take the left fork that drops into a small valley ending at Old Camp, said to be the site of an ancient Indian hunting camp. (The right fork dead-ends into the mountain.) Joplin Foot Trail, which climbs sharply up from Old Camp to Saddleback Mountain, is described in Ride 17.

Retrace your route back to your car after a thoroughly enjoyable ride.

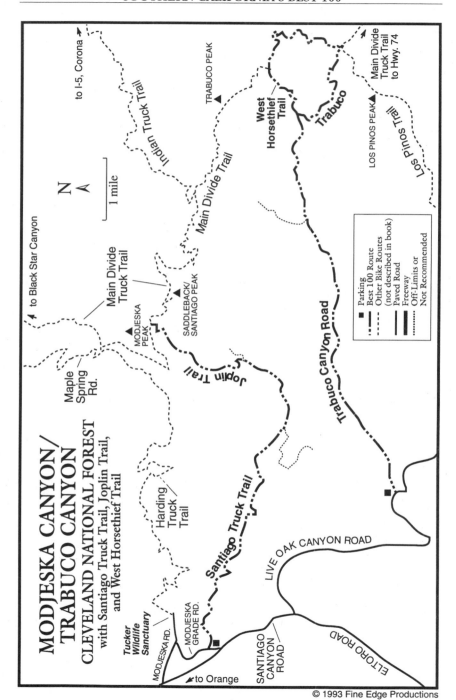

MODJESKA CANYON/ TRABUCO CANYON
CLEVELAND NATIONAL FOREST
with Santiago Truck Trail, Joplin Trail, and West Horsethief Trail

N

1 mile

to I-5, Corona

to Black Star Canyon

TRABUCO PEAK

West Horsethief Trail

Trabuco

Main Divide Truck Trail to Hwy. 74

LOS PINOS PEAK

Los Pinos Trail

Irujian Truck Trail

Main Divide Trail

Main Divide Truck Trail

MODJESKA PEAK

SADDLEBACK/ SANTIAGO PEAK

Maple Spring Rd.

Joplin Trail

Trabuco Canyon Road

Harding Truck Trail

Santiago Truck Trail

LIVE OAK CANYON ROAD

Tucker Wildlife Sanctuary

MODJESKA RD.

MODJESKA GRADE RD.

SANTIAGO CANYON ROAD

EL TORO ROAD

to Orange

Parking
Best 100 Route
Other Bike Routes (not described in book)
Paved Road
Freeway
Off-Limits or Not Recommended

© 1993 Fine Edge Productions

16 Trabuco Trail/ West Horse Thief Trail

Distance: 11.5 miles
Difficulty: Moderately strenuous, technical
Elevation: Begin/end 1,900'; high point 4,200'
Ride Type: Loop on singletrack
Season: Year round
Topo Maps: USGS 7.5 minute series (Santiago Peak, Alberhill)

Getting There: Take I-5 to Mission Viejo. Exit on El Toro Road and head 7.6 miles east to where the road forks. Go right onto Live Oak Canyon Road (S19). Approximately 2 miles later you pass O'Neill Regional Park and find an open creek bed to your left. A dirt road enters the creek's flood plain area. This is the entrance to Trabuco Canyon. If your car has low clearance, park at the canyon entrance.

Provided your vehicle has adequate clearance, drive up Trabuco Canyon and park your car 1 mile beyond Holy Jim Canyon at road's end (plenty of parking). Bring plenty of water since there is none en route.

Ride the rocky trail 1.8 miles to the junction of West Horse Thief Trail and Trabuco Trail. Take the right fork, which is much better for uphill travel than the West Horse Thief Trail, which is too steep and has soil conditions that make riding extremely difficult.

The lower portion of Trabuco Trail is very rocky. You ascend a small canyon and enter some of the lushest woodlands in the Santa Ana Mountains. Large bushes grow over the trail in many areas forming "Hobbit Tunnels" for you to glide through in the gloom of the darkened forest. The trails improve substantially for bike riding the higher you climb toward Los Piños saddle and the Main Divide Truck Trail.

You emerge from the forest onto 3S04 at Los Piños Saddle, 2.7 miles from the lower trail junction on Trabuco Creek. Turn left. In 3 miles of elevation gains and losses you find the West Horse Thief Trail (5401) on your left, which begins as a firebreak and becomes a footpath. At 1.9 miles down the mountain you struggle with an unending series of switchbacks, twisting and sliding on unstable shale soil. You might ask yourself, "Am I riding or skiing?" and you answer "Both" until you finally reach the valley bottom linking you with Trabuco Canyon Trail. From here you have a serene ride back to your car at the end of Trabuco Road.

17 Joplin Trail via Santiago Truck Trail

Distance: 20.4 miles
Difficulty: Strenuous, technical
Elevation: Begin/end 1,500'; high point 4,900'
Ride Type: Loop on dirt roads and singletrack
Season: Year round
Topo Maps: USGS 7.5 minute series (Santiago Peak)

Getting There: From Orange and the 55 Freeway, go east on Chapman, which becomes Santiago Canyon Road. Drive 14.1 miles to Modjeska Grade Road and turn left. In about a half mile you reach a metal pipe gate beneath several power line towers.

From the Mission Viejo area take I-5 to El Toro Road and head east 7.6 miles to where the road forks. Turn left onto Santiago Canyon Road. Drive 0.9 mile more to Modjeska Grade Road and turn right. Proceed about a half mile to the steel gate beneath the power lines.

Bring lots of water, since none is available here.

Pass the metal gate and ride the Santiago Truck Trail 7.5 miles through the hills. The road snakes its way around the contours of the land past some of Orange County's most eye-catching rock formations. At about mile 5.5 you'll see a road dropping sharply to the right off the Santiago Trail. This is the Joplin Road (not Joplin Trail), which dead-ends several hundred feet below Santiago Trail. Pass it by; there's no exit.

Two miles later you reach a fork in the road. Take the left fork, and the road drops into a small river valley. (The right fork dead-ends after about a mile.) This valley is the site of Old Camp, reputedly an ancient hunting camp used by local Indians. Follow the road into a small clearing. Look across the clearing (left) to an opposite hillside. (The hillside is part of a valley dropping into Old Camp from above.) Find and take a small footpath (there are no signs) that leads you up the valley 2.2 miles to the Main Divide Truck Trail (3S04).

The path is steep. Expert riders will streak upwards to the amazement and shame of the rest of us. Intermediate riders will "walk n' ride" steadily to the top. Large sections of the trail are well done, however, enabling you to realistically bike most of the distance. Not only is Joplin Trail beautiful, but you'll be pleased to note that few people use it. The day you ride there it will probably be your own private park. Returning to your car from the top of Joplin Trail is its own reward. You will bob, weave, brake and slide down this entire narrow ribbon of trail. Joplin Trail is "E ticket" riding material all the way. On completing the trip down, the only question in your mind will be, "When do we come back?"

From Old Camp on the Santiago Truck Trail, return 7.7 miles to your car.

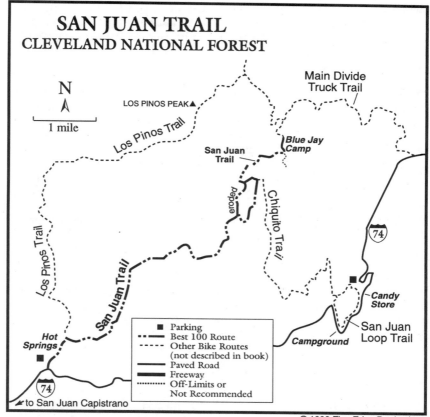

SAN JUAN TRAIL
CLEVELAND NATIONAL FOREST

N

1 mile

LOS PINOS PEAK▲

Los Pinos Trail

Main Divide
Truck Trail

San Juan
Trail

Blue Jay
Camp

eroded

Chiquito Trail

Los Pinos Trail

San Juan Trail

74

Candy
Store

San Juan
Loop Trail

Campground

Hot
Springs

■ Parking
-·-·- Best 100 Route
----- Other Bike Routes
       (not described in book)
―― Paved Road
━━ Freeway
········· Off-Limits or
       Not Recommended

74

to San Juan Capistrano

© 1993 Fine Edge Productions

18 San Juan Trail to Blue Jay Camp

Distance: 22 miles
Difficulty: Strenuous, technical
Elevation: Begin/end 800'; high point 3,300'
Ride Type: Out and back on singletrack
Season: Year round
Topo Maps: USGS 7.5 minute series (Cañada Gobernadora, Alberhill)

Getting There: Take I-5 to San Juan Capistrano. Exit on Highway 74 and drive east 12.5 miles. You'll see a sign for San Juan Hot Springs and notice some Forest Service buildings. Turn left here and drive down the canyon 1 mile to the trailhead. (There is plenty of parking in a grove of trees to the left.)

The trail begins as a series of

switchbacks going straight up the mountainside. Daunting as it looks, the trail is well-engineered and the grades are within the abilities of us "mere mortals."

Approximately 3 to 4 miles from the entrance of the trail you begin passing high ridges and mountain tops. The great valleys lie here and there. You see Highway 74 as a tiny line stretched across the mountains. The climb is sometimes steep and other times gradual, but always relentless to 3,000+ feet. I caution you to take the greatest care when you ride this route, especially on the down side. Every gnarly rock, root and pitfall imaginable exists on this wonderful trail. You'll note the path has lots of foot traffic, especially on weekends.

At mile 5.4 the trail forks, with an eroded old road (Route A) to the left and a continuation of the footpath (Route B) to the right. Both paths wind up at Blue Jay Camp.

Route A: At the San Juan Trail junction bear left on the deteriorated road. Follow this about 4 miles to a meadow area. You'll cross over another path and climb up a steep hill. (The soil is rocky and unstable.) Near the top of the hill is another footpath. Turn right and ride a mile or so to Blue Jay Camp.

Route B: At the San Juan Trail junction bear right. After riding the footpath to mile 9, you pass by Chiquito Trail on the right. Bear left on the path skirting the bottom of a hill. At the bottom you cross over an old road and take the gentle switchbacks up the hill to Blue Jay Camp. The camp area, which affords shade and usually has water, is a great spot to rest before your return.

Chino Hills State Park

Who'd have believed it? Twelve thousand acres of prime ranch country open to you and me in Orange County! One small corner of peace remaining in a too-fast world. Chino Hills is like all the other gorgeous oak-dotted hill country you've ever seen in California, the kind of place that makes you want to jump on your bike and ride off into the sunset.

Chino Hills is a land of seasons, fields of gold and brown most of the year. It's a world gone green in winter and spring, the optimum seasons for riding in the park when temperatures are moderate and air quality usually good. In summer and fall—when daytime temperatures are extremely high and when smog can obscure the views or be physically harmful—it's best to ride in early morning or evening.

Air quality permitting, views across north and south ridges are spectacular when snow covers the local mountains. Chino Hills State Park is a great place to ride and unwind; it's close to the city and easy to get to. For riding, views and open space, it is a key community resource.

The campground at the south end of Bane Valley has several water spigots by the side of the road. These are the only sources of drinking water in the park. The water available to you from these pipes is for emergency use only; because of its taste no one would willingly drink it! It's best to bring your own water—a minimum of 2 quarts per person.

19 Aliso Valley

Distance: 8 miles
Difficulty: Beginner, nontechnical
Elevation: Begin/end 700'; end of canyon 400'
Ride Type: Out and back on dirt road
Season: Year round

In terms of work and visual beauty, this is an ideal beginners' mountain bike ride.

Getting There: From north Orange County take the 55 Freeway to the 91 Freeway and head east toward Corona. At Prado Dam take the off-ramp for Highway 71 north (toward Pomona). Continue north on this busy, narrow road 6 miles to Pomona-Rincon Road. Turn left and continue along Pomona-Rincon a short distance north past a brick works to Soquel Canyon Drive. Turn left and drive another mile to Elinvar Drive. Turn left again. After a very short distance on Elinvar turn right onto a dirt road and begin driving up into the hills. In a mile you'll reach the boundary of the park. Continue through a gate and gently descend through Bane Valley.

At the end of Bane Valley you pass the campground up around a hill. In another quarter mile or so is the Ranger Headquarters with plenty of public parking.

A treat to see, the headquarters is the old Rolling M Ranch, whose buildings have been converted for use as public facilities. The former ranch house is the park office, and the former barn is used as a work area. The windmill water pumps still stand as reminders of the area's rich ranching history.

From Park Headquarters, take your bike south on the blacktop road. Just after leaving the ranch area you pass a dirt road on your right, the trailhead for Telegraph Canyon Trail. In another 100 yards you pass a second dirt road on the right. This is the beginning of South Ridge Trail, the park's longest trail.

Keep following the blacktop street around a hill and down toward the campground. Turn right into the camping area and ride the dirt road to a metal gate. Take your bike through the special opening in the gate and begin your ride.

Entering Aliso Canyon (south) is a visual experience. Vast expanses of the valley bottom are filled with lush fields of wild oats and large oak trees, gnarled and very old. The entire scene is strikingly beautiful, open and wide.

The main Aliso Valley Trail (north and south) is intersected by trails at many points. Trails from the east side of the valley all dead-end into private land—do not ride these trails. Trails from the west side of the canyon are okay to ride.

Half a mile from the camp area is the first connector trail, which leads to Water Canyon, Scully Ridge Trail and Bobcat Ridge Trail. Pass by this first set of trails and continue south into Aliso Canyon. As you ride you'll notice small roads dead-ending into gullies and at the base of hills. Often

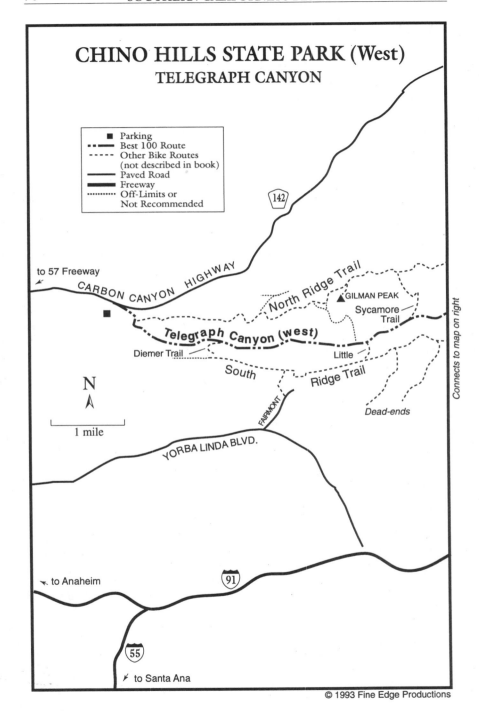

CHINO HILLS STATE PARK (West)
TELEGRAPH CANYON

■ Parking
━·━ Best 100 Route
--- Other Bike Routes
       (not described in book)
── Paved Road
▬▬ Freeway
······ Off-Limits or
       Not Recommended

142

to 57 Freeway

CARBON CANYON HIGHWAY

North Ridge Trail

▲GILMAN PEAK

Sycamore Trail

Telegraph Canyon (west)

Diemer Trail

Little

South

Ridge Trail

Dead-ends

N

1 mile

FAIRMONT

YORBA LINDA BLVD.

to Anaheim

91

55

to Santa Ana

Connects to map on right

© 1993 Fine Edge Productions

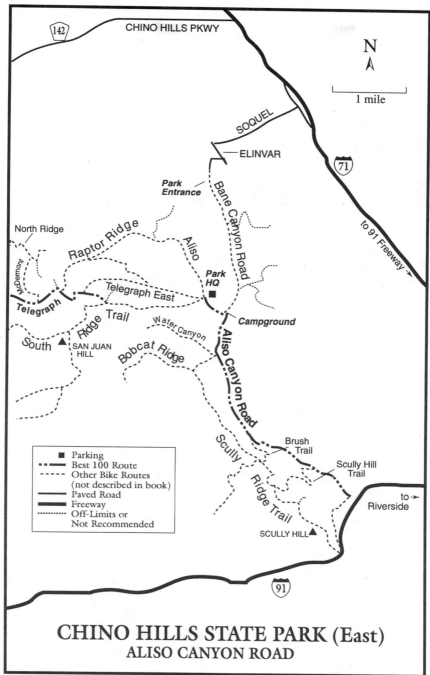

CHINO HILLS STATE PARK (East)
ALISO CANYON ROAD

is 300 feet, so gradual as to be nearly unnoticeable.

It's possible to link up with the Scully Ridge Trail from Aliso Valley beyond the park's southern boundary. Ride through the park entry gate down a dirt road for about a hundred yards until you come to a second dirt road. Turn right and ride a short distance to a stock gate. The gate opens out onto a large meadow. (Cyclists have permission to cross this land. Since horses are sometimes grazed here, you must re-lock each opened gate to prevent the loss of animals.) In less than half a mile the road passes south through the large meadow. The dirt road winds around the end of the West Ridge a short distance from some railroad tracks. On the right you'll find a blacktop road descending from the West Ridge above. Ride up the blacktop, which gives way to dirt higher up—the south end of the Scully Ridge Trail.

there are manhole covers at the end of the roads, water wells tended by the local water district. Beneath Chino Hills State Park is a rich aquifer whose waters supply Orange County.

Riding down the valley 1.8 miles from the campground entry you'll pass a second connector trail on the right. This is Brush Canyon Trail, one large switchback climbing to the top of the western ridge. (With over 400 feet of elevation gain, I recommend this climb to all muscle freaks and other like-minded mortifiers of the flesh. As you'd expect from such a steep trail the downhill run is hot, the kind that broken bones are made of. Caution advised: 15 mph limit.)

Riding farther south through Aliso Canyon, at 2.6 miles from the campground you pass Scully Hill Trail on your right. It rises abruptly to the Scully Ridge Trail with over 500 feet of elevation gain. Yes, it's definitely a challenging ride both up and down the Western Ridge.

Moving south from this last connector trail you come to the end of Aliso Valley at a well-marked metal gate. To return to the ranch area, retrace your steps up the valley. The elevation gain on your 4-mile return

Horses: I know nothing about horses; they intimidate me. But one day as I was riding with a friend, I passed a large group of horses in this meadow. My buddy showed me how to stop, then walk forward slowly so as not to frighten the animals. He put out his hands to reassure them and within a few moments several horses became downright friendly! We then rode slowly away without spooking any of the animals. This seemed like a good way to handle the situation. When you're in doubt, always ask the horseback rider.

20 Telegraph Canyon Trail to the Main Divide

Distance: 11 miles
Difficulty: Easy, nontechnical
Elevation: Begin/end 500'; high point 1,500'
Ride Type: Out and back on dirt road
Season: Year round
Maps: USGS 7.5 minute series (Yorba Linda, Prado Dam)

Getting There: This ride begins on the west side of Chino Hills State Park. In the Brea area of Orange County traveling on the 57 Freeway, exit at Lambert. Drive east until the street becomes Brea Canyon Drive. After 2.2 miles you'll see Carbon

Canyon Regional Park on your right.

Carbon Canyon Regional Park is the best place to park for your trip into the western Chino Hills. It's patrolled, cheap and easy to get in and out of (just bring two crisp Yankee Dollars to feed the "android" lot attendant).

Leave Carbon Canyon Park at the entrance and turn right, riding past an orchard. At a metal gate pass around and onto a blacktop road. The road dips into a creek bed. Most of the time there's water running in the creek, quite a bit in wintertime. The creek has a firm bottom so don't be afraid to roll on through. You rise out of the creek bed onto the other side and come upon another fence. Note the open entry and pass through. At this point you'll see one dirt road going right and another left. Take the right-hand road. The left road climbs into the hills to become the North Ridge Trail.

Continue on the right-hand trail a few yards until another dirt road breaks off to the left near some park displays. Turn left and begin the Telegraph Canyon Trail (west).

Telegraph Canyon Trail begins as a very narrow valley following the bed of a seasonal creek. The canyon widens as it twists its way deeper into the hills. At first the canyon is largely grasslands with a few scattered bushes and trees. This later gives way to larger stands of oak and huge sycamore trees that dominate the landscape. The entire ride through Telegraph Canyon has a nearly imperceptible elevation gain. In 5.5 miles you climb approximately 1,000 feet, but you hardly notice it due to its gradual nature.

There are many trails leading out of Telegraph Valley to other locations within the park. As you pedal up the valley road, you see the following connector trails:

Diemer Trail (named after the treatment plant up the hill on the right) leads from Telegraph Valley to the top of South Ridge. It begins on your right 1.5 miles from Carbon Canyon parking lot and climbs steeply up South Ridge. Little Canyon Trail, 1.8 miles beyond Diemer Trail, drops steeply from the South Ridge, connecting with Telegraph Canyon. Continue past this road. Sycamore Trail intersects Telegraph Canyon Trail from the left 0.5 mile beyond Little Canyon Trail. From the top of North Ridge it drops almost 500 feet in a very short distance, making it a downhill to remember. McDermont Trail comes in from the left 0.5 mile beyond Sycamore Trail. It leads up to the top of North Ridge and represents the very end of the North Ridge Trail. A few hundred yards beyond McDermont Trail is a crossroads of trails leading to various areas of the park. This is the Main Divide area.

You enter the Main Divide (west) on Telegraph Canyon Trail, several hundred yards east of McDermont Trail. What is the Main Divide? It is a north-south ridge, approximately 1,500 feet at its high point, that roughly separates the east and west sides of Chino Hills State Park, which is primarily comprised of ridges and valleys running generally east and west.

Find a dirt road off to your left (a dead-end). Next is a small footpath also on the left. Continue riding on Telegraph Canyon Trail past the footpath around a bend and over the crest of the Divide. You are now on the East Main Divide.

Shortly after passing over the Divide a trail on the left heads quickly downhill. This is the Telegraph Canyon Trail (east), which empties into Aliso Valley. Continuing on the Telegraph Trail, a few hundred yards after the last connection, there are three trailheads on the right. The left road is a dead-end. The right path going downhill is the South Ridge Trail and a wild ride to Aliso Valley below. The right path going uphill is the South Ridge Trail heading back (west) toward the Telegraph Canyon entrance to the park. This junction marks the end of Telegraph Canyon Trail (west). To return to your car simply reverse the previous directions.

For additional rides in this area, please refer to *Mountain Biking the Coast Range, Guide 11: Orange County and Cleveland National Forest*, by Robert Rasmussen, ISBN 0-938665-17-0 (see p. 304).

CHAPTER 3

Coachella Valley– Riverside County

By Paul Maag

Great mountain bike riding can be found in the mountains south of Palm Springs and in the general vicinity of Idyllwild. This is an area of great transition from low Colorado desert to high alpine terrain. The regions has been known for years to a small group of locals and pro riders, including Cindy Whitehead and other well-known early mountain bikers. The San Jacinto and Santa Rosa Mountains offer some of the finest riding in the nation, especially in the winter months. When the north country is locked in snow and even the southern California coast is locked in fog and drizzle, Coachella Valley offers clear blue skies and warm temperatures.

The lower Santa Rosa Mountains near Palm Springs are rugged, rolling hills with rocky, loose trail features. Most of the trails were built by equestrians, and many steep trails offer a gripping challenge for the mountain bicyclist. The landscape can look foreboding, something like a moonscape in very dry and hot years. Springtime riding along the ridges of the Santa Rosa Mountains can be most rewarding—1993 brought the most rain in many years and a wonderful burst of desert wildflowers.

The upper Santa Rosa Mountains and the San Jacinto Mountains offer a range of land types from brushy chaparral to cool pine forests. These higher rangers offer spectacular views from many of the trails described in this chapter. The singletrack trails here rate high when compared to many trails in Moab, Utah, or California's Sierra Nevada. Best of all, these trails are not crowded with other users. On many of them it is common not to encounter anyone else. This is a true mountain biking paradise!

Make sure you bring lots of water on rides in the desert. Three jumbo water bottles can sometimes last only an hour or two. Many cyclists have found that some of the new insulated water carriers can be very beneficial in addition to the standard two or three water bottles. You can never take too much water on a ride in this kind of climate, especially in warm months.

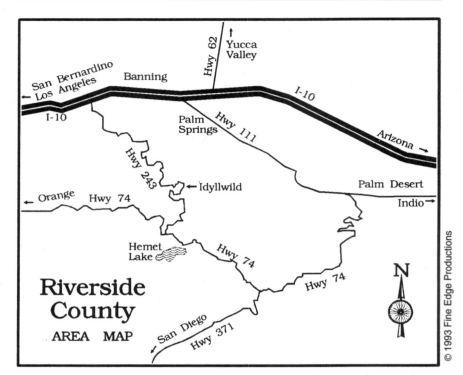

The weather can change quickly in both the higher mountains and the desert. The top of Mount Santa Rosa can be 40 degrees cooler than the desert below. Be prepared for such changes with the appropriate clothing, water and sun block.

The Coachella Valley Cycling Association offers weekly rides in the Santa Rosa Mountains. If you are not familiar with the area or are alone it is highly recommended that you hook up with the group rides. Members can give you knowledge about additional trail routes, times for travel, tips for bettering your skills and some good camaraderie along the trail. To reach a member just call 619-360-0761 or 619-320-7135, or stop in at one of the local bike shops.

The Santa Rosa Mountains National Scenic Area (SRMNSA) just south of Palm Springs, as well as areas managed by the Bureau of Land Management (BLM) and the National Forest Service, are not all owned by public agencies. The SRMNSA is a checkerboard of private, public and Agua Caliente tribal allotee lands. Land management policies and consequently biking access are under constant review.

Please check with the appropriate government office or land owner for current information:

Bureau of Land Management, Palm Springs South Coast Resource Area 63500 Garnet Ave., North Palm Springs, CA 92264 • (619) 251-0812

Coachella Valley Cycling Association
P.O. Box 2355, Rancho Mirage CA 92270

San Bernardino National Forest, San Jacinto Ranger District
P.O. Box 518, Idyllwild, CA 92349 (909) 659-2117

For topographical maps, visit the Desert Map Shop, 73612 Highway 111, Palm Desert, CA 92260.

Special Notes:

The Pinyon/Palm Canyon Loop and the Live Oak Canyon Trail are some of the best mountain bicycle riding in the country. However, both routes have their share of land access problems. With the help of the Coachella Valley Cycling Association and the International Mountain Bicycling Association, these issues are being addressed. Their value as spectacular routes outweighs the option of not mentioning these rides.

Both routes enter into the Palm Canyon drainage area and trail, which has been proposed as wilderness by the Sierra Club as of this printing. Wilderness status has been proposed for this area previously and has been rejected. Check with the U.S. Forest Service in Idyllwild for the current management status for these two trails.

You will also need to contact the U.S. Forest Service for Live Oak Canyon access through Penrod Canyon Road. This road crosses land owned by various individuals. Easement rights have been given to public access for all lands except for one small parcel. When in doubt, inquire first.

21 Pinyon/Palm Canyon Loop

Distance: 13 miles
Difficulty: Moderate, mildly technical
Elevation: 1,000' gain; high point 4,400'
Season: All year
Ride Type: Loop on dirt roads, singletrack, some pavement

This is one of the most enjoyable rides in this chapter. Be sure to bring extra water, especially in summer, and extra tubes.

Getting There: Start by driving 17.3 miles south from Palm Desert on Highway 74. Turn right on Palm Canyon Drive. Park at the dozer track behind the mailboxes.

Ride north on Palm Canyon Drive and at 3.3 miles turn left (west) on the unmarked road 150 feet after Chalet Drive (the last road before the two large upright posts). Follow the sandy road 0.2 mile, and at a big rock (the second dirt road on the right), take a right and then a left again. At 0.7 mile, just after a quick sandy jump, look left and find an unmarked singletrack along a fence line. Follow the singletrack south and then southwest through some very quick and technical turns. Continue over a ridge and then descend very steeply into Palm Canyon. Warning: This portion of the trail is very technical and requires that both front and rear brakes be applied almost to the maximum in some sections.

When you reach the bottom of the canyon (at 5.3 miles) look across Omstot Creek (dry much of the year) and find the trail going up the side of the hill. This is the Palm Canyon trail. Follow the trail south (left) and switch back up to the ridge top. Ride the

ridge until you descend to a cattle fence, making sure to close it after you pass. Continue south up a steep climb to a stack of cairns and turn right on the doubletrack. Continue through easy switchbacks to the Palm Canyon trailhead parking lot at 9.4 miles.

Turn left at Highway 74 and head east 3.6 miles. Turn left on Palm Canyon Drive to your car. Pretty good ride, huh!

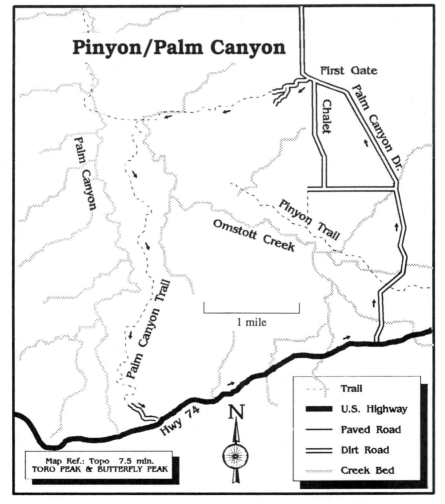

Pinyon/Palm Canyon

First Gate

Chalet

Palm Canyon Dr.

Palm Canyon

Pinyon Trail

Omstott Creek

Palm Canyon Trail

1 mile

Hwy 74

N

Map Ref.: Topo 7.5 min.
TORO PEAK & BUTTERFLY PEAK

	Trail
	U.S. Highway
	Paved Road
	Dirt Road
	Creek Bed

22 Live Oak Canyon

Distance: Approximately 21 miles
Difficulty: Strenuous, extremely technical
Elevation: 1,800' gain; high point 5,900'
Ride Type: One way with shuttle vehicle
Season: Spring, early summer, fall

This is a very difficult route. It's long, nasty and very technical with 21 long miles that seem like 40. It is also a fantastic ride for the experienced backcountry mountain biker. The trail is faint in many places because of its low usage. Its greatest reward is its wilderness experience. It's also an accomplishment to finish the trail. Be forewarned—it could be easy to get lost on this route and it may be advisable to first explore this trail with someone who knows it. All mileage mentioned is approximate. Take lots of water and tubes.

Important! See Special Notes, page 77, for additional information about access to this ride.

Getting There: This route can be reached by driving 19 miles north on Highway 74 from Palm Desert and parking a shuttle vehicle at the Palm Canyon trailhead parking lot. Drive the second car 7 miles on the highway to Penrod Canyon Road. Park along Highway 74.

Begin riding Penrod Road (dirt). Ride 0.8 mile along white fences and go left at the road fork. Continue climbing to a gate with numerous no trespassing signs on adjoining land (check with the U.S. Forest Service office in Idyllwild to find the land's current status). Continue on after closing the gate. At the

5.1-mile mark you reach Gold Shot Mine (private property). Veer right through the gate on trail #4E03. This trail heads east and at 5.7 miles turns south and quickly east with a tough and rocky hike-a-bike for approximately 0.5 mile where it meets the Pacific Crest Trail, which is off-limits to bicycles. Cross the trail and continue on a wonderful and technically difficult descent to Live Oak Spring at about 6.2 miles.

Water at the spring must be treated or filtered so plan to bring plenty of water for your start. Continue riding through consistently more brushy trail to a fork at approximately 7.4 miles. Veer right and continue east and down for approximately 6 miles to the Palm Canyon Trail. The trail is easy to lose in this

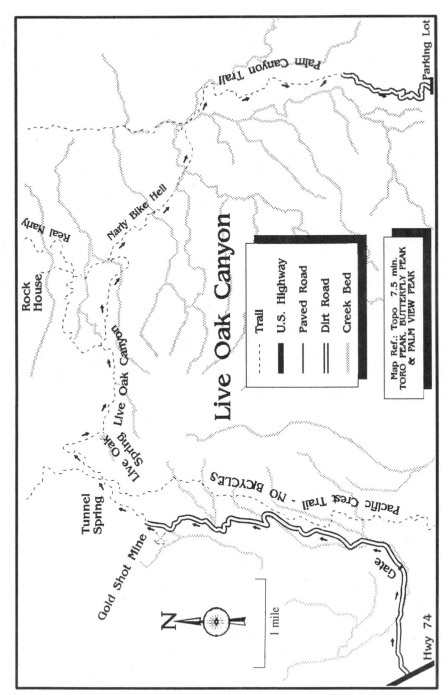

Live Oak Canyon

Parking Lot

Palm Canyon Trail

Narly Bike Hell

Real Narly

Rock House,

Live Oak Canyon

Live Oak Spring

Tunnel Spring

Gold Shot Mine

Pacific Crest Trail – NO BICYCLES

Gate

Hwy 74

N

1 mile

Trail
U.S. Highway
Paved Road
Dirt Road
Creek Bed

Map Ref.: Topo 7.5 min.
TORO PEAK, BUTTERFLY PEAK
& PALM VIEW PEAK

area. Look for rock cairns to find your way. There are many downhill hike-a-bike sections. The sensation of being lost is ever present, so you'll be glad you brought your topo map.

After reaching the Palm Canyon Trail turn right (south) and climb through a sandy plain to a trail heading due south and onto a ridge. Follow that trail via narrow switchbacks 5.0

miles to a fence (make sure you close the fence after crossing). Continue on doubletrack for 0.2 mile. When the doubletrack turns left, head straight up the mountainside on a faint trail for 0.1 mile. Turn right on a doubletrack and follow it switching up the hillside due south for 1.8 miles to your shuttle vehicle at the Palm Canyon trailhead.

23 Murray Peak

Distance: 12 miles
Difficulty: Strenuous, very technical
Elevation: 2,000'; high point 2,100'
Ride Type: Loop on dirt roads and trails
Season: Fall, winter, spring

Please be advised to remain on established routes only. Don't start a new trail by riding cross-country in this area. Even though the open, hardpan soil may look inviting, your tracks can damage the fragile desert environment.

Murray Peak is the highest peak in the area, and it gives you one of the finest views of the Coachella Valley and southward over Dunn Road. Birds always circle the peak to pick up thermals, and in fact, local hang gliders often fly to the peak to pick up extra lift to continue on to Mt. San Jacinto.

Getting There: Drive Highway 111 to Cathedral City and turn north on Bankside Drive. Park here.

Ride your bike half a block west on Highway 111 and turn left through the opening in the water control fence. Follow the broken pavement road to its end at an old building pad site. Continue via the singletrack to the

left. The singletrack follows 0.5 mile to doubletrack. An old dozer track continues west for 1 mile to the Eagle Canyon Wash. A network of trails here is referred to by locals as the Goat Trails.

From this point the rider can continue west past the wash by portaging bikes down the dry waterfall or swing back to Highway 111 by a side trail. To continue west, ride up the dozer track approximately 100 yards and make a hard right. Continue on through a series of turns and grunt climbs 0.3 mile to an intersection. A right turn will head back to Highway 111. Continue straight to explore more trail.

At 3.0 miles you come to a Y in the dozer track. Turn left and ride approximately 125 yards and turn right (west) on another dozer track. The doubletrack becomes singletrack and continues to an intersection. Turn left on the doubletrack and at 100 yards turn right (west) on another doubletrack. Continue riding 0.3 mile

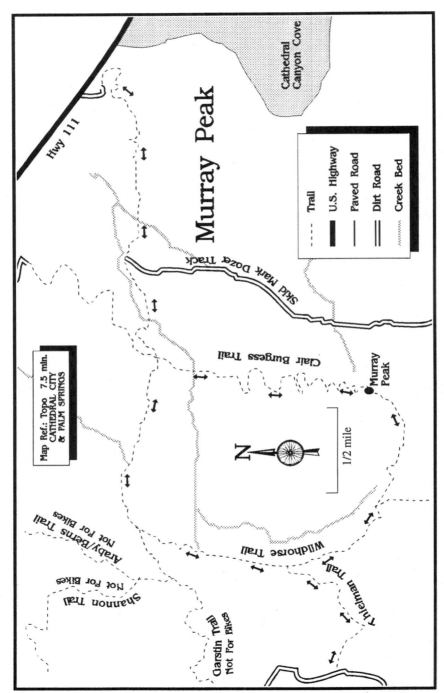

Murray Peak

Cathedral Canyon Cove

Hwy 111

Skid Mark Doza Track

Clair Burgess Trail

Murray Peak

Wildhorse Trail

Thielman Trail

Araby/Berns Trail
Not For Bikes

Shannon Trail
Not For Bikes

Garstin Trail
Not For Bikes

Map Ref.: Topo 7.5 min.
CATHEDRAL CITY
& PALM SPRINGS

1/2 mile

N

	Symbol
Trail	
U.S. Highway	
Paved Road	
Dirt Road	
Creek Bed	

and turn left on a side trail (in a dip) and follow the singletrack to the trailhead of the Wild Horse Trail.

There are great views of Palm Springs here, and it is a good place for less ambitious riders to turn around and return the way they came. You could also exit the mountains via the Thielman Trail (unmarked), which heads directly west down the mountains to Palm Springs. This trail is unmaintained and very rocky with difficult dropoffs. Veer left on the doubletrack and head out to the Andreas Hills development and then to Palm Springs. Loop back via city streets to your car.

To reach Murray Peak continue up the steep switchbacks to the cairns on Wildhorse Mountain. Follow down the ridge, which can be flush with wildflowers, 1.0 mile to cairns marking the Clair Burgess trail. Take the Clair Burgess trail east. It continues east and then south through a series of switches and rollers. You then come to a saddle at the foot of Murray Peak. Ascend the peak via 6 switches. The very pinnacle of Murray Peak is less than 1,500 square feet, giving you the feeling of being on top of the world!

To descend, follow the steep switchbacks down the north face. Most of the beginning switches are difficult to ride without a dab. Don't be embarrassed if you have to get off the bike and turn it around at the tight switchbacks (120° to 170° angles). Warning! The trail on the north face of Murray Peak is very steep, especially off the side of the mountain where the trail makes its tight turns. A mistake at the switchbacks can mean a long flying descent without your bike! Try these on the bike only if you are an experienced mountain biker with good working brakes and equipment.

At the bottom you intersect the goat trails just east of the Cathedral Canyon Wash. Turn east (right) and proceed back to the starting point.

This trail is under consideration for designation as a one-way trail. Please inquire about the direction of travel before you ride.

24 Mt. Santa Rosa Road

Distance: 13 miles one way
Difficulty: Moderate, nontechnical
Elevation: 4,200' gain; high point 8,700'
Ride Type: Out and back on dirt road
Season: Late spring, summer, early fall

Mt. Santa Rosa Road makes for great mountain biking. Long and with great vistas, it provides the rider with a medium incline. This is also a good climbing ride for those who don't like the radical. Yet the downhill can be very fast and wide open.

Getting There: Drive 18 miles from Palm Desert on Highway 74 and turn left on Mt. Santa Rosa Road. There is limited parking here or you can park 200 yards up the road in a turnout.

Begin riding up the road. Views will become apparent at about 1.0

mile as you look north towards Haystack Mountain and Mt. San Jacinto in the distance. Continue riding the road to reach a spring-fed creek and pine trees at 4.0 miles, a good resting spot. The road then begins to ascend the mountain in a series of switchbacks. At 8.0 miles you reach a short turnoff to Santa Rosa Spring, a good place to fill water bottles. This is usually where intermediate riders will start the return to their car.

Continue on up the road until you reach viewpoints at 9.0 miles, just after a turnout to a communication tower. Pinyon Flat, Mt. San Jacinto and even Mt. San Gorgonio can be seen from here as well as the switchback logging road far below. Continue riding past the upper Mt. Santa Rosa campground. At 12.0 miles take the narrower and rocky road to the right, reaching a gate at 12.8 miles. Continue as far as you can ride or until you reach the summit of Toro Peak, which has a communication tower on top. Here, at 8,716 feet elevation and 13 miles out, you have a tremendous 360-degree view over all of Southern California—truly one of the finest viewpoints in all of the Southland.

To return to your car, go back the way you came being careful to watch your speed. On some weekends there are many cars and trucks on this road. Watch for them!

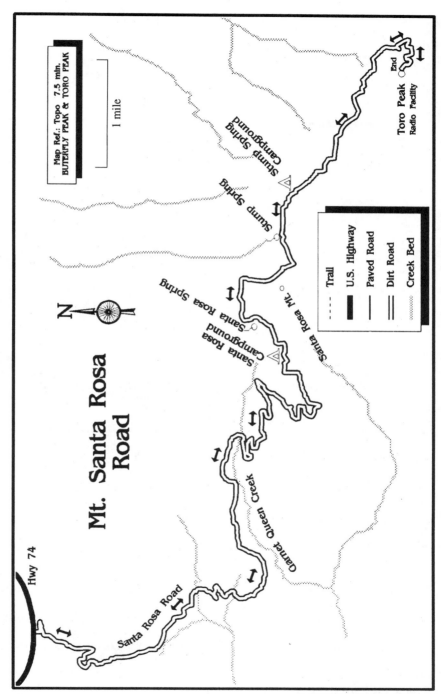

Map Ref.: Topo 7.5 min.
BUTERFLY PEAK & TORO PEAK

1 mile

N

Mt. Santa Rosa Road

Hwy 74

Santa Rosa Road

Garnet Queen Creek

Santa Rosa Campground

Santa Rosa Spring

Santa Rosa Mt.

Stump Spring

Stump Campground

Toro Peak
Radio Facility

End

Trail
U.S. Highway
Paved Road
Dirt Road
Creek Bed

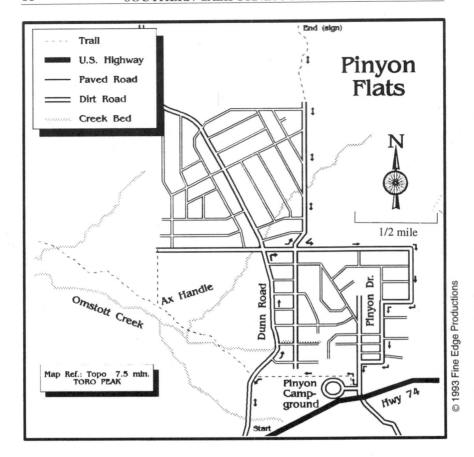

25 Pinyon Flats

Distance: 4 to 12 miles
Difficulty: Easy, nontechnical
Elevation: 500' gain
Ride Type: Loop on dirt roads
Season: All year

With lots of flat or nearly flat riding, this is a great area for beginners to practice their skills. The scenery is delightful among the pinyon pines and chaparral. There are constant views of Toro Peak and Mt. San Jacinto. Good camp spots are available at the Pinyon Flats campground.

Getting There: To reach Pinyon Flats, drive 17.3 miles from Palm Desert on Highway 74 (south) to Palm Canyon Drive. Turn right (north) and park at the dozer pad behind the mailboxes.

Begin by riding your bike 1.8 miles on Palm Canyon Drive before turning right (east) on Alpine Drive. Then ride 0.7 mile and turn left (north) on Jeraboa Street. Ride 0.5 mile to the road end and continue up the twisting doubletrack trail 0.5 mile to its end. You'll have great views here. Ride back down the way you came and continue down Jeraboa Street 1.0 mile and turn left (east) on Pinesmoke Street.

Ride Pinesmoke 0.8 mile and turn right (south) on Stonecrest Street. Ride 0.6 mile and turn right (east) on an unmarked road (Juniper). Then go 0.3 mile and turn left (south) on Santa Rosa Road. Continue 0.3 mile and turn right (east) on Indio Avenue. Then ride 0.2 mile and turn left on Pinyon Drive. It's 0.1 mile to the Pinyon Flats campground.

Turn right just after the entrance on the Pinyon Flats doubletrack and ride 0.7 mile to Palm Canyon Drive. Turn left (south) and continue 1.0 mile to the parking area.

Other routes abound. Just keep oriented to the location of your vehicle. Happy riding!

26 Fobes Ranch Trail

Distance: 12 miles
Difficulty: Moderate, somewhat technical
Elevation: 1,550' gain; 6,000' high point
Ride Type: Out and back on dirt road and singletrack
Season: Spring, summer, fall as snow permits

This is a great ride for views of Garner Valley and out to the vast desert of the Coachella Valley.

Getting There: To reach the trailhead drive 26 miles from Palm Desert on State Highway 74 and turn right (east) on Fobes Ranch Road (dirt). From Idyllwild, drive 9.5 miles on State Highway 74 to the turnoff. Park at the beginning of the dirt road.

Ride 0.3 mile and veer left at the intersection. Continue on, always taking a look back at Thomas Mountain and Mt. San Jacinto. The road continues as a medium climb on hard pack dirt for 4 miles. Turn right on the spur road (do not follow the road to Fobes Ranch—private property) and follow it to another intersection in 3/4 mile. Turn left and ride 400 feet to the singletrack junction.

This singletrack is short but sweet. It has its challenges but good riders can clean all the turns. The rest of us can just try to make the technical sections. Follow the trail on switchbacks and up good climbs for 1.5 miles until you reach the Pacific Crest Trail.

The view from the intersection is fantastic! You can see out towards the desert and Palm Springs 6,000 feet below and also towards Spitler Peak and Mount San Jacinto. The view is wonderful off to the west in the direction of Thomas Mountain. Notice the change in vegetation. This little pass gets much colder and receives twice the precipitation as the area just one mile below.

Be satisfied for now to look out on the beauty of the ridge top. Since the closing of the Pacific Crest Trail to bicyclists in 1987, this trail has been badly missed. Work is continuing to reopen this section south to Highway 74—you can help by staying off the Pacific Crest Trail.

To return to your vehicle, go back the way you came.

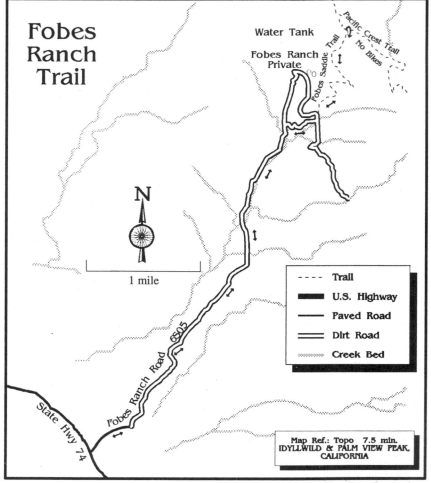

Fobes Ranch Trail

Water Tank

Fobes Ranch Private

Fobes Saddle Trail

Pacific Crest Trail

No Bikes

N

1 mile

- - - - Trail
U.S. Highway
Paved Road
Dirt Road
Creek Bed

Fobes Ranch Road 6S05

State Hwy 74

Map Ref.: Topo 7.5 min.
IDYLLWILD & PALM VIEW PEAK,
CALIFORNIA

27 Thomas Mountain Loop

Distance: 14 miles
Difficulty: Moderate, somewhat technical
Elevation: 1,700' gain; high point 6,200'
Ride Type: Loop
Season: Spring, summer, fall as snow permits

This is one of the most popular rides in the San Jacinto mountain area. It provides a moderate climb along a Forest Service road and a wonderful 5.5 mile descent from Thomas Mountain via great singletrack. It is also the site of the annual Thomas Mountain Classic mountain bike race.

Getting There: Drive 23 miles from Palm Desert on State Highway 74 and turn left (west) on Thomas Mountain Road. From Idyllwild, go 12 miles on State Highway 74 (approximately 3 miles past Lake Hemet) and turn right (west) on Thomas Mountain Road. Park here.

Ride on the paved road two long city blocks and turn left on Hop Patch Springs Road. Continue riding on pavement until it begins as a well graded dirt road. The road continues on flat and then rolling terrain through sugar pines. It then begins a relatively short but aerobic climb to a vista overlooking the town of Anza to the west. This is a good place to turn around for those who might find the first climb very difficult.

The road now turns due north and continues a moderate but constant climb through chaparral with occasional shade. Watch for views of the Anza Valley to the west and the San Jacinto ridge line to the north. Toro Peak can be seen from behind to the south. At 5.0 miles you reach Tool Box Springs Camp in tall pine trees. Turn right and follow the spur road downhill to Tool Box Spring—a good place to fill water bottles.

Ride north on the road 100 yards to its end to start the Ramona Trail (unmarked). Watch for some short dropoffs at the beginning (keep that weight back). The trail starts by switchbacking through sugar pines and alder. This is singletrack paradise! Some of the switchbacks are technical, but with a little brake action you can make it!

The trail descends out to chaparral and no shade as it becomes more rocky. Some turns are sharp with lots of small boulders and rock water bars in place. Continue along more sandy trail on a ridge line and out to the trail end. Follow the primitive dirt road east to State Highway 74, making sure you close the gate.

Turn right on the highway and follow it 3.5 miles before turning right on Thomas Mountain Road and returning to your vehicle.

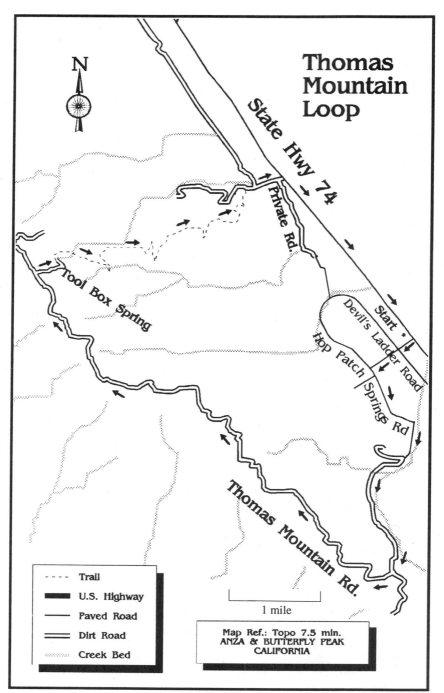

Thomas Mountain Loop

Legend:
- – – – Trail
- ▬▬ U.S. Highway
- ——— Paved Road
- ═══ Dirt Road
- ·········· Creek Bed

1 mile

Map Ref.: Topo 7.5 min.
ANZA & BUTTERFLY PEAK
CALIFORNIA

28 Black Mountain Road

Distance: 5.5 to 12 miles one way
Difficulty: Moderate, nontechnical
Elevation: 2,000' gain; 7,600' high point
Ride Type: Out and back on dirt road
Season: Late spring, summer, early fall

Black Mountain Road is an excellent ride in beautiful forest. This is a good pick when other areas are too hot for riding—shade is present for the majority of the route. The road gains 2,000 feet in a short 5 miles. It is well constructed, with switchbacks making up the side of the mountain with a good constant grade. Some of the road has been paved to reduce dust from motorized vehicles, and this is to the advantage of cyclists. The descent is fast and furious. Don't forget that there are vehicles on the road! The views are spectacular from about 6.5 miles. Mt. San Gorgonio looks magnified from the Black Mountain Rim.

The U.S. Forest Service is surveying this area for a singletrack loop to be identified and constructed in 1994 or 1995. Contact the Idyllwild Ranger Station for information. There is good camping at Black Mountain Camp and other camps close by.

Getting There: Drive State Highway 243 from Banning 18 miles or drive 8 miles north of Idyllwild, reaching a wide dirt turnout with a sign that reads *Black Mountain Road 5.5 miles*. Park here.

Start your ride through cool forest with partial sun and intermixed dirt and paved road. The road switches constantly, but the climb is never too extreme. At 2.5 miles good views can be seen back towards the southeast and the city of Idyllwild. You also get good views of the east face of Mt. San Jacinto and Taquitz Peak.

Keep on, and soon you reach Cinco Poses Spring, a good place to fill water bottles with ice cold mountain water. At 5 miles is the turnoff to Boulder Basin Campground and Black Mountain Fire Lookout—a pleasant side trip for spectacular views.

Continue on past this junction for your first downhill, a welcome relief from the climb. You ride up and down through old forest past Black Mountain Group Camp. At 6 miles you reach the Black Mountain Lookout and some of the most fantastic views of Mt. San Gorgonio and Banning Pass. On very clear days Mt. Wilson and Mt. Baldy can easily be seen. This is a good place to turn around if you feel tired from the climb. The return down the road is very fast. Approach the switchback turns with caution. Weekend motorized traffic can be a hazard.

Those who don't turn back here can continue past the lookout and start a slow descent on the Black Mountain Rim, passing the Pacific Crest Trail in 0.75 mile (no bikes allowed). Follow the road downhill, crossing many small seeps, and heading out to a small, sloping valley. The road switches on hardpack and soft dusty soil to the road end and the start of the north section of the Pacific Crest Trail at 6,400 feet (mile 10). To return, follow the road back up to the rim and out to your starting point at State Highway 243.

For additional rides in this area, please refer to *Mountain Biking the Coast Range, Guide 12, Riverside County and Coachella Valley,* by Paul Maag and Robert Shipley, ISBN 0-938665-24-3 (see p. 304).

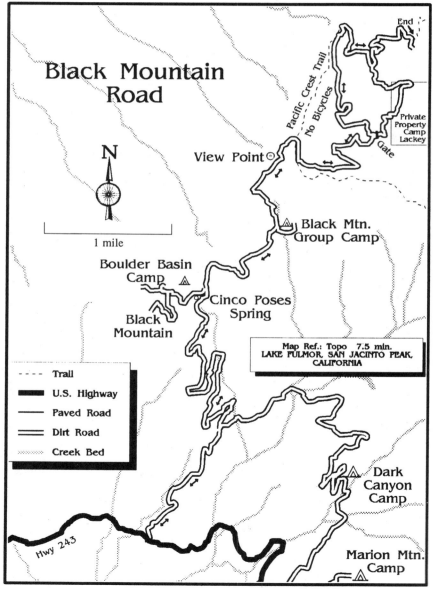

Black Mountain Road

N

1 mile

Pacific Crest Trail
No Bicycles

End

View Point

Private Property Camp Lackey

Gate

Black Mtn. Group Camp

Boulder Basin Camp

Cinco Poses Spring

Black Mountain

Map Ref.: Topo 7.5 min.
LAKE FULMOR, SAN JACINTO PEAK, CALIFORNIA

- - - - Trail
▬▬▬ U.S. Highway
──── Paved Road
════ Dirt Road
∷∷∷∷ Creek Bed

Dark Canyon Camp

Hwy 243

Marion Mtn. Camp

CHAPTER 4

San Bernardino Mountains

By Robert Shipley and Allen Thibault

These mountains are a truly wonderful playground. And the modern mountain bike has given us access to almost every stream and peak, meadow and trail sprinkled throughout this magnificent forest. Discover for yourself what thousands of Native Americans, prospectors, ranchers, hikers and vacationers have known for countless decades—the call to explore.

You'll come to know all types of terrain from the high desert of 3,500 feet to spectacular mountain peaks above 9,000 feet. You'll amble along rivers, pedal around high mountain lakes, splash across countless streams, clamor up to active fire lookout towers, whisper along more than 40 miles of singletrack and ponder dozens upon dozens of breathtaking vistas.

The principal riding areas in this chapter are around Silverwood Lake, Big Bear Lake and along the Santa Ana River Canyon north of Angeles Oaks. Along the western edge of this national forest is Silverwood Lake State Park, with a casual paved bike path bordering half its shoreline. There are excellent recreational facilities here for the entire family, including swimming, boating, fishing, hiking, picnicking and of course, memorable bike riding.

By far the most popular mountain biking area in the entire forest is around Big Bear Lake. On the north side is the ghost town of Holcomb Valley and the quaint community of Fawnskin. Butler Peak and Snow Slide Road offer challenges and views you'll not soon forget. On the south side of the lake, the no-effort ride on the chair lift to the top of Snow Summit has to be experienced! Once you get to Skyline Road you gain access to mile after mile of roller coaster riding beyond compare.

If you lust for real trail riding, you'll find the longest singletrack in the forest along the Santa Ana River Canyon. You can choose among five options for this ride, requiring skill levels from beginner to advanced gonzo. From tight hairpins clinging to sheer cliffs to deep river crossings, you'll know you've tested your abilities and will be hot to tell the disbelievers back home of your exploits.

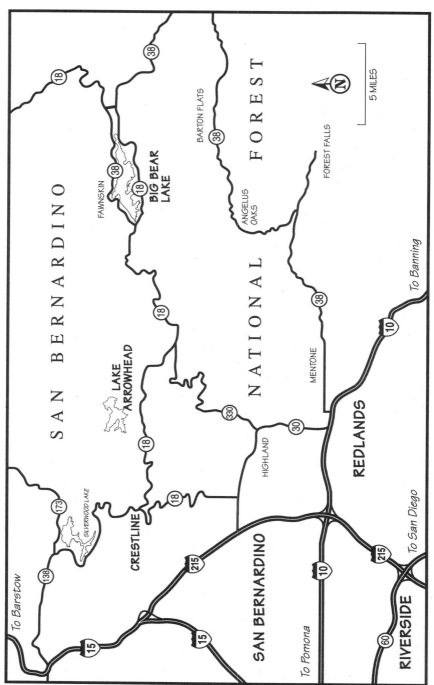

If you'd like to camp on your vacation, there are numerous campgrounds in the forest. Among the most convenient are Barton Flats, Coldbrook, Green Valley, Hanna Flats, Holcomb Valley, Pineknot, San Gorgonio, Serrano and South Fork. Fees range from $6 to $15. Serrano is the only campground with showers. For a complete listing, see the American Automobile Association (AAA) map of Central and Southern California Camping.

29 Silverwood Lake Bike Path

Distance: 12.5 miles
Difficulty: Easy, nontechnical
Elevation: 3,400'
Ride Type: Paved bike path, out and back
Seasons: Spring, summer, fall

This is an excellent destination for the entire family because of the extensive recreational facilities at the lake shore. You can windsurf, swim, fish, launch your own boat or just walk the dog. There is something here for everyone. In fact, it's so popular, I recommend you do this ride before Memorial Day or well after Labor Day, and avoid the weekend crowds in particular.

You'll find a roller coaster, paved, smooth (sort of), two-lane bike path following the shore. In some spots the path is badly eroded, making it more challenging as well as unsuitable for the skinny tired bikes for which it was probably first built. Unfortunately, the path doesn't circle the lake; this is an out-and-back ride. For more experienced riders, there is a rather technical, sometimes ugly singletrack at the end of the paved path on the north side of the lake. Beginners need not apply (at least for the dirt part).

Getting There: Take I-15 north of San Bernardino to Highway 138 east to Silverwood Lake Park entrance.

There's a day use fee ($6/car) but it's well worth the price. Plan on taking picnic food, arriving early and making a full day of the outing. There's water available at the picnic area. Nearest services are in Crestline or Summit. Drive to Lot #1. Park and ride to the bike path, which goes in both directions around the lake.

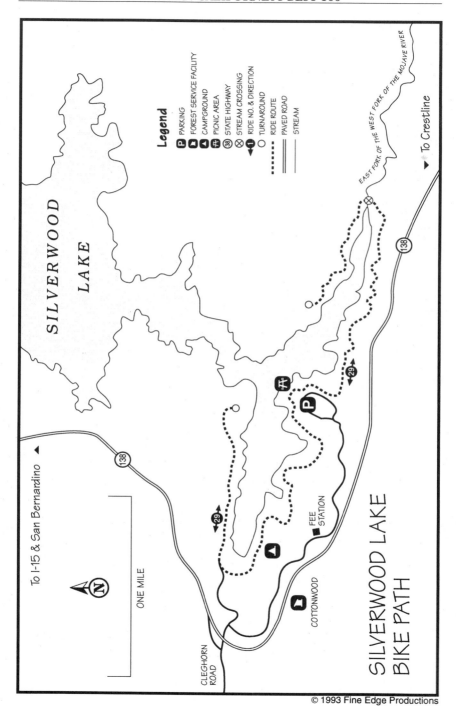

Legend

- **P** PARKING
- **◢** FOREST SERVICE FACILITY
- **◄** CAMPGROUND
- **⛱** PICNIC AREA
- **138** STATE HIGHWAY
- **⊗** STREAM CROSSING
- **1** RIDE NO. & DIRECTION
- **○** TURNAROUND
- ┈┈┈ RIDE ROUTE
- ═══ PAVED ROAD
- ─── STREAM

SILVERWOOD
LAKE

EAST FORK OF THE WEST FORK OF THE MOJAVE RIVER

To Crestline

138

29

To I-15 & San Bernardino

ONE MILE

N

138

29

FEE
STATION

COTTONWOOD

CLEGHORN
ROAD

SILVERWOOD LAKE
BIKE PATH

© 1993 Fine Edge Productions

This bike route will take you east, return you to the lot, head west and return again to the lot. You can find the path by heading toward the lake behind the restrooms—turn right beyond the boat launch and continue past the east edge of the parking lot. You'll see a paved path climbing up the slope.

After 0.6 mile of steep climbing you come to a junction and a small restroom building. Turn left up the slope to the gate. This is a typical gate designed to allow passage of bikes (and people). A lot of people don't like to use this gate so they have worn a path around it. The choice is yours. Turn left and coast down the hill to another gate. The twisting, swooping path crosses numerous wooden bridges as it hugs the shoreline. Through the trees you can catch fleeting glimpses of ducks, gulls, bald eagles in the winter and people fishing from boats and from the shore.

At 2.1 miles the path crosses a steel grate and concrete apron where the East Fork of the West Fork of the Mojave River enters the lake basin. The path loops to the north of the lake and heads west. Move through (or around) another gate at 2.3 miles, go up onto the paved road (not down to the dirt path to the left of the gate) and ride east. At 2.5 miles there is another restroom, a sign indicating Serrano Beach and the return of the bike path just beyond a wood bridge.

After 3.0 miles the paved portion of the path ends. Beginners should turn around here and retrace their route. Experienced riders can elect to continue on the singletrack leading off the end of the cul-de-sac. But if you get queasy clinging to sheer dropoffs, don't bother. For about 0.3 mile the path is rideable, but barely, in spots. It gradually climbs up the face of the slope, giving you a progressively better view of the lake. This path looks for all the world like a burro track and it probably should have stayed that way. But gonzo bike riders being what they are....

At 5.5 miles (if you didn't ride the singletrack) turn right at the top of the paved road to return through the locked gate. If you miss this turn you can still find your way back to your car by following the road down toward the lake. At 5.8 miles you will be back to your car.

You can elect to end your cycling here, but if you have the time and energy for more, continue west on the bike path as it winds its way through several picnic areas.

After the path dumps you onto another parking lot, it turns right through a locked gate. Follow the path down and then up a slope to a Y. Take the left branch and continue up the hill to an attractive, somewhat remote campground. The path continues just a few feet to the right of where you enter the lot. Take this down the hill, around the campground back toward the lake. At the gate, turn right and head east. You can take the bike path on the far side of the road or ride the road to the picnic and beach area.

At the next parking lot take the path along the beach and then through the next locked gate up the side of the hill to the overlook. This is the other end of the paved bike path. The Los Animas hiking trail takes off from this cul-de-sac. Bicycles are not permitted on this trail.

Turn around and retrace your route. Go straight through the first gate, turn left to go through the second gate and stay to your left on the path as it hugs the shoreline. At 12.5 miles you are back at your car.

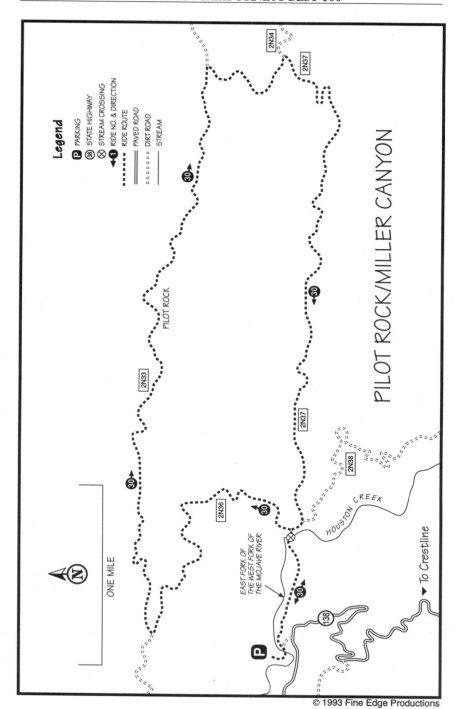

PILOT ROCK/MILLER CANYON

30 Pilot Rock/Miller Canyon

Distance: 11.8 miles
Difficulty: Moderately strenuous, mildly technical
Elevation: 3,400'
Ride Type: Loop on fire roads
Seasons: Spring, summer, fall
Topo Maps: Silverwood Lake, Lake Arrowhead

Almost all of the climbing on this ride occurs during the first 3 miles. The rest of the ride roller coasters in a general descent back to the start. There are a few challenging sections but nothing really difficult or technical. A note of caution: These roads tend to be popular with motorcycle riders and 4WDs, so you may want to avoid summer weekends. It can get pretty warm here in the middle of summer, too, so be sure to bring at least 2 water bottles and food on this ride. An even safer plan would be to just avoid it altogether during the heat of the summer between Memorial Day and Labor Day.

Getting There: From I-15 north of San Bernardino, take Highway 138 to Silverwood Lake. Continue east past the park entrance staying on 138 to the Miller Canyon Unit turnoff and go down to the entrance (fee station) to the picnic area. The entrance to the conservation camp is to the right. Park here. Water is available at Silverwood Lake beach/picnic area. The nearest services are in Crestline or Summit Valley.

Ride back up the paved road 0.1 mile and turn left on Miller Canyon road (if you get all the way to the highway, you went too far). The road follows the south boundary of the correctional facility (minimum security prison), crosses Houston Creek and ends at the junction of 2N36 and 2N37 (0.9 mile from the start). Take 2N36 to the left. At 2.9 miles, 2N36 ends at 2N33. Take the right branch of the junction heading east.

There are a few steep, technical sections but they are short and fun riding. The views of the Mojave River basin, Hesperia and Silverwood Lake are spectacular. Take time to stop and gaze down on the high desert. Ponder the changes humans have wrought in this region. What might this spectacular country be like in 100 years?

At 4.1 miles 2N17X takes off to the left. Continue past this side road. You come to a gate at 6.7 miles, just before the junction of 2N33 and 2N34. Turn right onto 2N34 to ride an enjoyable rolling road through pines, oak, sage and manzanita. At 7.3 miles turn right again onto 2N37. This is Miller Canyon Road. There are some short, steep, winding, rocky sections here that will challenge beginners. Take it slowly and you'll have no problem. After 8.7 miles you come to a junction where you take the right branch down the hill.

At the junction of 2N37 and 2N38 turn right for 0.1 mile to the junction of 2N37 and 2N36. Turn left onto the road you came in on. Continue past the conservation camp to the pavement. Turn right and ride down the hill back to your car.

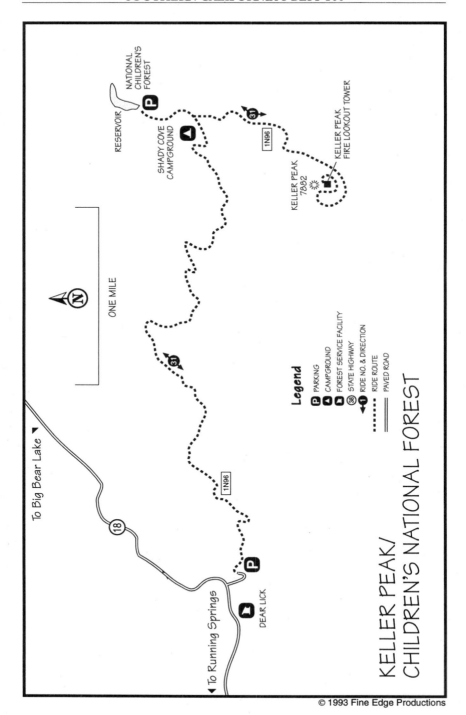

KELLER PEAK/
CHILDREN'S NATIONAL FOREST

Legend

P PARKING
◢ CAMPGROUND
■ FOREST SERVICE FACILITY
(38) STATE HIGHWAY
➤➊ RIDE NO. & DIRECTION
•••• RIDE ROUTE
═══ PAVED ROAD

ONE MILE

N

To Big Bear Lake ▼
To Running Springs ▼

RESERVOIR
NATIONAL CHILDREN'S FOREST
SHADY COVE CAMPGROUND
KELLER PEAK 7882
KELLER PEAK FIRE LOOKOUT TOWER
DEER LICK
1N96
31
18

31 Keller Peak/ National Children's Forest

Distance: 12.5 miles
Difficulty: Moderate only because of the long climb, nontechnical
Elevation: Start 6,080'; gain 1,882'
Ride Type: Out and back on paved road and dirt fire road
Seasons: Spring, summer, fall
Topo Map: Keller Peak

This out-and-back ride climbs a steep, smooth, paved, two-lane road from 6,000 feet to 7,882 feet at the top of Keller Peak. In some spots the road is just wide enough for two cars to pass, so be sure to stay to the right, especially on the curves. The view from the peak is breathtaking and easily worth the climb, not to mention the white-knuckler swooping downhill back to your car. Another wonderful part of this ride is the National Children's Forest. This is a unique forest fire study area dedicated to thousands of children nationwide who have helped reforest our country's burned timber. No water is available at the ride start. Nearest services are in Running Springs.

Getting There: From Highway 18 at the east end of Running Springs, turn right onto 1N96. After 0.2 mile there are two small parking areas. Park in one of these. Note: If you don't want to bicycle up the paved road to the beginning of the dirt section below the peak, drive the 4.2 miles to the intersection described in the next paragraph to begin your bike ride.

Begin your climb from the parking lots. At 2.5 miles there's a turnoff to a primitive campground. You reach the junction to Keller Peak at 4.2 miles. Turn to the right for the dirt road climb to the lookout tower.

The road levels out around 5.4 miles and you get a fantastic view of the Santa Ana River basin below and the San Bernardino/Redlands/Yucaipa areas farther to the southwest. You can also see the Morton Peak fire lookout above Mentone. Near the Santa Ana River you can see miles and miles of good dirt roads snaking along the slopes.

The road continues west to wind around the peak, climbing again to the top 6.0 miles from the start of the ride. In addition to the fire lookout, you can see a vast array of broadcasting towers and microwave antennae bristling from the massive boulders. If the gate to the fire lookout tower is open, ride up to the base of the tower, park your bike, climb the stairs and say hi to the ranger. He or she will probably give you a short, fascinating tour of the tower and explain what a fire lookout does.

From this vantage point you can see the top of the chairlift at Snow Valley, Lake Silverwood to the west, and the towns of Hesperia and Apple Valley to the north.

When you have finished your snack and explored the peak, ride back down the dirt road to the junction and turn right. Ride 0.2 mile up a short hill to the parking lot of the National Children's Forest. Park your bike and take the short walk along the Phoenix Trail; this is an excellent interpretive tour through a once burned forest. Under no circumstances may you ride your bike on the narrow, paved walking path. One of the reasons is that many blind people walk this interpretive trail and the sound of a bike close to them could be frightening. After your walk, collect your bike and return back down the hill to your car.

32 Snow Slide Road/ Green Valley Lake

Distance: 30.4 miles
Difficulty: Strenuous, nontechnical
Ride Type: Fire road and a little pavement, out and back
Elevation: Start 6,744'; high point 7,520'; gain 1,296'
Seasons: Spring, summer, fall
Topo Maps: Keller Peak, Butler Peak, Fawnskin

On this ride you crank and coast through hilly, heavily forested, remote country and cross several streams trickling from springs. It's a wonderful forest jaunt that takes you from one quaint little town to another (Fawnskin to Green Valley Lake). Take two water bottles and carry plenty of food.

Getting There: Park behind Fawn Lodge in the town of Fawnskin (north shore of Big Bear Lake). The lodge is on Navajo Street across from the fire station.

Turn left onto Navajo Street. Then turn right, heading northwest, onto Rim of the World Drive in front of the State of California fire station. The road is paved and begins climbing. At 0.5 mile the road turns to dirt and 3N14 begins. It is open to vehicles so be sure to stay to the right, especially as you approach the curves. Continue climbing. After 1.4 miles you come to the junction of 3N14 and 2N68. Stay to the right on 3N14 toward the YMCA Camp Whittle. At 1.8 miles 3N12 branches to the right but you continue on 3N14. Immediately after the driveway into Camp Whittle take 2N13 to the left. Continue on through the open gate and stay on 2N13 past the junction with 2N13A. Continue on 2N13, ignoring the lesser trails branching off to

the left. The road is in good condition and allows a brisk ride through the undulating terrain.

As you pass unmarked junctions with lesser roads, continue on the more heavily traveled road. At 4.0 miles 2N13C cuts to the left. Stay right on 2N13 as it becomes steep, a bit rocky and eroded and then level and delightful. At 5.6 miles you crest a summit to view Mt. Baldy in the San Gabriel Mountains some 45 miles to the west and Cajon Canyon closer in. You begin a long, rocky, sandy descent, crossing Avalanche Spring and then climbing a short, steep grade through stands of Douglas fir and ponderosa pines.

After crossing Snow Slide summit you begin the challenging drop toward Green Valley Lake at 6.8 miles. At 8.0 miles continue straight past a spur to the right, then onto 2 miles of outstanding roller coaster riding through the forest. At 10 miles 2N13 cuts hard to the right and 2N13 curves left. Take a break and go straight ahead up a short slope to an overlook near an old concrete water tank. Have a drink and a snack as you survey the hills and canyons around you. Look back along the road that brought you here and contemplate your achievement.

Scoot back down to 2N13 and continue southwest. At 10.6 miles, enter a clearing where Craft Peak,

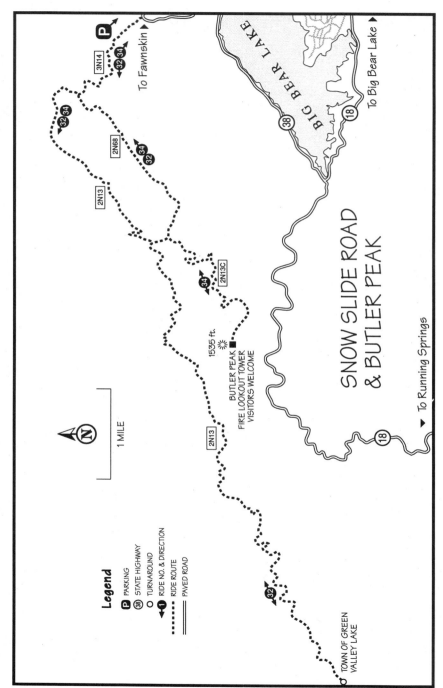

SNOW SLIDE ROAD & BUTLER PEAK

BIG BEAR LAKE

To Big Bear Lake

To Fawnskin

To Running Springs

BUTLER PEAK
FIRE LOOKOUT TOWER
VISITORS WELCOME
1535 ft.

TOWN OF GREEN
VALLEY LAKE

3N14
32 34
32 34
34
2N68
2N13
34 2N13C
2N13
2N13
32

18
38
18

Legend

- **P** PARKING
- **38** STATE HIGHWAY
- **O** TURNAROUND
- **1** RIDE NO. & DIRECTION
- ••••• RIDE ROUTE
- ═══ PAVED ROAD

N

1 MILE

© 1993 Fine Edge Productions

Snow Slide and Middle Earth cross-country ski trailheads begin. Turn right and ride down the road among the massive ponderosas to the junction with 2N54 at 10.9 miles. Stay to the left on 2N13 for another 0.7 mile where you hit the pavement of Green Valley Road. Go right again and coast into the town of Green Valley Lake.

This is your turnaround point, but first take time to explore the town. Park your bike and pop into the Green Valley Lake Market across from the lake for a drink and snack. After your rest, head back up the paved road past the Lodge Steak House. Make a left turn onto 2N13 (dirt) and toward Fawnskin just under 15 miles away. Stay right at the junction with 2N54, left at the ski trailhead area (2N13), right at the junction below the concrete water tank.

At 20.6 miles from the start, turn right on 2N13C at the junction with 2N13. Ride through the

gate and turn left onto 2N68Y. Turn left onto 2N68, continue past Graves Peak Group Camp and pass 2N80. At 3N14 turn right to coast back down to your car in Fawnskin.

33 Butler Peak

Distance: 13.7 miles
Difficulty: Somewhat strenuous, nontechnical
Elevation: 6,800' to 8,535'; 1,735' gain
Ride Type: Fire roads, loop ride below the short leg to the peak
Seasons: Late spring, summer, fall
Topo Maps: Fawnskin, Butler Peak

The highlight of this ride is the fabulous view from the fire lookout on top of Butler Peak. This is an out-and-back ride you'll want to tell your friends about, especially if you climb the short distance to the tower itself and visit with the volunteers.

Getting There: Park behind Fawn Lodge in Fawnskin (north shore of Big Bear Lake).

Begin by following the directions for the Snow Slide Road/Green Valley Lake ride. At 4.0 miles take

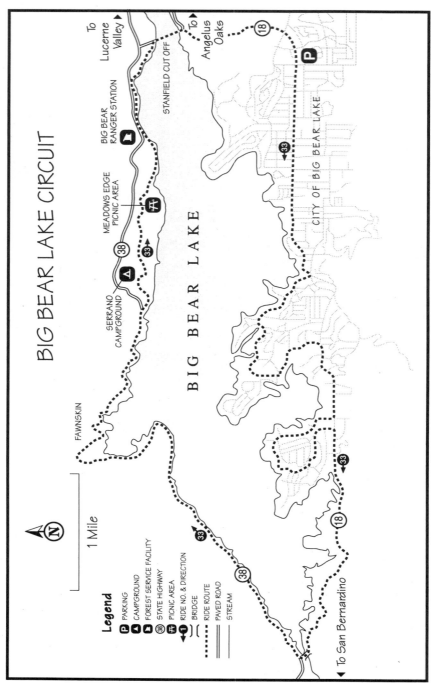

BIG BEAR LAKE CIRCUIT

BIG BEAR LAKE

© 1993 Fine Edge Productions

2N13C to the left (through the open gate) and begin a long climb up the rocky road. At the junction with 2N68Y stay right on 2N13C. At 7.0 miles you round a bend to be greeted by a breathtaking view of the Inland Empire—more than 7,000 feet below and 30 miles away—as well as the slopes of Snow Valley near Running Springs and Keller Peak to the south. Around the next bend you suddenly see your destination: the fire lookout tower precariously perched atop a massive rock outcropping. The road gets steep and rocky, and it may be rutted. Ride past a spur off to the left and continue up to the parking area below the tower at 6.9 miles.

Park your bike. Please observe and respect the notice about visitors before you hike up the short trail (right side of propane tank) to the tower. On the tower you have an absolutely fabulous view of Keller Peak to the south, Mt. Baldy in the San Gabriels to the west, San Gorgonio Mountain to the southeast, Big Bear Lake, Silverwood Lake, Apple Valley and (if the air is clear) Lake Perris. If you're shaky about heights, you may not want to climb up here. Imagine what it must have taken to build this tower on these rocks some 60 years ago.

Return back down to the junction and turn right onto 2N68Y at 9.6 miles. Turn left onto 2N68, continue past Graves Peak Group Camp and pass 2N80. At 3N14 turn right to coast back down to your car.

34 Big Bear Lake Circuit

Distance: 18 miles
Difficulty: Easy, nontechnical
Elevation: Start/end 6,800'; 80' gain
Ride Type: Loop on highway and paved bike path
Seasons: Late spring, summer, fall

You certainly don't need a mountain bike for this ride, but if you do use one, pump your tires to their maximum rated pressure to minimize your effort. This pleasant 18-mile ride takes you into part of the business district of Big Bear Lake, through the intriguing residential districts of the south shore and Boulder Bay, to Fawnskin, and on a delightful bike path along the north shore. Summer weekend traffic tends to be heavy but not fast. Be sure to stop in the rustic town of Fawnskin for a food and drink break.

Getting There: Drive to Big Bear Lake on Highway 18 from Running Springs or on Highway 38 from Angeles Oaks. Park in the Vons shopping center at the east end of the town of Big Bear Lake on Highway 18. There's a bike store near Stater Bros. in the shopping center across the street if you need supplies.

From the Vons parking lot, turn right onto Big Bear Boulevard heading west. At the third signal, continue straight onto Lakeview Drive (Big Bear Boulevard turns left at this

signal and heads into the main business district). Turn right, staying on Lakeview Drive. Turn left at Edgemoor Drive, right on Big Bear Boulevard, and left onto Cienega Road, which becomes Waterview Drive. Continue through this peaceful residential district, where you can see that most of the homes on your left have appealing lake views.

Turn left on Blue Jay Road, right on Catbird Lane, left on Landing Road, right on Blue Jay Road, and right on Big Bear Boulevard. This portion takes you through the neighborhood called Boulder Bay, and from the rock formations you will see why. Now you enter the only hilly part of this ride. The climb is short, the road is winding, and there may be a good bit of traffic here. Then the road drops back down to the lake and crosses the dam. At the junction with Highway 38 turn right.

You are now heading east. If it is afternoon you will probably be pushed along by a delightful tail wind. The road winds along the north shore of Big Bear Lake here, affording you a wonderful view of San Bernardino peak to your right. If it is early in the year there will probably be a lot of snow on the mountains. A brisk tail wind, the gorgeous lake and the snow covered mountains in the distance make for nearly ideal cycling.

Next you cruise through the picturesque little town of Fawnskin, a fine spot for "refueling." There are several places to eat, including a restaurant and a small grocery. You can also picnic on the fire station lawn and use the restroom.

The ride continues east on Highway 38. Watch for the North Shore turnoff. Turn right on North Shore Drive toward the observatory. After about one block turn left onto the bikeway.

This is a Class 1 paved bikeway. It winds through the trees with a large picnic area and campground on your left and the lake on your right. The bikeway crosses the entrance to the Serrano Campground. Then it crosses the highway so watch for traffic. It then follows the lake shore in a curving, roller coaster ride for several miles. Usually there is a brisk tail wind every afternoon.

The bikeway ends across from the entrance to the North Shore Elementary School. Turn right on Standfield Cutoff and cross the landfill at the east end of Big Bear Lake. Turn right on Big Bear Boulevard and into the town of Big Bear Lake. Continue on to the parking lot and your car.

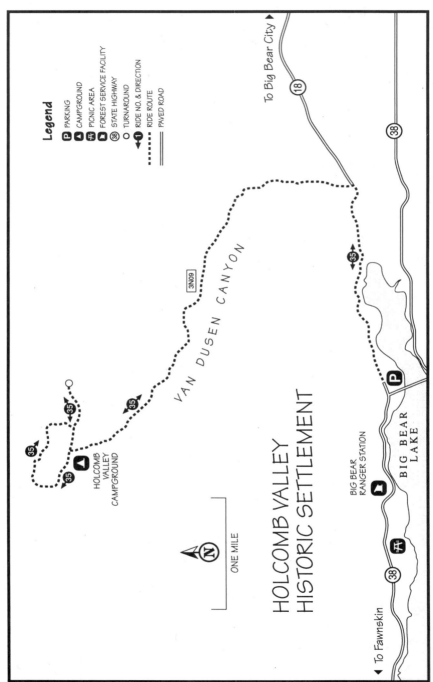

HOLCOMB VALLEY
HISTORIC SETTLEMENT

ONE MILE

VAN DUSEN CANYON

HOLCOMB
VALLEY
CAMPGROUND

BIG BEAR
RANGER STATION

BIG BEAR
LAKE

To Fawnskin ▶

To Big Bear City ▶

Legend

P PARKING
🏕 CAMPGROUND
🅟 PICNIC AREA
🏠 FOREST SERVICE FACILITY
38 STATE HIGHWAY
○ TURNAROUND
↞● RIDE NO. & DIRECTION
••••• RIDE ROUTE
═══ PAVED ROAD

© 1993 Fine Edge Productions

35 Holcomb Valley Historic Settlement

Distance: 13.8 miles
Difficulty: Easy, nontechnical
Elevation: 6,800' to 8,120'; 1,320' gain
Ride Type: Out and back on fire roads and pavement
Seasons: Late spring, summer, fall
Topo Maps: Fawnskin, Big Bear City

This trip visits the beautiful, historic Holcomb Valley. If you are at all adventurous, not afraid of ghosts wielding picks and shovels, have plenty of water and food and a few hours, consider exploring side roads in addition to the route listed here. There are many miles of Forest Service roads leading to old mining claims, picnic spots and just plain interesting places to explore.

Getting There: Park at the North Shore School parking lot (on the north shore of Big Bear Lake). Note: if you start your ride at the end of the pavement on Van Dusen, subtract 2.0 miles from each of the distances given in this description.

To begin your ride, turn right (east) on Highway 38. Ride 2.0 miles and turn left (north) on Van Dusen Canyon Road. At the end of the pavement the road becomes 3N09. The road climbs gradually and is in good condition. It may be heavily traveled by vehicles, especially on weekends during the summer, so stay to the right.

At 5.6 miles turn left at the T with 3N16. Pass the Holcomb Valley Campground. Turn right at 3N05 (sign of the pick and shovel) at 5.9 miles to begin the ride through the remains of the historic settlement. At each of the markers ride through the opening in the split rail fence and slowly cruise past each of the remains. Be careful not to disturb any of the remains, interfere with hikers or stray from the established paths. Local sights include the remains of Two Gun Saloon, Jonathan Tibbets Grasshopper Quarts Mill and Hangman's Tree (be careful of the four very aggressive ghosts at the base of the tree).

Turn left on 3N16 at 7.0 miles. Be sure to check the Original Diggings. Continue east (left) on 3N16 to 7.4 miles and turn left to the old log cabin. Park your bike here. Explore the cabin on foot and try to imagine what it must have been like to live here during the gold mining days, especially during a hard winter without TV and an electric blanket.

This is the turnaround point. When you're done exploring and perhaps having a snack, reclaim your bike from the ghost miner by the railing. Take a right on 3N16, turn left on 3N09 and ride back down to Highway 38. Turn right on the highway for the 2.0 miles to your car in the school parking lot.

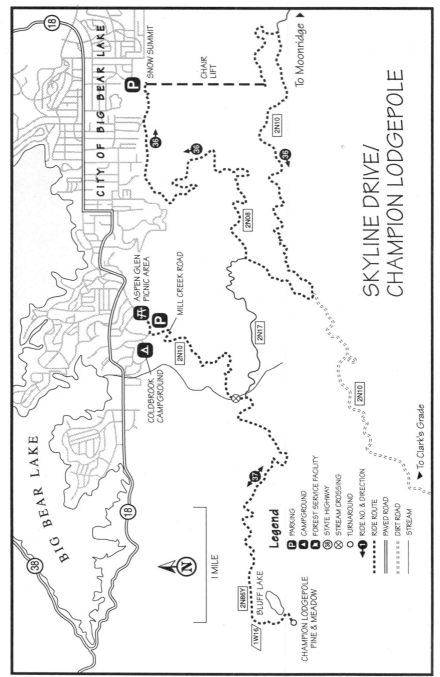

SKYLINE DRIVE/
CHAMPION LODGEPOLE

Legend

🅿	PARKING
◢	CAMPGROUND
🅕	FOREST SERVICE FACILITY
38	STATE HIGHWAY
⊗	STREAM CROSSING
○	TURNAROUND
➊	RIDE NO. & DIRECTION
••••••	RIDE ROUTE
———	PAVED ROAD
======	DIRT ROAD
———	STREAM

36 Skyline Drive via Sky Chair

Distance: 9 miles
Ride Type: Loop on fire roads and singletrack
Difficulty: Moderate, mildly technical
Elevation: 6,960' to 8,120'; 1,180' gain by chairlift
Seasons: Late spring, summer, fall
Topo Map: Big Bear Lake

Skyline Drive is an ideal ride for the beginning mountain bike rider who wants a few thrills, a fairly short ride, a little climbing, a lot of downhill and fabulous mountain views high in the forest. Except for a few roller coaster sections, the ride is mostly downhill—virtually all of the elevation gain is achieved with the chairlift. This may be a bit scary for someone who has never ridden one, but it's totally safe. The lift takes you and your bike (in separate chairs) to the top of the ski run. To ride the lift, obtain your ticket ($7) and sign a waiver in the Team Big Bear bike shop at the foot of the lift. You can also rent a bike and a helmet here, but I recommend you bring your own.

The route described here is the easiest option, and you can find additional routes on the map you get when you buy your lift ticket. (You can obtain a map from the counter even if you don't buy a lift ticket.) If you want a more challenging ride, stay on 2N10 to 2N08 rather than taking the 2N51Y turnoff from 2N10 to 2N08 (see map on facing page).

Getting There: Park in the Snow Summit lot at the upper end of Summit Boulevard in the town of Big Bear. Find the Team Big Bear bike shop, get your lift ticket and take your bike to the bottom of the lift. Step off the lift at the top, retrieve your bike.

Start your odometer and head east on the trail marked for bikes. It descends quickly, turns south and then hits 2N10 (Skyline Drive) just after you go around the locked gate. Turn right. Caution: This is a regularly used Forest Service vehicle road, so be sure to stay to the right, especially as you careen downhill through the left hand turns. To your left across the Santa Ana River canyon, you can see San Gorgonio Mountain (highest in Southern California) and to the southwest, the tip of the Inland Empire thousands of feet below and some 60 miles away.

At 1.7 miles continue straight at the junction with 2N51Y (may not be marked). Stay on 2N10 past the next spurs on the left. At about 2.7 miles, looking due west, you can see Butler Peak with its lookout tower perched on a massive rock outcropping. At 3.8 miles angle right at the junction onto 2N08. Just before you hit 2N08, a singletrack to a lookout (Grand View) climbs to the left and another singletrack takes off to the right. At 4.6 miles go right on 2N08 where it joins 2N17 and begin a great downhill ride. When you reach the unmarked junction at 6.3 miles continue straight on 2N08. Then at 7.6 miles watch for a trail taking off between two large boulders on your right as the road sweeps around to the left. (If you miss the turn you hit pavement in 0.2 mile. Just turn around and go back up the hill, looking for the singletrack entrance on your left.)

This is the Town Trail back to Snow Summit, and it's a great roller coaster ride through quick turns, around rock outcroppings, and over streams. Go past the gate at the end of the buildings and cruise into the "bike jungle" outside Team Big Bear's shop where you started this escapade.

37 Champion Lodgepole/ Bluff Mesa

Distance: 10.4 miles
Difficulty: Moderately strenuous, mildly technical
Elevation: 6,870' to 7,600'; 730' gain
Ride Type: Out and back on fire roads, singletrack and pavement
Seasons: Late spring, summer, fall
Topo Map: Big Bear Lake

On this trip, you'll find what is believed to be the largest lodgepole pine standing guard over a serene mountain meadow. The route is hilly, remote, and heavily forested in spots. It courses past beautiful rock formations on the way to the tree. The ride includes 2 miles of an easy, delightful singletrack. This is a two water bottle ride. Be sure to carry food.

Getting There: Park your car at Aspen Glen Picnic Area on Mill Creek Road just off of Bear Boulevard on the west end of the lake.

Begin your ride by turning left on Mill Creek Road. Ride 0.2 mile, turn left at the junction of Mill Creek and Tulip and begin climbing on 2N10. The road is paved, steep and winding. Be careful to stay to the right. You pass small, old wood cabins set well back from the road; they are privately owned but on land leased from the Forest Service. Because of the large lots, these owners enjoy far more privacy than do most of the residents in Big Bear.

Just before the pavement ends after 0.8 mile, there is a junction. Stay left because the branch to the right goes to the Cedar Lake Christian Camp. When the dirt road begins, you pass through an open gate. Remember, this is a regular Forest Service road used by cars and trucks, so stay alert for them and ride as close to the right as is safe. There are many good views of Big Bear Lake to your right as you climb up from the valley.

At the next junction, 1.3 miles from the start, 2N17 to Skyline Drive begins, but you continue straight ahead on 2N10. You ride through a beautiful grove of old growth ponderosa pines as you continue to climb. You begin seeing lesser dirt roads branching off 2N10, but don't take any of them unless you feel adventurous. At the next junction 2N52Y goes left, but you continue to the right around the bend. At the next junction 2N10B goes right, but once again, continue straight on 2N10.

After 2.6 miles of steady climbing with only a few level sections, you finally reach the top of the majority of the steep sections. Now there are several well-earned descents through the forest and past extensive rock formations. Except for some washboard sections the road is in fine condition, and you can maintain a pretty good speed along the right hand side. To the right you can catch glimpses of the lake and valley through the thick stands of trees. The road levels out and even takes you on some descents. After 3.6 miles you come to a junction with 2N86. Look for the sign announcing the Bluff Lake YMCA Camp, 2 miles, and the Lodgepole Pine, 3 miles, both to the left. Take 2N86 to the right. It's a dead-end road, but you turn off before it ends.

On both sides of the road are massive boulder formations that invite exploration. If you look closely you can see numerous small double tracks (jeep roads) meandering off into the forest among these formations. If you have the time and inclination, explore these roads but be sure to stay on them. Don't cut new trails here or  anywhere else. At the junction of 2N86A and 2N86 continue left on 2N86A. After 0.1 mile bear right at the unmarked Y. After 4.2 miles look for a small sign on your left indicating the Bluff Mesa Trail, Champion Lodgepole Pine, 1 mile. Turn left off the road onto Trail 1W16.

This is a fun, beautiful, only slightly technical singletrack. It should be no problem even for a beginning mountain bike rider. Watch for hikers and be ready to yield to them. Coast down to a small stream crossed by a narrow, short wooden bridge.

Cross the bridge and immediately turn right, where you can see a beautiful meadow ringed by trees and large rock formations. On your left is a split rail fence encircling the base of the Champion Lodgepole.

Park your bike and take a respectful walk around the fence to ponder the height and beauty of this spectacular conifer. If you planned ahead and brought along a picnic lunch, this is the perfect place to eat it. The meadow is a peaceful, spiritual place that deserves quiet and appreciation for its natural beauty.

After your pause here, the route returns to the starting point at Aspen Glen Picnic Ground. You can continue past the Champion Lodgepole either to the east or to the west. The Siberia Creek Trail begins here. The trail to the west (left) takes you either to the Bluff Mesa YMCA camp or out to 2N10, depending on which branch you take.

The return to Aspen Glen retraces your route. Take the singletrack back to 2N86A, turn right, stay to the left at the next unmarked junction and at the junction with 2N10. Stay right at the junction with 2N85 and continue on 2N10 (past junction with 2N17) through the open gate and onto pavement (requires good bike handling on the steep descents.) When you get to the pavement be sure to control your speed because the steep, sharp turns can lead you right into oncoming traffic if you aren't careful to stay on the right side of the center line. At the T, turn right to return to the campground and your car.

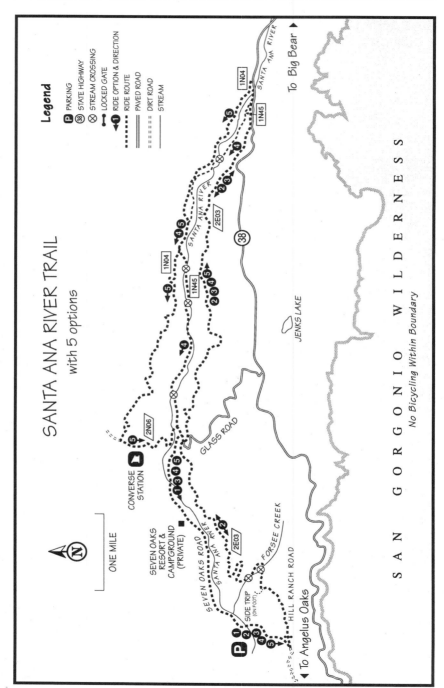

SANTA ANA RIVER TRAIL

with 5 options

38 Santa Ana River Trail

Distance: See listed options
Difficulty: See listed options
Elevation: 5,000' to 6,200'; gain 1,200'
Ride Type: Depends on option taken
Seasons: Late spring, summer and fall

This is the longest singletrack in the forest and it's one of my favorites. (It's also part of the Santa Ana River Corridor Trail System that starts in Heart Bar and, when completed, will eventually go all the way to the ocean.) You have the option of doing this ride as an out-and-back trip or as four different loops. In fact, since every option is a great ride, consider doing each one during the course of the season. You'll catch magnificent vistas of the Santa Ana River valley and mountain ranges, cross several streams and cruise through small meadows. And you'll ride through miles of beautiful ponderosa pine, lodgepole pine, California black oak and Engleman oak forest canopies. The downhills are fast and exciting while some of the climbs are short and steep but not difficult.

Take plenty of food and at least two water bottles for these rides.

Caution: The trail options listed below are thrilling and just a touch risky in spots. This trail was designed and built for hikers and horses—very slow movers! Portions of the singletrack twist sharply while clinging to the sides of very steep slopes. In addition, during the fall, many of these same sections are carpeted with acorns. Ever ridden on marbles? Here's your opportunity! So, if these turns are taken at more than a mere crawl, or if you slip, you may be launched into space. It's a long way

down and I see no way for you to get yourself *and* your bike up to the trail—even if you wanted to.

Getting There: From Angelus Oaks (nearest services) on Highway 38, drive down toward Seven Oaks via Middle Control Road (dirt, starts 0.5 mile east of Angelus Oaks). Following are the ride descriptions for the beginning of all the options. Park off the road on either side of the river (popular parking area for fishermen).

Start by riding back up Middle Control Road. At 0.9 mile look for a dirt road angling back to the left. Take this up to and over the locked gate. This is Hill Ranch Road or 1N07 (formerly Forsee Creek Road). At 2.7 miles there's a spur taking off to the left that dead-ends at the top of a plateau. If you feel like a short hike, this is perfect. If not, continue around to the right, down a short slope to the Santa Ana River Trail marker, 2E03, branching left. Drop onto the trail here to begin your singletrack adventure.

The trail crosses Forsee Creek (look for the log). The flow could be heavy and deep, depending on the snow runoff and time of year. At 3.2 miles, Seven Oaks Resort is to your left at the bottom of the canyon. Look for manzanita (Spanish for little apple—the red berries are edible in the fall and taste like apple), desert sage and occasional holly. You also ride through small stands of incense cedar (red, stringy, gnarly bark) and past many pines that have been killed by the bark beetle. The infestation became epidemic because years of drought weakened the trees.

At 4.0 miles, you cross two streams (they can be deep) and then cross Glass Road at 5.4 miles.

You have a number of options with this ride. (The mileages given here are ride totals.)

Option 1:
9.6-mile loop
Turn left onto the pavement (watch for cars coming down the road!). Turn left again at the junction with Seven Oaks Road. Continue on Seven Oaks Road to the resort. If you have the time, stop in for refueling. This is a quaint old place and well worth a visit. Take Seven Oaks Road back down to your car.

Option 2:
23 miles out and back
The trail picks up on the other side of the road about 60 feet down the pavement and continues east. At 7.0 miles the trail bends sharply to the right as it clings to the sheer, exposed slope with an open vista to the left. At 8.9 miles continue straight through an unmarked junction. (The branch to the right heads up 1 mile, goes over the ridge and drops into Barton Flats Campground. The left branch drops 1 mile to the Santa Ana River and 1N45.) Continue the roller coaster, hill-hugging escapade another 2.6 miles to the pavement and a small parking area adjacent to Highway 38 and opposite the South Fork Campground. This is the turnaround point for two of the five optional return routes. Retrace your route, getting back on 2E03, staying

on the singletrack until it joins Hill Ranch Road (after crossing Forsee Creek). Take the old road back to and around the locked gate, turn right on Middle Control Road and ride 0.9 mile back down to your car.

Option 3:
21 miles, out and back with loop
From the turnaround point in Option 2, retrace your route just to Glass Road (at 17.2 miles from the start). Turn right on the pavement. Then bear left at the junction with Seven Oaks Road. Continue on Seven Oaks Road to the resort and then to your car.

Option 4:
20.4-mile loop
This is particularly attractive on a hot day when you'd like to get wet! From the turnaround point in Option 2, return on the pavement, 1N45, but do not get back onto the singletrack. The road soon becomes dirt. For the next 5.5 miles you parallel and cross the river four times, passing a few cabins and private camps for the next several miles. Many of these cabins are on government leased land. You'll also see several rugged old stone homes built from native rock some 60 or more years ago.

After 12.5 miles, you come to the first of four wet crossings of the Santa Ana River. You can either carry your bike across, hitch a ride in a passing car or truck or try riding it. If the water is no more than 8 to 10 inches deep, you'll probably be able to ride it. The stream bottom is rocky, not sandy or slippery. The only thing to be concerned about is getting water into the bearings of your bike. If the hubs, bottom bracket and pedals are sealed, you should have no problem—unless you slip and dump yourself and your bike. The choice is yours. Just before the river crossing, there's at least one trail to the right that leads to well shaded, stream-side picnic spots.

At 14.0 miles, the road splits. Take the left branch, 1N45. At 14.4 miles, you come to the second stream crossing. Another 0.4 mile brings you to a third river crossing. At 16.2 miles, cross the river the last time. This becomes Seven Oaks Road and is paved. At 16.6 miles, 2N06 takes off to the right. Continue straight 0.1 mile (note the massive old incense cedar on the northwest corner). Turn right at the junction with Glass Road, heading toward Seven Oaks Resort and back to your car.

Option 5:
24.1-mile loop

If you want to stay dry and you have the energy to climb a little, return via 1N04 and Converse Station. Ride out of the parking area to the highway and cross the highway. Turn left, and then cross the bridge over the Santa Ana River. Watch for traffic as you cross the highway again to the left. Enter 1N04 (0.2 mile from the parking area on the other side of the river). Ride west on a gentle climb on 1N04 to its junction with 1N45 at 14.2 miles. At the next junction turn right onto 1N04 again and continue the climb to 6,000 feet. At 18.0 miles turn left at the unmarked junction (Radford Road). If you miss this you quickly come to another junction, which is 2N06. Turn left here. Either road will get you to Converse Station and the beginning of a paved downhill cruise.

At the bottom of Radford Road turn right onto Seven Oaks Road. Bear right at the junction with Glass Road, past Seven Oaks Resort (stop for refueling if you want). In another 1.5 miles you're back to your car.

For additional rides in this area, please refer to *Mountain Biking the Coast Range, Guide 10: San Bernardino Mountains,* by Robert Shipley and Allen Thibault, ISBN 0-938665-16-2 (see p. 304).

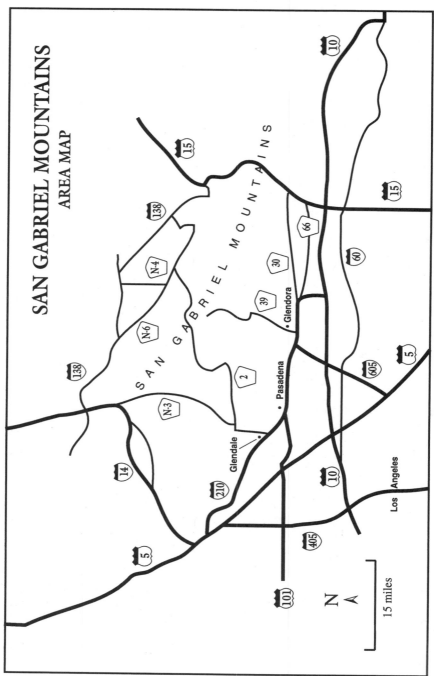

SAN GABRIEL MOUNTAINS
AREA MAP

CHAPTER 5

San Gabriel Mountains

By Mike Troy

Imagine yourself at 6,000 feet elevation in the San Gabriel Mountains, just an hour above Los Angeles, one of the largest cities in the United States. To the horizon, peak after peak of craggy mountains give way to rugged canyons. Lying west to east along the northern boundary of the Los Angeles Basin, the San Gabriels offer recreational opportunities to millions of people. Your mountain bike can take you to a place where you can forget the rush and noise of the sprawling city far below.

Although the San Gabriels provide some of the most strenuous and technical biking in Southern California, they hold something for every level of mountain cyclist. What's your preference? An easy cruise up the beautiful and historic lower Arroyo Seco or a 9-mile climb to the top of Mt. Wilson? Something in between? It's here.

For over 100 years, people have visited these mountains to seek solitude and recreation. They came first on foot, then by horse and mule or wagon; later by railroad (yes, railroad!) and automobile. Now, the rugged and sophisticated mountain bicycle provides a near-perfect vehicle for exploration and quiet, non-polluting, low impact recreation.

Today the highways, roads and trails that crisscross the area make visiting the forest an easy task. There is plenty of room for exploration and enough space to find solitude if that's what you're seeking. Thousands of acres to pedal will challenge, thrill, and reward you for years to come.

The Arroyo Seco front range is easily accessible, very scenic, and contains some of Southern California's most challenging climbs and best singletrack. It is also dotted with the ruins of historic hotels and lodges. The Arroyo Seco backcountry, on the northern side of the mountains, is less crowded but still accessible. Its higher elevations and cleaner air make it a good choice in the hot summer months.

Those who enjoy desert environments will want to visit the Valyermo

District. Its relatively small network of roads is uncrowded and offers some of the best riding in Angeles National Forest. The Crystal Lake area in the Mt. Baldy District is unique in the Angeles, containing the only natural lake in the San Gabriels. Beautiful stands of cedar also grace the area.

The San Gabriels are urban mountain biking at its best!

39 Mt. Gleason Area: Roundtop/Mt. Pacifico

Distance: 19 miles
Difficulty: Very strenuous, technical if you take the 4WD loop option
Elevation: 2,400' gain
Ride Type: In and out on fire road
Season: Spring, summer, fall
Topo Map: Pacifico Mountain, Chilao Flats

Rising out of the northern section of the Tujunga, Mt. Gleason's broad shoulders offer fine roads for exploring the pine forest. The 6,500-foot elevation brings relatively cool temperatures year round. During most winters, the slopes of Mt. Gleason are covered with snow. The paved road (3N17) from Mill Creek Summit allows easy auto access to the top of Mt. Gleason and lends itself well to cycling, although it involves two good climbs to get there.

For families, driving the road to the summit of Mt. Gleason and exploring the area by bicycle would be a great adventure. For more information on the Tujunga District, contact the USFS at 12371 N. Little Tujunga Canyon Road, San Fernando, CA 91342, (818) 899-1900.

A sister mountain to Mt. Gleason, Mt. Pacifico is 7,000 feet high and just as lovely. It is crisscrossed with jeep roads and hosts the desirable Pacifico Campground. You reach the summit by way of a long and very constant climb.

This ride also visits Roundtop and Granite Mountains as optional side roads.

Getting There: The ride begins at Mill Creek Summit Rest Area, located on Angeles Forest Highway. Here, 3N17 descends from the east face of Mt. Gleason and crosses An-geles Forest Highway before heading up toward Pacifico. Mill Creek Rest Area has toilets in case you want to start in comfort. You may start from here or drive up 3N17 through Mill Creek Station and park at the end of the pavement at the parking lot. There are restroom facilities here and good water. The parking lot is for day-use only, and the gate at Angeles Crest Highway may close at dusk. If you plan to take a long time on your trip, it would be best to check this out or park at Mill Creek Rest Area.

Starting from the upper parking area, go up 3N17 past the gate and onto the dirt. This isn't a really difficult climb, but it is constant and gives you little rest. One of the nicest things about riding the north side of the range at these higher elevations is the nifty view into the Antelope Valley and on rare, clear days, to the Tehachapis and beyond. The patchwork of the valley floor is quite a sight. At 3.2 miles you reach the intersection with the road to Roundtop Mountain. The trip out to Roundtop and back is a worthwhile diversion if you're not too tuckered out, and it offers a different perspective of the Pacifico area.

As you are standing there at the crossroads munching your Power Bar and deciding which way to go, you can see a time-worn and decrepit trail

MT. GLEASON AREA

to Alton

Aliso Canyon Rd.

to Highway 14

N

1 mile

to Mt. Gleason

3N17

MT. PACIFICO

Mill Creek
Summit

GRANITE MTN.

Angeles Forest Hwy

ROUNDTOP

to Highway 2 and
Glendale/Pasadena

■ Parking
▪-▪- Best 100 Route
---- Other Bike Routes
          (not described in book)
—— Paved Road
▬▬ Freeway
········· Off-Limits or
          Not Recommended

© 1993 Fine Edge Productions

that takes off to the left of the sign that points the way to Mt. Pacifico. This "trail" skirts the north side of the mountain and is not rideable, but a short and careful scramble out a ways offers you an outstanding look down Tie Canyon towards Aliso Canyon Road.

Feeling up to the challenge of a little side trip? Good. Then Roundtop it is. Turn right on 3N90 where a sign reads *Granite Mountain - 1 Mile, Roundtop Mountain - 3 Miles*. (The campground on Roundtop no longer exists.) This is a roller coaster of a road and a good workout up to the road's end 6.2 miles later on the 6,300 foot Roundtop Mountain. From here, you have a clear view over Chilao Flats and Angeles Crest Highway into the San Gabriel Wilderness.

There is no place to go but back the way you came. A right turn on 3N17 towards Pacifico continues the ride. At 9.1 miles go past a steep 4WD road. (A return option that uses this road is discussed later.) At 10.3 miles turn left and up. At 11.4 miles you pop up on top of Pacifico.

There are numerous paths to explore, but if you keep left and continue climbing a little more, you reach Pacifico Campground at 11.9 miles. Situated amidst boulders large and small and well shaded by large pines, this is a lovely campground where you can have lunch and scramble around. There are tables and pit toilets here. Looking down towards the desert floor, Little Rock Reservoir is the small blue puddle 4,000 feet below. When you tire of clear, thin air and solitude (if you ever do), returning to your vehicle is a downhill joy as you retrace your path down the mountain.

If you're looking for a more adventurous and technically challenging route off Pacifico, the 4WD road you passed on your way up at 9.1 miles will do nicely. Ride down the main road off the mountain, until at 13.1 miles (about 1 mile from the campground), you can take a branch road off to the right. You know you are on the right road if you see the Pacific Crest Trail crossing nearby. (The Pacific Crest Trail is closed to bicycle traffic.) Follow the 4WD road for steep, challenging climbs and nasty downhills. At 13.7 miles turn left, then right again and continue west along the ridge. At 14.2 miles you pop up on a small hill and can see down to Mill Creek Summit.

From here it gets somewhat confusing as there are numerous paths to choose from. However, you can see 3N17 below you to your left and with a little searching, the path down to it is obvious. It is also rough, rocky and knee deep in whoop-dees. When you drop onto 3N17, turn right and enjoy a really fun and rapid cruise back to your car at Mill Creek Summit. At 18.6 miles you are there!

Arroyo Seco Front Range

Encompassing the front range of the San Gabriels above the foothill cities of La Canada, Altadena and Sierra Madre, and extending northeast along Angeles Crest Highway to Krakta Ridge, the Arroyo Seco District is perhaps the most heavily used area in the San Gabriels. Angeles Crest Highway is like a magnet drawing people to the trails and camping areas easily accessed along its winding path through the mountains. Some of the most popular rides in the San Gabriels are found here. On any fair weather weekend, the Arroyo Seco, the Mt. Wilson Toll Road, Mt. Lowe and many other popular routes bring together cyclists, hikers and equestrians all seeking the same benefits the forest environment supplies. The easy access and high quality riding means you will seldom be alone as you ride. With all the heavy traffic, it's no wonder that mountain bike land access in the San Gabriels first became an issue here, giving birth to one of the first mountain bike trail building and land access groups—the Mt. Wilson Bicycle Association. Working with the Forest Service, the Mt. Wilson group has played a major part in keeping these areas open for

our enjoyment. As you ride here, keep their efforts in mind and ride responsibly. For the latest trail information, contact the USFS Arroyo Seco District, Oak Grove Park, Flintridge, CA 91011, (818) 790-1151.

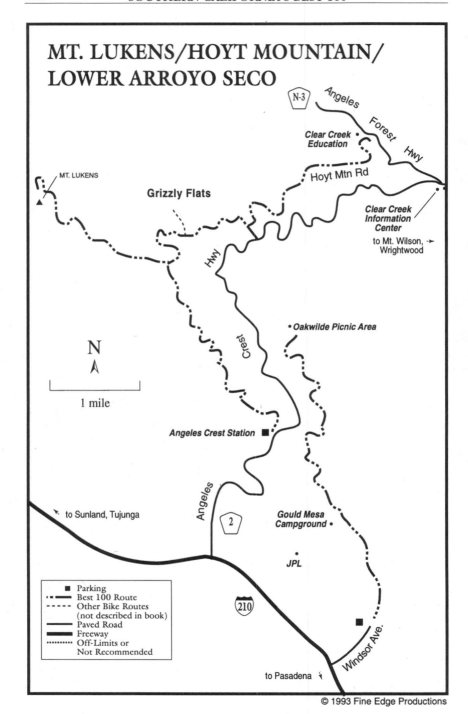

MT. LUKENS/HOYT MOUNTAIN/
LOWER ARROYO SECO

N-3

Angeles Forest Hwy

Clear Creek Education

Hoyt Mtn Rd

MT. LUKENS

Grizzly Flats

Clear Creek Information Center

to Mt. Wilson, Wrightwood

Hwy

Oakwilde Picnic Area

N

1 mile

Crest

Angeles Crest Station ■

to Sunland, Tujunga

Angeles

2

Gould Mesa Campground

JPL

210

Windsor Ave.

to Pasadena ↓

■ Parking
∙∙—— Best 100 Route
- - - - Other Bike Routes
        (not described in book)
——— Paved Road
━━━ Freeway
∙∙∙∙∙∙∙∙∙∙ Off-Limits or
        Not Recommended

© 1993 Fine Edge Productions

40 Mt. Lukens/Hoyt Mountain

Distance: 16.2 miles
Difficulty: Very strenuous, nontechnical; technical if you take the Hoyt Mountain option
Elevation: 2,700' gain
Ride Type: Fire road loop
Season: Most of the year, but summer can be hot and smoggy
Topo Map: Pasadena, Condor Peak

This is a very popular front-country workout. The climb to the top of Mt. Lukens is a stiff one, but the view is dramatic if the air is clear enough to see any distance at all. Mt. Lukens is named for Theodore P. Lukens, who helped shape the Angeles National Forest and introduced the concept of reforestation to the slopes of the often fire-ravaged San Gabriels. Today, electronic towers crowning the mountain top that carries his name are the objects to shoot for on this ride. The top of the mountain is city property and bristles with antennas instead of trees.

Getting There: Begin at Angeles Crest Station off Angeles Crest Highway. This is not far up from the city and is easily found on the left of the highway. Park here, making sure your auto will not block any emergency vehicles.

Fire road 2N76 begins at the back of the station property, so if you follow the road through the station you come right to the fire road. The road is signed 2N76A. Up toward Mt. Lukens you go. The climb is steep in some places and is lousy with washboard from the vehicle traffic up to the electronic sites. At 3.1 miles you intersect with the Earl Canyon motorway coming up from La Crescenta. Keep right. At 3.3 miles

keep left at the Grizzly Flat Road turnoff. It's still pretty tough climbing for a while until the road levels off a little bit.

At 5.2 miles keep right. The end of the hard work is in sight, and 6.0 miles finds you at the top. The heat of the lower part of the ride is abated by a cool breeze and there is plenty to look at if the day is clear enough. The views over the valley and into the backcountry of the San Gabriels are your reward.

The return is simple if you just want to retrace your steps to Angeles Crest Station. To add some fun and mileage, make a loop out of this ride by taking the Grizzly Flat turnoff on the way down the mountain. Bounce down 2N76 from the top of Lukens until at 9.3 miles you are back to the Grizzly Flat turnoff. Turn left and descend a fun and twisty fire road blissfully free of washboard, but covered with loose rocks.

At 11.3 miles keep right where the road splits to drop onto Grizzly Flats. It's a little up and down until you come to a fork at 12.4 miles and a water tank. Angeles Crest Highway is visible below; keep right and head for it. At 13.1 you reach the highway. Turn right and ride the highway back to Angeles Crest Station. This is all downhill and is an easy cruise. Keep an eye out for would-be Mario Andrettis—the shoulder here is narrow. At 16.2 miles you have finished.

The more advanced rider may want to try climbing to Hoyt Mountain. The singletrack on this option is the remains of a decaying roadbed, now narrowed into a rocky and brushy singletrack. Don't let the few nasty sections worry you, though—this is still a great ride. The fire road uphill at the start is all the real climbing you will do, and the fast return on Angeles Crest Highway is a fitting end. *Caution:* Be very aware of vehicle traffic on the highway return.

Riding up 2N76 toward Mt. Lukens from Angeles Crest Station to the Grizzly Flats road, 2N80, and then following 2N80 to Hoyt Mountain would be a total loop of 18 miles or so and would add much more climbing. This is a great addition if you are up for the increased mileage.

Coming down 2N80 you come to a water tank and a fork in the road. Take the left fork and continue past the gate on a little-used fire road. Following power lines, this is a pretty steep climb but doesn't last long. You top out at 1.8 miles. It seems that the road ends here, but if you look past the tower on the left, there is a distinct trail heading off around the side of the mountain.

The trail starts out on several three-foot-deep rollers and then begins to wind its way through the rocks and brush. Except for some sections where rock slides have encroached onto the trail, this is great fun. Little yucca plants bite at your ankles and low branches swipe at your head. After a bit, the trail improves and comes to a small wooden creek crossing. Cross over this bridge and follow the road up to the pavement at the back of Clear Creek Outdoor Education Center. Turn right up the pavement. Soon you are at Angeles Forest Highway. Turn right again and work your way up to Angeles Crest Highway at 4.9 miles. You are near the road to Josephine Peak and right by Clear Creek Station. Turn right on Angeles Crest Highway and enjoy a quick downhill all the way back to your starting point.

41 Lower Arroyo Seco

Distance: 12 miles
Difficulty: Easy and mildly technical
Elevation: 600' gain
Ride Type: In-and-out trail
Season: Year round
Topo Map: Pasadena, Condor Peak

With the exception of the Mt. Wilson Toll Road, this forest access is without a doubt the most well used in the front country. Due to its easy beginning and scenic beauty, the lower Arroyo Seco is a magnet for trail users of all kinds. This trail is usually done by less experienced riders from the bottom, in as far as their skills allow. The first few miles are pretty easy and are very lovely. Past Oakwilde Camp, the going gets very technical and demanding. The top part of the trail pops out at Switzer's Camp and continues up canyon to Red Box. Convenient access by auto to both the top and bottom of the trail allows an easy car shuttle and has resulted in many cyclists using the Arroyo Seco as a thrill ride, increasing tensions between cyclists and other users. The true mountain cyclist looks at the uphill as "dues" and is willing to pay them before enjoying the downhill to come. If people in your group suggest a shuttle blitz on the Arroyo Seco, point out the error of their ways before you flatten their tires.

Getting There: From the Arroyo Boulevard exit at the 210 Freeway turn left onto Windsor Avenue and drive toward the San Gabriels for a few blocks. There is a parking area on the left that sits above the dry wash of the Arroyo Seco across from Jet Pro-

pulsion Lab (JPL) and is a good staging area. This parking lot will nearly always be busy with cyclists gearing up for the ride up the Arroyo.

From the parking lot, ride north up Windsor Avenue to a sharp bend in the road. The road splits at this bend and goes three ways. Take the middle path around a gate where a sign announces this as a part of the Gabrielino National Recreational Trail, 11W14. Drop down a paved road. At 0.7 mile keep right. You don't have to wait long for the ride to turn lovely. Ornate bridges framed with boughs of alder cross the creek, now alive with a small singing brook. The going is easy and relaxing as you travel the remains of the roadway placed here to service the resorts that were formerly located in the canyon. For many years the sylvan retreats of Oakwilde and Switzer's traded upon the beauty of the Arroyo Seco to draw people to the comforts they offered.

At 1.3 miles keep left from the Brown Mountain access road and continue up canyon under large sycamores. Pedaling easily, you soon pass Gould Mesa Campground. The trail gets just a touch trickier in bits and pieces but is still very enjoyable. At 3.1 miles you pass Nino picnic grounds. Past Nino the going gets a little more challenging, rocky and wet with stream crossings aplenty. Bounce, splash and dab as little as possible to 4.3 miles, where the trail divides at Paul Little Picnic Area.

This marks a decision point. If the preceding miles were challenging enough, then this is a good stopping point. Otherwise, continue on up to Oakwilde. Either way, you should take a little detour to the left through Paul Little and follow a well worn trail a short distance to the base of a nifty waterfall coming from the Brown Canyon debris dam, an especially nice snack stop.

Back on the trail split at Paul Little, if you are returning to your car, please watch your speed down the Arroyo Seco. If you are continu-

ing (now at 4.7 miles if you made the detour to the waterfall), push your bike up the sandy, steep section of the Gabrielino as it climbs up along the Brown Canyon debris dam and just as quickly drops down again to creek bed level. From here to Oakwilde Camp it is more of the same, simply lovely and enjoyable singletrack, and just technical enough to keep an experienced rider grinning and your plebe buddies flailing.

At 6.0 miles you reach Oakwilde Camp. In 1911 J. R. Phillips built a resort at this spot. Improving an old road from the mouth of the canyon to his doorstep, he made the trip to Oakwilde a possible, although adventurous, trip by auto with lots of

creek crossings. The road, subject to frequent washouts, had to be rebuilt nearly every year. The resort was a great success until the great flood of 1938 washed the road away for the last time. Oakwilde Camp closed in the early 1940s; now it's simply a nice place to rest and consider the rest of the trip.

To continue up the trail from here requires a lot more work than you put out to get to Oakwilde. Unless you feel very confident about your abilities and fitness, I would recommend that you turn around here and enjoy the trip down-canyon.

42 Mt. Lowe/ Echo Mountain Loop

Distance: 12.5 miles
Difficulty: Very strenuous, nontechnical to very technical
Elevation: 2,800' gain
Ride Type: Loop on pavement, fire road and singletrack
Season: Year round
Topo Map: Pasadena, Mt. Wilson

There is a lot of history in this highly recommended ride. The first 2.5 miles of steep pavement is by far the most difficult. Once you hit the dirt, the grade eases considerably. This ride can easily be broken up into shorter (and easier) rides, but no matter what, you need to make it past the brutal pavement section. For example, riding out to the ruins at Echo Mountain would be 3.5 miles one way and would be a doable, albeit strenuous, beginner ride.

Getting There: From the 210, take Lake Avenue north to its end. Go left and continue for a few miles until you see a yellow light. This marks Chaney Trail. Turn right and climb to the top of Chaney Trail (at Sunset Ridge) where the road splits to drop left into Millard Campground and right up to Mt. Lowe. The road to Mt. Lowe is gated at this intersection. Parking here is limited and fills up quickly on the weekends. If full, you can start from the Millard Campground parking lot, although this would add a tough climb up from Millard to the gate at the Mt. Lowe Road.

Even though it is paved, the first section of the roadway up to the Cape of Good Hope is by far the most strenuous of the trip. Plug along, enjoying the view of the city below, and I'll tell you a story about a man and his vision.

In 1888, Professor Thaddeus Sobieski Coulincourt Lowe (Thad to his friends), Civil War balloonist extraordinaire and self-made man, settled in Pasadena with retirement in mind. Professor Lowe was no couch potato, however, and he felt like a man without a mission. Looking up into the San Gabriels every day from his home, Lowe was inspired to do something. He just didn't know what. In 1890, he had a fateful meeting with another visionary, David MacPherson, an engineer by trade. Together they hatched a plan to build a railway to the summit of Mt. Wilson, carrying folks up into the heights of the front country for a modest fee.

Problems with easements dashed their hopes of ascending Mt. Wilson, so they turned their attention to a lesser peak, Echo Mountain. MacPherson oversaw the construction of a cogwheel railway from Rubio Canyon up to Echo Mountain, a marvelous feat of engineering. The Great Rubio Incline exceeded a 60 percent grade in some places and rose some 1,300 feet in a little over half a mile—real pixie ring stuff. At the end of the incline, Professor Lowe built a hotel, a small observatory and a zoo. All this came to be known as the White City. In 1893, the first public trip was conducted on the railway. To much fanfare, honored guests were winched up the incline by a 3,000 pound cable attached to a great bullwheel, all located on the top of the mountain.

The Echo Mountain complex was a great success, and Professor Lowe set out to continue his railway up into the San Gabriels to the summit of Mt. Lowe. The railway never quite reached the top of Mt. Lowe, but it did follow a winding and scenic four-mile course up to Crystal Springs, a beautiful oak-shaded cove on the side of Mt. Lowe, where he constructed Ye Alpine Tavern, a Swiss chalet-style resort. Scores of people rode the railway into the mountains and hiked, rode horses, played tennis or just lounged around the tavern, enjoying the remote beauty of the quiet forest.

Although seemingly very successful, the endeavor placed a great financial strain on Lowe and he lost his beloved railroad to mounting debts. Although operated by other parties into this century, an unsure economy and changed interests on the part of the public brought a gradual decline to the railway. Fire and other natural disasters spelled the end for Professor Lowe's dream, and by the late 1930s, the Mt. Lowe Railway had ceased operation.

Back to the ride! Still on the pavement, at 1.5 miles stay right. At 1.7 miles you pass a gate and a sign that reads: *1.5 Miles - Echo Mountain 3.5 Miles - Mt. Lowe Campground 1.7 Miles - Mt. Wilson Road.* Just past here there's a roadside map showing the old railway route. A little more cranking brings you to the beginning of Sunset Ridge Trail (on the left). This nicely technical trail takes you back to the gate at Chaney Drive.

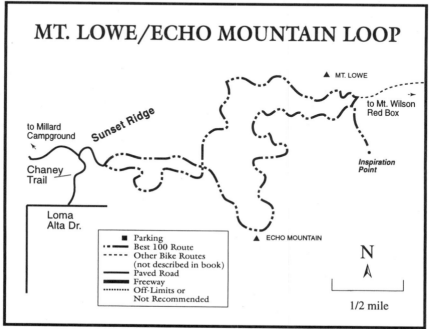

MT. LOWE/ECHO MOUNTAIN LOOP

▲ MT. LOWE

to Mt. Wilson
Red Box

to Millard
Campground

Sunset Ridge

Inspiration
Point

Chaney
Trail

Loma
Alta Dr.

▲ ECHO MOUNTAIN

N

■ Parking
▪▪▬ Best 100 Route
▪▪▪▪ Other Bike Routes
     (not described in book)
▬▬ Paved Road
▬▬ Freeway
▪▪▪▪ Off-Limits or
     Not Recommended

1/2 mile

Past Sunset Trail on the right is the Echo Mountain Trail to—surprise, surprise—Echo Mountain. Both of these trails are ridden on the return trip, but anyone who is too pooped to pedal uphill anymore would be well advised to ride out to Echo Mountain and explore the ruins of the White City before returning home.

A little farther up the Mt. Lowe Road the pavement ends at the Cape of Good Hope and you begin to ride on the route of the original railway. This is a nice railroad grade and is much easier than the pavement behind you. As the miles pass by, you ride through history, passing such noted locations as the Circular Bridge (3.3 miles), where the railway negotiated a sharp curve by means of a trestle over the canyon below, and the Granite Gate (4.4 miles), where the railway bed was blasted through solid rock. Some of the original electrical wires that supplied power to the railway cars are still visible here.

At 5.2 miles you reach the Mt. Lowe Campground, built on the site of the Alpine Tavern. This is a fine lunch spot since the climbing is mostly over and the ruins of the tavern are fun to sit on as you try to imagine the way it was in its heyday some 90 years ago.

Back on the Mt. Lowe Road, ride a little bit farther uphill (0.3 mile) to an intersection with the road to Inspiration Point and the Idlehour and Sam Merrill trailheads. Mt. Wilson is plainly visible and the Mt. Lowe Road continues around San Gabriel Peak before intersecting with the road to Mt. Wilson and Red Box. Stop climbing here and take a quick little jaunt out to Inspiration Point before hitting the Sam Merrill Trail.

Take a right up the fire road and ride the short distance out to

some ruins, where sighting tubes point out distant landmarks like Venice, the Rose Bowl and Los Angeles. Unfortunately it is a rare clear day that a peek through the pipes provides anything other than haze. Note: The Castle Canyon Trail which takes off from here is *not recommended* as a bike trail.

Return to the trailhead for the Sam Merrill, on the left now at 6.0

miles, and then turn left onto the singletrack. This trail has many personalities in its 2.6 miles to Echo Mountain. It is lovely and shaded, then exposed and rocky, and mostly always technical and challenging. On many of the large rock outcroppings in the lower part of the trail, I suffered my first double pinch flat of the year, a dubious accomplishment indeed. There are also many sharp switchbacks to negotiate, and proper riding techniques are required to reduce the impact on the trail structures. Some are better walked than ridden. Don't brakeslide! As always, ride softly and watch for other trail users.

At 8.6 miles you reach the ruins at Echo Mountain. As you intersect with the Echo Mountain Trail (to the right), the Sam Merrill continues on down the mountainside. This section is very narrow, tight and exposed, and it is *not recommended* for bikes. If you like, take a left and ride out to the ruins of the White City, past the great bullwheel and the ruins of the power house. There are still remnants of the railroad tracks heading toward the precipice into Rubio Canyon.

To continue the ride, follow the Echo Mountain Trail back out to the pavement of the Cape of Good Hope, visible to the west. This short section of railroad bed makes a fine trail, although there is some exposure, so use caution. There are also a lot of hikers using this and the Sunset Ridge Trail to come, so be good boys and girls.

Back on the pavement now at 9.6 miles, turn left and ride 150 feet or so to the trailhead for the Sunset Ridge Trail. Turn right and proceed onto the trail. Still a technical trail (winding above Millard Canyon), it is more shaded and damp than the Sam Merrill. Watch for poison oak! It thrives here. As with the Sam Merrill, there are several tight switchbacks to negotiate. At 10.6 miles you come to a paved spur road from the Mt. Lowe Road. Continue straight ahead on the trail. This last section of trail is mellow and rolling. At 11.6 miles stay left. At 12.1 miles you are back at the pavement of the Mt. Lowe Road, and a right turn brings you down to the gate and your starting point after 12.5 miles.

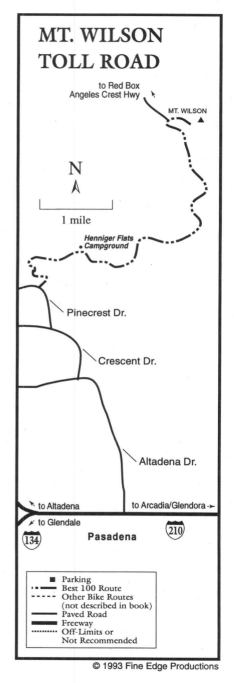

MT. WILSON TOLL ROAD

to Red Box
Angeles Crest Hwy

MT. WILSON

N

1 mile

Henniger Flats
Campground

Pinecrest Dr.

Crescent Dr.

Altadena Dr.

to Altadena

to Glendale

to Arcadia/Glendora →

134   Pasadena   210

- ■ Parking
- ·-■-· Best 100 Route
- ----- Other Bike Routes
  (not described in book)
- —— Paved Road
- ▬▬ Freeway
- ·········· Off-Limits or
  Not Recommended

© 1993 Fine Edge Productions

43 Mt. Wilson Toll Road

Distance: Varies from 5.5 to 18 miles
Difficulty: Very long and strenuous, fairly technical due to steep grade on the return
Elevation: 4,500' gain maximum
Ride Type: Fire road, in and out
Season: Year round, but there can be snow in winter
Topo Map: Mt. Wilson

This is one of the classic Southern California mountain bike rides and is a benchmark for anyone wanting to test his or her fitness level against the consistently steep grade of the Toll Road. The large amount of variance in riding time and mileage takes into account that this is not an all-or-nothing ride. Many cyclists make Henninger Flats Campground their goal and leave the summit of Mt. Wilson to hardier folks. This is certainly not the ride to do on a hot smoggy day.

Note: The amount of traffic that any weekend brings to the Toll Road has resulted in some incidents involving cyclists and equestrians. This is a *heavily* used pathway and demands the utmost in caution when you are coming back off the top. The prolonged, steep grade makes high speeds readily attainable, but there is a posted speed limit of 15 miles per hour. Don't be a "bonehead on a bike." Save the heroic high-speed antics for some less-traveled back-country route, or better yet, use the race course.

Getting There: The entrance to the Mt. Wilson Toll Road is off Pinecrest Drive in Altadena. The easiest way to get there from the 210 Freeway is to exit at Sierra Madre and turn left on Altadena Drive. Follow Altadena Drive to Crescent Drive. Turn right,

then turn right again on Pinecrest Drive. There is an entrance on the right of the road at a gated chain-link fence that drops into Eaton Canyon and heads up the Toll Road. It is a little obscure, but chances are you will see other folks milling about the entrance.

Ride through the gate and drop down into Eaton Canyon, cross the bridge, and begin to climb the Toll Road. Steep, isn't it? Get used to it. Learn to love it. There are 9 miles to go. You will quickly gain elevation and before long, Altadena will be far below. There are many turnouts where you can look around you. Let's stop at one and talk about some of Mt. Wilson's history.

Mt. Wilson is named after Benjamin Wilson, owner of a local vineyard. He considered Mt. Wilson as a source of lumber for fencing and wine barrels. Later, looking to exploit the mountain in a different way, a private enterprise built the first developed pathway to the top with the intent of charging for passage. In 1891 the Toll Road opened to the public as a trail with the toll being 25 cents for foot traffic and 50 cents for individuals on horseback. The Toll Road was a popular but rugged trip, and many hardy souls reached the summit by way of it.

As years went by, the trail was

widened to accommodate vehicle traffic and the transport of a 60-inch telescope to the top of the mountain. Later, bigger and better observatories were designed and a bigger and better road was required to transport the equipment, resulting in the final width of 10 feet. All this road widening was done by hand! As you suffer along, think about that. Maybe it will make you feel better.

All through this time, the Toll Road drew scores of people to Wilson. This was a grand time in the history of the mountain. A hotel was built on top, meeting the needs of weary travelers who arrived on foot, horseback, or in more comfort by private car or bus.

The late 1920s saw a slow decline for the Toll Road. Angeles Crest Highway was pushing its way into the forest and, when it reached Red Box, soon gave the public an easy option to the top of Wilson. There was no way the Toll Road could compete with a modern, public highway, and it soon ceased operation and was turned over to the Forest Service. The hotel was torn down in 1966 to make way for the Skyline Park.

Back to our ride. At 2.7 miles you come to Henninger Flats Campground. Named for "Captain" William K. Henninger, an early rancher-farmer in the area around 1880, Henninger Flats is a lovely campground and is the destination for many travelers on the Toll Road. There are water and restrooms here. Henninger Flats is operated by Los Angeles County, which allows camping by permit. There is also a restored log cabin and lookout tower here. If you are feeling a little the worse for wear, this is a good spot to turn back.

To continue on, the Toll Road picks up again through the campground and to the right. At the road to the heliport, turn right and continue up. The worst part of the climbing is behind you, but the road is still pretty tough. Unlike the bottom 3 miles, the scenery along the upper section of the Toll Road is at times well shaded and always quite lovely. At 3.4 miles you go by Idlehour Trail. At 7.5 miles you pass the Little Santa Anita Trail, and just as you pass the trailhead, you can look up ahead to the communication towers on Wilson. Every TV station in Los Angeles and many radio stations broadcast from here, and the mountaintop fairly bristles with them.

A little more grinding brings you to the pavement at 9 miles. This is a steep little section that takes you to a small gate. With towers on the right and towers on the left, ride around the gate and onto level pavement. Turn right and ride through the gate to Skyline Park. Here there is a broad parking lot with great views into the valley and beyond. Yes, you really did ride all the way up here, you animal you. The observatories are visible as bald-headed buildings in the distance.

The return trip down the Toll Road is potentially very fast and furious. Please use common sense and control your speed at all times. To return to your starting point at Eaton Canyon, simply retrace your route down the mountain.

Arroyo Seco Backcountry:

44 Silver Moccasin Loop from Charlton to Chilao

Distance: 13 miles
Difficulty: Strenuous, technical
Elevation: 1,000' gain
Ride Type: Loop on fire road, pavement, trail
Season: Spring, summer, fall
Topo Map: Chilao Flat, Waterman Mountain

The Arroyo Seco backcountry is less crowded than the front range but is still quite popular. The extra distance from civilization yields clearer air, and the higher elevation provides an environment for heavy stands of pine trees instead of chaparral.

The trail section of Silver Moccasin Trail earns this ride the technical rating. Sandy with stair-stepped sections, Silver Moccasin is a well used hiking trail and demands the utmost in courtesy and caution with regard to other trail users.

Getting There: Charlton Flats Picnic Area on Angeles Crest Highway, south of Chilao Flats, is a good staging area for this ride. Begin here by parking in the picnic area proper or at the information area near the entrance to Charlton. Note: If you follow the paved road into Charlton and keep right, you reach a dead end at a gate in the roadway. This is a nice shady place to park, and it is where you come out off of Silver Moccasin Trail.

From the entrance to Charlton Flats, ride the 2 miles of easy pavement up Angeles Crest Highway toward Chilao Flats Campground. There are two entrances to Chilao. You want to enter the lower, most southern one just past the Cal Trans

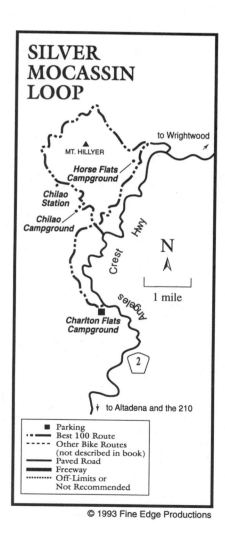

© 1993 Fine Edge Productions

yard located on the right (east) side of the highway.

Turn left into Chilao Flats and follow the paved road toward Manzanita Meadow Campground. At 2.4 miles stay straight ahead. You are heading toward road 3N14. At 2.8 miles bear left. The right road leads to the visitor center. Ride straight through the Chilao Station and at 3.7 miles the road turns to dirt. This now becomes a little tougher ride, but I had no trouble keeping it in the middle chainring. Enjoy the climb and the nice look at Pacifico Mountain, Granite Mountain and Roundtop to the northwest. After 6.2 miles you come to a paved road. Turn right. The pavement is actually steeper than the dirt road that brought you to this point. Persevere, you sweaty pilgrim, to the trailhead at 8 miles.

The Christian camp on your left is a good place to seek some shade. Water is available here, also. This was the staging area for the Angeles Crest Stage Race, a mountain bike race that used much of the roads and trails you are riding today.

Across from the camp on your right is where the Silver Moccasin Trail takes off. Below, and on the right of a yellow gate, the trail begins its sandy and switchbacked course towards Chilao Flats. Note: This trail is heavily traveled by all trail user groups. Please help save the trails for all of us by not brakesliding into the corners and contributing to erosion and trail damage.

Down the trail a half mile near Bandido Flats Campground, there is a split. Take the middle path and continue on across an abruptly steep and challenging creek crossing. Grab your granny. At 9 miles you intersect with Horse Flats Campground. Keep left and continue down. Ka-thud, ka-thud, ka-thud goes your bike as you negotiate lots of peeler log waterbars, placed there to control erosion. Many are on blind corners in a switchback, so be skillful or the next ka-thud may be *you,* not your bike.

After 10.1 miles you come to the upper road into Chilao Flats. Look 100 feet or so to your left to pick up the trail as it drops into a wide creek bed. The trail is mellow for a while but it's all a ploy to lull your massive quads into relaxing before a really steep climb along the side of a hill. Complete with roots to cross, it does its best to hurt you. Make it up without a dab? I knew you could.

At 12.2 miles you reach the lower road into Chilao Flats. The trail picks up directly across the pavement up a short and sandy push. Soon it becomes vague. Stay right and head toward the campground below. At the pavement, turn left for 30 feet, then left again on the trail. There is more stair-step downhill, the best

yet, and then the trail exits onto a fire road. Go left. It's a climb, but you are almost there. At 12.7 miles, you reach a gate. Go left onto the pavement and continue on to Charlton Flats Picnic Area and your vehicle.

If you started at the entrance to Charlton at Angeles Crest Highway, follow the paved road through the picnic area and turn left at the T intersection. This brings you out of the campground.

45 *Valyermo District:* Blue Ridge Loop

Distance: 18.5 miles
Difficulty: Fairly strenuous, somewhat technical
Elevation: 1,600' gain
Ride Type: Loop on pavement, fire road, trail
Season: Spring and summer best
Topo Map: Mt. San Antonio, Mescal Creek

Although this district is often passed over as desert or forgotten completely by mountain bicyclists from the front country, it deserves better. In fact, in my opinion, it contains some of the best riding in the Angeles National Forest on its relatively small network of roads and trails. Plus it's uncrowded, compared to well-known areas such as the Arroyo Seco. The Valyermo District is long and narrow and runs from its western border near Little Rock Reservoir to the eastern border at Wrightwood. To the north lie Valyermo and Pearblossom and the expanse of the Mojave. The San Gabriel and Sheep Mountain Wilderness Areas line its southern border.

It's the northeastern corner of the Valyermo that contains the bulk of the riding, and this area is well known to snow bunnies since it

contains several ski areas. The fun really begins when the snow melts, uncovering a network of roads and trails that pass through beautiful forest with thin, clean air. While the rides are not long, they are of high quality and will keep you coming back for more. Obviously, winter is not the prime time to ride in the higher elevations; you can expect the majority of these rides to be at their best in spring and summer.

The district contains one of the highest peaks in the San Gabriels, Mt. Baden Powell at 9,399 feet. Located within the Wilderness Area, it is not open to bicycle travel, but offers fine, strenuous hiking. The limber pine, with twisted branches and needles that resemble a bottlebrush, is found on the summit of Mt. Baden Powell and is considered to be the oldest living thing in the National Forest.

For further information about this area write the Valyermo Ranger District, P.O. Box 15, Valyermo, California, 93563.

Getting There: Begin at Inspiration Point, a scenic overlook located off Angeles Crest Highway, 2 miles west of the intersection of Angeles Crest Highway and Big Pines Highway. There is ample parking , and a plaque nearby gives you a guided tour of the peaks and valleys around you.

Starting and ending in the shadow of Mt. Baden Powell at Inspiration Point, this ride takes you to the doorstep of Mt. San Antonio (Old Baldy) and returns you by way of one of the finest singletracks in the forest. The trail may be omitted to make this an easy in-and-out ride for beginners.

East Blue Ridge Road, 3N06, is a paved road heading east from the parking area on the east side of the Angeles Crest Highway. Got that? It's easy to find. The road is level at first, then tilts more and more, making you work a little to continue. The slow pace up 3N06 gives you ample time to examine the many roadside flowering plants, some still in bloom in late September. You pass under some of the ski lifts of Mountain High Ski Resort before you come to Blue Ridge Campground and the end of the pavement at 2.4 miles.

This is the upper end of the Blue Ridge Trail. Continue on 3N06 onto the dirt. This is a lovely ride and improves as the miles pass and you distance yourself from the noise of

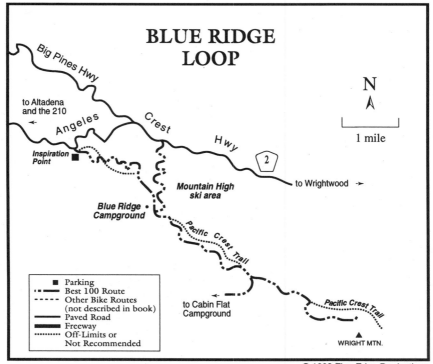

BLUE RIDGE LOOP

N

1 mile

Inspiration Point

to Altadena and the 210

Angeles Crest Hwy

Big Pines Hwy

Mountain High ski area

Blue Ridge Campground

Pacific Crest Trail

to Wrightwood →

to Cabin Flat Campground

Pacific Crest Trail

WRIGHT MTN.

Legend:
- ■ Parking
- ▪▪▪ Best 100 Route
- ---- Other Bike Routes (not described in book)
- ——— Paved Road
- ▬▬▬ Freeway
- ·········· Off-Limits or Not Recommended

the highway. After a short downhill, you reach the turnoff to Guffy Campground at 5.2 miles. Stay right and continue on 3N06.

At 5.6 miles you reach another intersection. Road 3N39 drops steeply right toward Lupine and Cabin Flat Campgrounds, then ends at the Wilderness boundary. This is a 1,000 foot drop and there is nowhere to ride but back up the way you came. To keep pain at a minimum, bypass this road and continue left on 3N06. At 7.4 miles you pass the trailhead for the Devils Backbone Trail to Mt. San Antonio (*not a bike trail!*). The road ends at 8.2 miles on the east side of Wright Mountain. Many small paths lead to viewpoints of the Antelope Valley and Valyermo.

When you are ready, turn around and retrace your steps to Blue Ridge Campground. On my computer, 14.1 miles put me back at the campground and at the Blue Ridge trailhead. If you opt for this trail, it will demand more uphill to return to your vehicle at Inspiration Point, but unless you are totally fried it's worth it. This is a great singletrack down to Angeles Crest Highway. Wide and smooth, the trail is signed as being maintained by the Wrightwood Mountain Bike Club. Good job, guys and gals!

You'll still be grinning as you reach Angeles Crest Highway at 16.3 miles. A left turn brings you to the rustic Big Pines Visitor Station, complete with restrooms and water. This building was part of the complex that was the Big Pines County Park. In the 1920s, Los Angeles County purchased 760 acres with the intent of

making a winter playground in the forest. Big Pines County Park was an immediate success and the Forest Service extended the limits of the park to include Jackson Lake. Throughout the 1920s and into the 1930s, the complex grew more deluxe with skating rinks, campgrounds and developed trails.

The Great Depression of the

1930s hit the park hard, and it became too much of a burden for Los Angeles County to maintain. Through the next few decades, the Forest Service gained control of the properties. Although the Big Pines area is not the deluxe mountain amusement park it once was, the natural beauty is still a draw to folks year round.

To return to Inspiration Point, turn left on Angeles Crest Highway (west) and continue past Mountain High West and Big Pines Highway. After 2 miles of relatively easy pavement climbing, you are back at your starting point.

46 Crystal Lake Area: South Mt. Hawkins

Distance: 12 miles
Difficulty: Strenuous; trail loop option adds a very technical section
Elevation: 1,900' gain
Ride Type: Fire road in and out with trail loop option
Season: Year round
Topo Map: Crystal Lake

The Crystal Lake area of the San Gabriels is, in many ways, quite different from any other part of the forest. An amphitheater for nature programs, a small supply store, a visitors' center and extensive camping areas make this seem more like a national park. Contributing to this feeling are the trees—big ones—excellent stands of stately cedar trees that somehow escaped the logging that was rampant in the early days.

Having the only natural lake in the San Gabriel Mountains, the Crystal Lake area, originally called Pine Flat, was a haven for wildlife. According to early reports it had more than its share of grizzlies. Hunting and vacation cabins were built in the area and the arduous trek up from Coldbrook Camp was offset by the abundant game and beauty of the area. In the late 1920s, Los Angeles County leased land from the Forest Service and established Crystal Lake County Park. It was a huge success and drew crowds of people seeking recreation for better than a decade. World War II ended the parade of campers driving to Crystal Lake, since more prudent demands on gasoline made the long journey difficult. The area was turned back over to the Forest Service to administer, which they do to this day. The Crystal Lake Store is a holdout from those bygone days, dating back to 1934.

Mountain biking in the Crystal Lake area is somewhat limited, but there is enough to keep a person busy for a camping and/or cycling weekend. This is an especially nice family camping area. There is an extensive trail system here that is open to mountain bikes (with the exception of the Pacific Crest Trail). However, some of the trails are not really appropriate nor do they provide enjoyable cycling. I feel the one to South Mt. Hawkins is the best. In any case, please use utmost caution and observe the proper trail etiquette towards other trail users. Don't you be the cause of closing this area to bikers.

For more information on trail conditions, contact the Mt. Baldy Ranger District, 110 N. Wabash Avenue, Glendora, CA 91740, (818) 335-1251.

Getting There: This ride originates from the parking lot near the visitors' center and store located in the heart of the campground. Following the turnoff for Crystal Lake from Highway 39, the road into the campgrounds passes by a toll booth, where a day use or overnight fee is collected, then leads directly to the visitors' center. There are area maps available here, along with program information for the campgrounds.

This ride takes you to the top of South Mt. Hawkins, where a fire lookout tower still stands watch over the forest. This tower is being refurbished and in the future will be a visitor attraction. There is a trail register at the top of the mountain for peakbaggers. This is bighorn sheep country, so keep sharp and maybe you will see one of those rascals.

From the visitor center, ride up the pavement toward Deer Flats Campground. There is a sign at the visitor center showing this in detail. This is the main road through the campgrounds and is easy to follow. You wind along on this paved road past campsites until at 0.4 mile you reach the gate to Deer Flats. Ride around the gate and continue toward Deer Flats, which is arrived at with 0.9 mile on the clock. It gets a little steeper now but is still paved and is a very pretty ride.

At 2.2 miles you come to the campground proper. There is an unmarked dirt road dropping off to the right of the paved road you are now on. (If you miss it, you continue

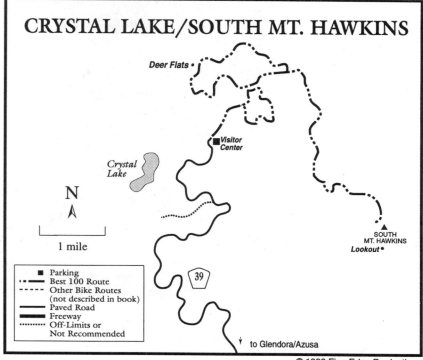

CRYSTAL LAKE/SOUTH MT. HAWKINS

Deer Flats •

■ Visitor Center

Crystal Lake

N

1 mile

SOUTH MT. HAWKINS
Lookout •

39

■ Parking
•—■— Best 100 Route
– – – Other Bike Routes
(not described in book)
———— Paved Road
▬▬▬ Freeway
•••••••• Off-Limits or
Not Recommended

↓ to Glendora/Azusa

into Deer Flats Campground and end up circling back around to this point anyway.) Take the dirt road and begin to climb towards South Mt. Hawkins. The climb is never very steep—no more so than the pavement you rode to this point—but it is rocky in sections and had been freshly graded the day I rode it, increasing the sweat factor by two.

Soon you reach a sign that tells you this is Road 3N07 and you have 5 miles to the lookout. Very near the top, the road splits. Stay right and ride the last 0.4 mile to the summit. From here you have an incredible view into the Sheep Mountain and San Gabriel Wilderness Areas, down to the San Gabriel Reservoir, and to such high peaks as Mt. Wilson and Mt. Baden Powell. The trail register is located under a pile of rocks north of the lookout tower.

To head down, you can follow the fire road you came up on or take a short section of singletrack that takes off at the south end of the mountain and rejoins the fire road 0.3 mile later. Either way you head back down 3N07. At a little under 4 miles from the top of the mountain, you come to where the Windy Gap Trail crosses 3N07. You may have seen this on the way up. A left turn on this trail takes you down to the pavement near the visitors' center, and it is highly recommended for the well-skilled rider.

Along with trees, this area also has lots of rocks, and this trail proves it. Bunches of rock waterbars will test your skills and make you want suspension in the worst way. You cross the pavement 0.7 mile into the trail and pick it up again on the other side. Finally, at 11.7 miles you spill out onto the pavement at the lower Windy Gap trailhead and turn right towards the visitors' center, reaching your starting point at 12.1 miles.

For additional rides in this area, please refer to *Mountain Biking the Coast Range, Guide 9, San Gabriel Mountains, Angeles National Forest* by Mike Troy, ISBN 0-938665-11-1 (see p. 304).

CHAPTER 6

Saugus District
of Angeles National Forest
& Mt. Pinos

By Mike Troy, with Mt. Pinos section by Kevin Woten

The northernmost section of Angeles National Forest, the Saugus District, has a different character than the rest of the Angeles—rounder and not so rocky and rugged, and lacking the elevation of the San Gabriels to the southeast. Still, the Saugus District has much to offer the mountain cyclist. The lesser elevations generally make for easier climbs and the area is far less traveled than the heavily used San Gabriels.

The Liebre and Sawmill Mountains section of the Saugus District contain the best scenery and the highest elevations (5,000 feet plus), along with fine mountain biking possibilities. On an especially clear day, the top of 5,700-foot Burnt Peak can show you the glimmer of the distant Pacific Ocean. Sawmill and Upper Shake Campgrounds are two of the most beautiful campgrounds in the district, and the higher elevations of Sawmill Mountain bring with them large pine trees that whisper in the cooling breezes.

This area provided lumber for the construction of nearby Ft. Tejon, an early army establishment and key outpost along the trading route to the San Joaquin Valley below. Today the Pacific Crest National Scenic Trail (closed to bikes) crosses much of the area.

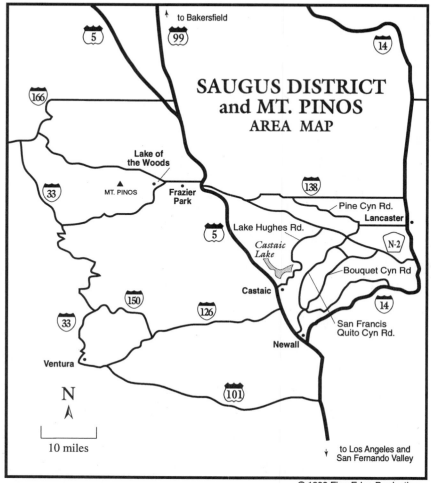

© 1993 Fine Edge Productions

The northern tip of this range, Liebre Mountain (the name comes from the Spanish word for cottontail), shoulders fine stands of black oak woodland and is especially rewarding to ride in the fall when the leaves are turning color and carpeting the forest floor.

Summer temperatures are milder here than in the lower forest, but still expect midday highs into the upper nineties. There is no water available in this area, so bring plenty with you. Winter can bring snow to Liebre and Sawmill although this generally will not be heavy or long lasting. In general, this area lends itself to year-round exploration if you avoid the extremes of the seasons, with spring and fall being particularly fine times to ride.

47 Liebre Mountain/ Golden Eagle Trail

Distance: 16.2 miles
Difficulty: The full loop is strenuous and fairly technical. The level of difficulty can be varied by shortening the loop into smaller loops or driving to the top of the mountain.
Elevation: 1,500' gain
Ride Type: Fire road and trail loop with small pavement section
Season: Spring, summer, fall
Topo Map: Liebre Mountain

This fairly long climb on a good fire road up the west shoulder of Liebre Mountain offers excellent views. The return on Golden Eagle Trail is fun and not too difficult, with some of the finest legal singletrack in the entire range. There is no water, so come prepared.

Getting There: Travel north on the Interstate 5 from Castaic and exit at the Highway 138/Quail Lake off-ramp. Drive 4.2 miles to the turnoff for the Old Ridge Route Road. Turn right. Drive uphill on 8N04, a paved road, for 2.6 miles to the ruins of Sandbergs Resort on the right. Park here. These foundations are all that's left of one of the greatest rest stops on the Old Ridge Route.

After unloading, return to the pavement of 8N04 and continue south. Cruise along on the broken pavement until at 2.6 miles you intersect with 7N23. The sign on the left reads *Castaic 25 mi., Bear Campground 9 mi., Sawmill Campground 14 mi.* Turn left on 7N23. Except for a short section near the top, the first mile is the steepest of the entire ride. Don't lose heart, it gets easier. At 3.2 miles keep left, bypassing 7N22. (7N22 to Knapp Ranch is not recommended, since it leads to a ranch located on private property. The ranch is used for cattle and the area is fenced.)

Settle in and enjoy the climb, because the road improves considerably and the views start to come into their own. Beyond Pyramid Lake to the south are White Mountain, Black Mountain and Cobblestone Mountain. Looking more westerly you see Hungry Valley, Frazier Mountain and the rolling Gorman Hills.

At 6.5 miles you reach the first summit and begin to roll along more gradually. There are too many roads branching off of 7N23 to mention, but the main road is always clearly defined. The terrain becomes strikingly pretty as you move into lovely oak woodland. Keep an eye out for golden eagles soaring on the thermals above you, a reminder of the solitude the backcountry can offer.

At 7.8 miles a short rocky climb brings you over the top. Roll along to 9.8 miles, and just after a small rise in the road, a doubletrack takes off to the left. This path leads to Horse Camp Canyon, 17W01. Down this jeep road 0.1 mile is a sign at a crossroads that reads *Bear Camp 2 mi., Burnt Peak Junction 10 mi., Wilderness Camp 1 mi., Oakdale Canyon Road 5 mi.* Road 17W01 down Horse Camp Canyon is the Pacific Crest Trail (PCT), which is closed to bicycle traffic. Standing in front of the sign and facing south, look for the beginning of Golden Eagle Trail

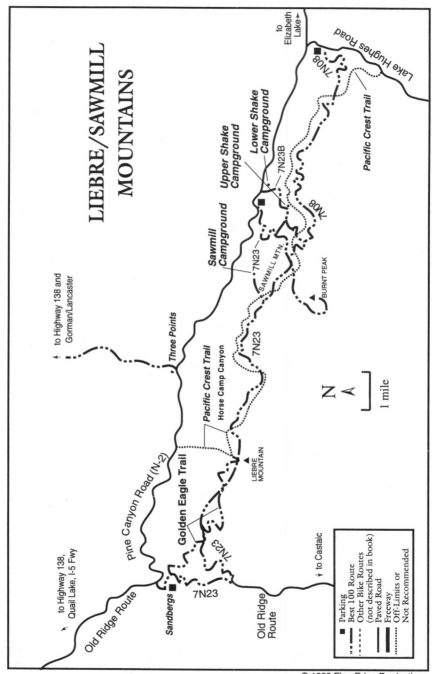

LIEBRE/SAWMILL MOUNTAINS

to Elizabeth Lake→

Lake Hughes Road

7N08

Pacific Crest Trail

Lower Shake Campground

Upper Shake Campground

7N23B

Sawmill Campground

7N08

SAWMILL MTN.

7N23

BURNT PEAK

to Highway 138 and Gorman/Lancaster

Three Points

Pacific Crest Trail

Horse Camp Canyon

7N23

N

1 mile

LIEBRE MOUNTAIN

Pine Canyon Road (N-2)

to Highway 138, Quail Lake, I-5 Fwy

Golden Eagle Trail

7N23

Sandbergs

7N23

Old Ridge Route

Old Ridge Route

to Castaic

■ Parking
▪▪▪ Best 100 Route
— — Other Bike Routes (not described in book)
——— Paved Road
■■■ Freeway
····· Off-Limits or Not Recommended

© 1993 Fine Edge Productions

about 30 feet up a fading road. Taking off on the right (west), the trail seems only a game path through the trees, but it soon opens to a good trail winding through the oaks.

The ride is easy now and runs slightly uphill. Except for some occasional brush and fallen limbs, beginners will have little trouble on this section. At 10.6 miles you cross 7N23 and pick up the trail on the other side to the southwest. The route has some brushy areas but is still a good, clean trail. At 11.8 miles you cross a spur road from 7N23 and continue straight across this road on a doubletrack for 300 feet or so. On the right, with a massive old oak in the background, the trail picks up again. There should be a stake with a yellow ribbon marking the trail.

After a little more riding, you drop into a gorgeous oak forest as the trail roller coasters along a hillside. (Watch for little nubs of oak root sticking up out of the trail. They are hard to pick out of the shadows and could easily cause a flat.) After leaving the oak forest, the trail opens up as you roll toward a lovely grass knoll with a great view of Pyramid Lake.

At 13.7 miles you cross 7N23 again. From here the going becomes much more difficult with brush crowding over the trail. If you are wearing a long sleeve shirt, long fingered gloves and tights, the trail is passable, although sandy and narrow. Without the proper clothing, it's comparable to riding through a shredder. If you like, turn left on 7N23 and enjoy a fun fire road descent on 7N23 back to the Old Ridge Route. *Caution: This is a long, fast descent, so control your speed at all times.* To continue on the trail, cross 7N23 and follow the singletrack. At 16.2 miles the Ridge Route Road is visible to the left. Drop down to the road, turn right and ride the last 100 feet to your vehicle.

Sawmill Mountain

This area is accessed by two Forest Service fire roads, 7N08 and 7N23. Both of these routes will be used to explore this area, creating rides of varying difficulties. Road 7N23 is the most direct route to Sawmill Mountain and Sawmill campground, and it is usually open to vehicle traffic. Although roads in the forest are subject to rapid and unannounced changes in surface quality, 7N23 from Pine Canyon Road is navigable by most any vehicle. The road to Upper Shake campground is gated and often closed. For up-to-date information on these roads and campground facilities, contact the district Forest Service office at (805) 296-9710.

48 Upper Shake Campground

Distance: 6 miles
Difficulty: Easy and nontechnical; more technical with trail loop option
Elevation: 600' gain
Ride Type: Fire road in and out with trail loop option
Season: Spring, summer, fall
Topo Map: Burnt Peak

This is an easy ride (good for beginners) with some uphill. A loop return option, Upper Shake to Lower Shake Loop, adds some technical sections that beginners may need to walk. Note: This area is subject to a gated closure, so check with the Forest Service before riding.

Getting There: We get to this ride via Castaic/Lake Hughes Road, but you can get here from many directions (consult your map). From the intersection of Lake Hughes Road and Lake Elizabeth Road, turn left (north) and you immediately find yourself on Pine Canyon Road. Continue north until at approximately 4.4 miles you see an area on the left with a sign and a dirt road leading into the mountains. The sign reads *Upper Shake 3 mi., Sawmill Campground 5 mi., Burnt Peak 7 mi.* Park here at this dirt area.

Jump on your bikes and begin climbing immediately up 7N23 past the sign to Upper Shake. This section is a constant uphill, but for the average rider it is an entirely manageable grade. As you continue on you come to an area that gives some views of the valley to the east toward Rosamond, and as you keep climbing, you can look ahead and up towards the Sawmill and Burnt Peak areas, with their stands of oak and pine trees.

You won't go that far on this route, though, for at 2 miles and 20 minutes of riding you reach a junction of three roads and your first turnoff. Straight ahead and uphill lies Burnt Peak. To your left are two roads. The farthest road to the left is gated shut and is not shown on the USFS map. Take the middle road (7N23B, also gated) and descend toward Upper Shake Campground. Upper Shake is very pretty, and it is well shaded by large pines. In summer the area is cool, while winter may bring a good covering of snow. To return to your vehicle, simply retrace your steps back up the fire road.

There is an alternative return to your starting point once you have reached Upper Shake Campground— a technical and challenging trail that connects Upper Shake and Lower Shake Campgrounds. This adds some time and a challenge to your day, but it is a nice loop. The canyon you ride through is very pretty and most of the year carries enough water in its stream bed to get your feet wet.

To find the unmarked trailhead, look to the north end of the campground near the creek. There is a steeply descending trail that drops you into the creek and heads into a narrow canyon. This is not a difficult trail, but it throws a little bit of everything at you to test your abilities. Have fun! By the way, you do know what poison oak looks like, don't you? A friendly word of warning to those who slept through science class: poison oak is here. Trust me.

This is a beautiful trail, and the canyon you are riding through is well shaded and cool. It is a quick ride, but a good trail for honing your technical abilities. It drops into Lower Shake Campground, which is sadly scarred by vandalism. Follow the dirt road out to Pine Canyon Road and turn left. After a short climb on pavement, you are back to your starting point.

49 Sawmill Campground

Distance: 9 miles
Difficulty: Fairly strenuous climb, but not technical; fast descent, watch for rocks
Elevation: 1,500' gain
Ride Type: In and out on fire road
Season: Spring, summer, fall
Topo Map: Burnt Peak

This ride takes you up to a very pretty campground in the Sawmill Mountain area—lots of pines and great views.

Getting There: As in the ride to Upper Shake, start from the intersection of Pine Canyon Road and 7N23.

Head up the mountain on 7N23 past the sign that reads *Upper Shake 3 mi., Sawmill Campground 5 mi., Burnt Peak 7 mi.* Climb past the turnoff to Upper Shake (7N23B) and continue up the mountain on a steeper grade. The surroundings become less and less like the usual brushy hills of the Saugus District as you ride past large pines and oaks. Several viewpoints along the way give you the opportunity to see the west end of

Antelope Valley and points north.

At 3.1 miles you reach the saddle at Burnt Peak. Here you are at a junction of three fire roads. Ahead of you is the tallest peak in the range, 5,788-foot Burnt Peak, crowned with microwave towers. The ride up to the top is worthwhile and is a good workout, being just under 3 miles (one way) and nearly 600 feet in elevation gain from the intersection of 7N23, 7N23A and 7N08. The peak provides an excellent view of the Saugus District backcountry; on one clear, winter day, with the ground frozen beneath our feet, a companion and I could see the faint glimmer of the Pacific Ocean 70 miles in the distance.

If you wish to add this to your trip, allow one hour and add your mileage (about 5.5 miles round trip) to the total trip distance.

Back at the three-way intersection at the saddle, a sign informs you that Sawmill Campground is 1 mile ahead along 7N23. Follow this direction and continue on 7N23. You go uphill for just a little longer, as you move along into a nice, grassy grove of black oaks that turn vivid colors in the later part of the year—flaming reds, oranges and browns from nature's palette.

At 4.5 miles, after a short downhill, is the turnoff to Sawmill Campground. Taking off to the right, the road descends into a cool and shady picnic area with tables. Here on the north side of Sawmill Mountain at 5,200 feet, the wind is nearly a constant companion, and the sound of the pines being gently stirred by these breezes is soothing. This campground sees some use, although it has never been occupied by more than three or four campers in the times I have been there.

Return to your vehicle by retracing your steps down 7N23. It is very nearly all downhill on the return leg. It's a great downhill, too, with challenging corners and reasonably good surfaces. There are some loose rocky sections, so use caution. Watch for vehicle traffic, since this road is an access used by many visitors.

50 Sawmill Mountain Truck Trail

Distance: 18 miles
Difficulty: Fairly strenuous climb, nontechnical
Elevation: 2,200' gain
Ride Type: Fire road loop with trail option and pavement return
Season: Spring, summer, fall
Topo Maps: Lake Hughes, Burnt Peak

On this lovely ride you get great views off the east side of Sawmill Mountain. The climb is long but never very difficult, and the return half of the loop is mostly downhill. There is an option to take a trail from 7N08 to Upper Shake, then to Lower Shake Campground on the return leg. This adds a moderate-level technical rating to the ride.

Getting There: On Lake Hughes Road, 0.3 mile south of Pine Canyon Road, fire road 7N08 takes off to the west. Located among some houses, it would be difficult to recognize it as an entrance to one of the most beautiful areas of the Saugus District if it weren't for the sign. Park your vehicle along the beginning of this road, being careful not to block access to any of the residences.

Sawmill Mountain Truck Trail is in excellent condition, and it is mostly a middle chain ring ride as you work your way up the shoulder of Sawmill Mountain. At a little over 2 miles and 800 feet of elevation gain, you pass a television antenna site. Spring brings a carpet of wildflowers among the small pines planted here. At 3.9 miles you come to a fork in the road. Take the left road and descend. To the right are great views of Elizabeth Lake and the surrounding community. It is easy traveling

for a while, and at 4.2 miles you pass by some beautiful black oaks. You begin climbing again at 5.5 miles, passing mature pines, and the view to the east is striking at times. At 7.8 miles look left for a fantastic view of four consecutive mountain ridges all the way to the San Gabriels. Here you work a little harder —the grade increases and the road is sandy in places.

At 8 miles or so all the work is over as you roll over the shoulder of Sawmill Mountain. You have worked your way up 2,200 feet of elevation gain and can cruise downhill for a while until, at 9.8 miles, you reach an intersection with roads 7N23 and 7N23A (you are traveling on 7N08). To the southeast is Burnt Peak, with microwave towers perched atop its 5,700-foot crown. Ahead: Sawmill Campground and the road to Atmore Meadows and Liebre Mountain.

Rest here if you like and enjoy the beauty of an area that is very much out of character with the rest of the Saugus Range. Instead of scrub oak and buckthorn, deciduous oaks and pines surround you. Smog? Only what is below you obscuring the valleys from view. While summer is a fine time to ride here (it is usually cooler at this elevation), fall is the best time to visit. The air is clearer and the leaves are turning. Late in the winter though, expect snow.

Now you have several choices.

Burnt Peak is 2.7 miles to the south and requires more climbing. Sawmill Campground is one mile ahead on 7N23, a little more climbing. To your right 7N23 dives down to Pine Canyon Road. Downhill. Aahhh.

There is, however, another option. It involves a little backtracking if you have come this far, but adds a great little section of singletrack to the loop. A half mile back along 7N08 (the way you came up) there is an unmarked trail that takes off to the left. It is not too difficult to locate. As you are backtracking, at the first sweeping right hand corner in road 7N08, look left. The trail dives off from a wide spot on the left and heads due east. About 25 feet down you cross the Pacific Crest Trail. It is clearly marked and easy to distinguish from the trail you are on. Note: Avoid riding on the Pacific Crest Trail; it is off limits to bicycle travel.

Continuing straight ahead and down, you pass a sign that reads *Upper Shake 1 mile, Lower Shake 2 miles*. Just past this sign is a sharp switchback to the right. Control your speed at all times, since the top section is full of these beauties, some rideable, some not. Use caution—they tend to sneak up on you. One of these is reached at 0.6 mile and is a sharp, sharp switchback to the left. Walk your bike around. If you overshoot this one, you will run right over the edge into a very painful drop.

After the switchbacks, the trail narrows and follows along a hillside. There is fair exposure here, so watch your speed and choose your lines carefully. As you move along, the grade eases a little and the trail opens up and becomes truly fine. There is little brush to contend with, and a series of bumps in the trail discourages vehicles and makes for a high

grin factor. Some of the bumps are quite high, so be very careful lest you fly more than God intended you to. At 2.0 miles you come to the road to Upper Shake Campground, 7N23B.

From here you can turn left and ride a short uphill to 7N23, then turn right and continue the ride down to Pine Canyon Road, following the rest of the Sawmill Mountain Truck Trail (7N08) back to your vehicle. Or, you can ride one more section of singletrack by following the trail down to Lower Shake Campground (see Upper Shake Campground: 7N23, 7N23B), exit on Pine Canyon Road, turn right and resume the loop ride.

If you ignore both of these options, turn right on 7N23 and continue down, down, down. One mile brings you to the turnoff to Upper Shake Campground. Two miles later you reach Pine Canyon Road. Turn right onto Pine Canyon Road and follow the pavement back down to Lake Hughes Road. Turn right and ride a short way back to your vehicle. The pavement return is all downhill and is fast enough to spin out the big chain ring for nearly the entire distance. A final right turn on 7N08 and you are finished.

The Old Ridge Route

This section of Angeles Forest is bisected by a road that is little used today—the Old Ridge Route Road. Otherwise known as the Grapevine, it had a relatively short but busy history. In 1909, legislation calling for better highways prompted engineers to plan a shorter route from Newhall to Gorman, bypassing the trip around Elizabeth Lake and Pine Canyon. They surveyed a road directly along a ridge top, hence the name Ridge Route. Interestingly, the name of the man to survey the route was Lewis Clark. With its completion in 1915, the new highway was hailed by the Automobile Club of Southern California as "the last word in scientific highway building."

Be that as it may, the road soon developed a reputation as a killer with its steep grades and narrow lanes. Sharp curves bordered steep dropoffs into canyons near the edge of the roadway. Many travelers found their motorcars at the bottom of these ravines due to failed brakes or miscalculations.

Still, it was heavily traveled and a good many roadside rest stops and gas stations sprang up along the route to cater to the needs of weary travelers, places with names like the Tumble Inn, Halfway Inn, Lebec, and the most gracious of all, Sandbergs Motor Inn. Little remains of these sites except crumbling foundations. Bypassed in 1933 by the faster and wider Highway 99, travelers saved time and effort and avoided the torturous Ridge Route. The road is seldom traveled today.

For mountain bikers, this is a pleasant area to ride. Driveable by auto, the road is maintained from Castaic to Templin Highway. North of Templin Highway it is gated to vehicle traffic. Because there is no water available on any of these routes, take ample supplies with you.

51 Castaic to Templin Highway

Distance: Varies, 30 miles one way if done in its entirety
Difficulty: Easy to strenuous, nontechnical
Elevation: Gain varies with distance traveled
Ride Type: In and out on pavement
Season: Year round
Topo Maps: Liebre Mountain, Whitaker Peak, Warm Springs Mountain

The Old Ridge Route is such a long ride that few people travel its full length in one trip, even though it is certainly possible to do so. Instead, excursions from one end into the middle and back out again are the norm. If you want to make the whole journey in a day, I recommend that you have someone shuttle you to the north end to start and that you ride south to Castaic. This is by far the easiest way to go. The upper reaches of 8N04 are remote, but they are used quite often and vehicle traffic is always a possibility.

If you ride from Castaic north

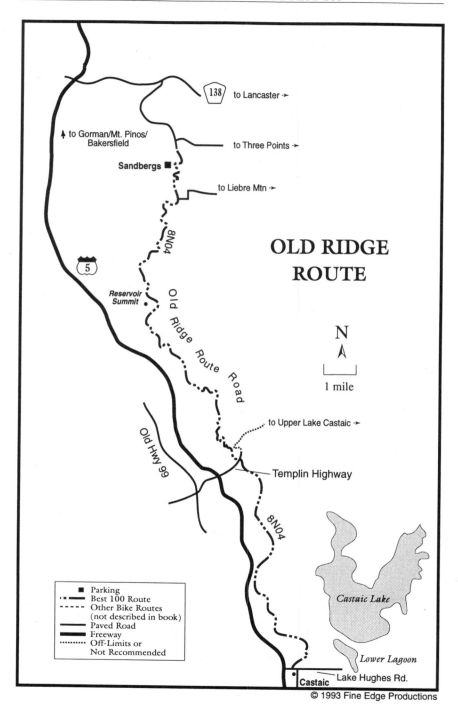

138 to Lancaster →

to Gorman/Mt. Pinos/
Bakersfield

to Three Points →

Sandbergs ■

to Liebre Mtn →

8N04

5

**OLD RIDGE
ROUTE**

Reservoir
Summit

Old Ridge Route Road

N

1 mile

to Upper Lake Castaic →

Old Hwy 99

Templin Highway

8N04

Castaic Lake

Lower Lagoon

■ Parking
▪▪▪ Best 100 Route
--- Other Bike Routes
       (not described in book)
—— Paved Road
▬▬ Freeway
······ Off-Limits or
       Not Recommended

Lake Hughes Rd.

Castaic

© 1993 Fine Edge Productions

toward Templin Highway, 8N04 is a good paved road suitable for any type of bicycle. On any given weekend you will likely encounter a number of cyclists on the road. Oh, one little thing: From Castaic to Templin Highway is 7.5 miles uphill. It is still not too difficult, being a good paved road, so don't be put off by this.

Getting There: To start this section, there is convenient parking at the Fisherman's Landing parking lot on the corner of Lake Hughes Road and The Old Ridge Route Road in the town of Castaic.

Follow The Old Ridge Route Road north past the west side of the lower lagoon of Castaic Lake. Continue past the workings of the Castaic Brickyard and on toward Templin Highway. For part of the time you parallel I-5. This portion of 8N04 is not as remote as the upper sections, but it is still quiet and peaceful for a paved road. At 7.5 miles you reach the intersection with Templin Highway. You can ride on as your heart and legs desire, but be advised that the road soon deteriorates past this point. The rest of The Old Ridge Route from the opposite end is described in the following ride. Oh yes, getting back to your vehicle is incredibly simple. Just turn around and enjoy a 7.5-mile downhill!

52 Sandbergs to Reservoir Summit/ Templin Highway

Distance: 16.8 miles round trip
Difficulty: Moderate, nontechnical
Elevation: 4,164' to 3,500' to 3883', then reversed
Ride Type: In and out on pavement
Season: Year round
Topo Maps: Liebre Mountain, Whitaker Peak, Warm Springs Mountain

Getting There: Take I-5 north from Castaic and exit at the Quail Lake/ Highway 138 off-ramp. Drive 4.2 miles to The Old Ridge Route turn-off on the right. It is a couple of miles to the National Forest boundary, so keep driving for a little bit up the paved road. At 2.2 miles, now within the National Forest, you reach the intersection of 8N04, Pine Canyon Road, 8N05, and the road to the Bald Mountain weather station. Here a sign tells you Castaic is 28 miles away. Continue 2.6 miles up 8N04 to the site of Old Sandbergs Resort. This is a lovely spot and is a good place to park and start your ride.

The foundations that lie before you have an interesting history. Opened in 1916 by Herman Sandberg, the Sandberg Hotel and Motor Inn was styled as a grand Swiss chalet. Along with meals and lodging, rumor has it there was gambling and vice of a more feminine nature available at Sandbergs. The main building burned down in the early 1940s, although traffic had long since bypassed the Old Ridge Route with the opening of Highway 99 in 1933.

From Sandbergs, continue down 8N04. The pedaling is easy on the road surface of broken asphalt. In some sections you ride on the original surface of steel reinforced concrete. At 2.7 miles you reach the turnoff for 7N23. Continue on 8N04, still easy going. After 500 feet or so, a road to the right takes you to what is shown on the topo map as the Tumble Inn Campground, although there are no facilities. At 3.9 miles you come to the ruins of the Tumble Inn, another one of the rest stops along the Old Ridge Route. A sign here indicates that it is 5 miles to Reservoir Summit and 23 miles to Castaic. Here also the south end of 8N05 heads down into Liebre Gulch.

At 5.3 miles 8N01 takes off to the right. At 6.2 miles, just before you pass under the high voltage lines that cross 8N04, the turnout on the left is the site of the Halfway Inn, yet another one of the rest stops that sprang up along the road to meet the needs of weary travelers. Nothing remains of this one except scattered bits of broken glass and china.

You descend for a short time before beginning the climb to Reservoir Summit, one of the highest points on the Ridge Route. The climb is not very difficult and 8.4 miles finds you at the summit. Road 7N27 heads up to a small plateau and a stand of pines. There was a lookout station here at one time, but now there is only the wind through the pines. 7N26 takes off near here and drops steeply into Posey Canyon heading towards Pyramid Lake. Reservoir Summit makes a great lunch stop, with good views of Liebre Mountain, Red Rock Mountain and on down to Warm Springs Mountain. This is a good spot to turn around and ride the easy 8.4 miles back to your vehicle at Sandbergs.

If you want to continue ahead, it is mostly downhill to Templin Highway. At 13.7 miles you come to the final set of ruins. This was the Hiway Inn, and the steps and partial foundation are located on your right under the ever-present power lines. 19 miles of cranking brings you to Templin Highway, and 7.5 miles farther along is Castaic.

Mt. Pinos

Mt. Pinos, the tallest peak in the small White Mountain Coastal Range, is quickly becoming one of the premiere mountain bike areas in Southern California. Located midway between Los Angeles, Lancaster and Bakersfield, its pine-covered slopes, cool summer temperatures and magnificent vistas beckon to the urban cyclist.

Mt. Pinos has an excellent network of hiking and cross-country ski trails to challenge cyclists of all abilities. The McGill, Mt. Pinos and Chula Vista camps can be used for parking to ride a favorite trail or as base camps for a weekend of exploration. There are 109 campsites with piped water and restroom facilities, with easy access to riding trails. Weekends are usually uncrowded, but visitors should arrive early on holidays to get a campsite. The nearby communities of Frazier Park, Pine Mt. Club and Lake of the Woods can provide food and camping supplies. Mt. Pinos receives heavy snow in late fall and winter, so visitors should plan trips from late April to late November.

Much of Mt. Pinos is included in the new Chumash Wilderness. The Wilderness was created in 1992 to keep this area unspoiled for future generations. Visitors can ride from the Chula Vista parking lot to the Condor Peak Summit but should return the same way since *all* trails from the summit enter Wilderness, where mountain bikes are prohibited. Another point of interest to visitors is the reintroduction of the California condor to the area. These magnificent birds make their homes in the Sespe Wilderness visible to the south of Mt. Pinos. The condors have a very large feeding range, so it is possible to see them flying overhead from either the Condor Peak Lookout or Iris Point Vista.

The trails on Mt. Pinos are also popular with hikers and equestrians, so remember to control your speed and use courtesy towards other visitors.

53 McJeff Trail Warm-Up

Distance: 1.4 miles
Difficulty: Moderate
Elevation: Start/end 7,429'; 151' gain/loss; high point 7,580'
Ride Type: Trail, road and skid road
Season: Late April to November
Topo Map: Cuddy Valley

This is a good warm-up ride for the McGill Trail. A nice short ride in itself, it can help you get in tune with the quiet tranquillity of the mountain.

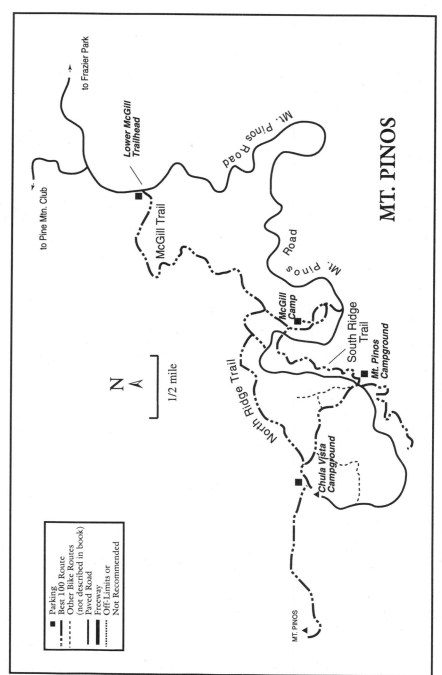

MT. PINOS

to Frazier Park

to Pine Mtn. Club

Lower McGill Trailhead

Mt. Pinos Road

McGill Trail

McGill Camp

Mt. Pinos Road

South Ridge Trail

Mt. Pinos Campground

North Ridge Trail

Chula Vista Campground

MT. PINOS

N

1/2 mile

■ Parking
▪▪ Best 100 Route
▪·▪· Other Bike Routes
        (not described in book)
─── Paved Road
═══ Freeway
····· Off-Limits or
        Not Recommended

© 1993 Fine Edge Productions

Getting There: From Interstate 5, exit at Frazier Park and head west (left) up the mountain. About 15 miles up the road is McGill Campground on the right. Park here at the day use lot to the right of the entrance. To the left of the entrance is the McGill trailhead.

Ride up (northwest) the McGill Trail, climbing gradually to the junction at 0.2 mile. Turn left (northwest) on "Skater" Trail to reach Mt. Pinos highway at 0.4 mile. Go right, climbing Mt. Pinos Road to an unmarked Jeffrey Pine Flat road on your right at 0.6 mile. Take that to a junction at 0.7 mile. Turn right (east) on the McJeff Trail, marked by a small jump. Ride down McJeff, using caution on the large jumps. You may wish to ride around some of these. Continue to the McGill/Skater Junction at 1.1 miles. Take the center left trail (McGill Trail) to return to McGill Camp at 1.4 miles.

54 McGill Trail

Distance: 8.3 miles
Difficulty: Moderately technical, strenuous if ridden as a loop
Elevation: Start/high point 7,429'; low point 6,203'; 1,226' loss/gain
Ride Type: Trail with pavement loop return; can also be done as a shuttle, or rider can return up the trail
Season: Late April to November
Topo Map: Cuddy Valley

This excellent trail can be ridden alone as a loop or combined with the North or South Ridge Trails to link the mountain from top to bottom. This trail is also popular with hikers and equestrians, so please control your speed and use proper mountain biking trail etiquette.

Getting There: Park in McGill Camp at the day use lot to the right of the entrance. (See previous ride for directions). The McGill trailhead is left of the main entrance. The sign at the trailhead shows the Whitehorn Nature Trail and the McGill Trail. The Whitehorn Nature Trail is for handicapped use only; no bikes. Sign reads *McGill 3 3/4 miles to Mt Pinos Road* at the bottom of mountain.

Ride up the McGill trail, climbing gradually. At 0.2 mile you reach a junction. Take the trail to the right (northeast). As you ride, you can see the paved Whitehorn Trail to your right downslope. At 0.3 mile you come to another trail junction and sign. The sign indicates McGill Trail to the left and Whitehorn Trail to the right. Go left, down the McGill Trail.

The trail is a very clean singletrack, gradually falling through the pines and whitehorn. Slow at 0.8 mile to look at Frazier and Alamo Mountains to the east and the far walls of the Topatopa Mountains to the south. Continue descending, dodging the occasional patch of rocks or lone roots. To the northeast, Antelope Valley can be seen at 1.3 miles.

Below on your right at 1.6 miles, you can see Cuddy Valley and regions beyond the Tehachipi Mountains looming past Tecuyah Mountain.

Resume your descent to the base of Mt. Pinos. The singletrack is exceptional; clean for the most part, although stones, small thickets and the odd fallen tree will keep riders from sightseeing too much. The trail to several private camps appears on your left at 2.5 miles. Please stay to the right. The trail descends steeply after this. Beware of more trail users. Here oaks begin to appear more fre- quently as you descend the last stretch to reach Mt. Pinos Road at 3.6 miles.

You now have several options to return to McGill Camp: 1) If your ride is a shuttle, jump in the car and motor back. 2) You can ride up the pavement, a moderately strenuous climb to reach McGill Camp. 3) You can do what many local riders do and ride back up the trail. This can be strenuous and is steep at the bottom. The reward is more singletrack and a shorter round trip of 7.2 miles. Any way you return, you'll want to ride this trail again.

55 South Ridge

Distance: 2.7 miles
Difficulty: Easy to mildly technical
Elevation: Start/high point 7,800'; low point 7,509'; 291' loss/gain
Ride Type: Trail, with a pavement loop return
Season: Late April to November
Topo Map: Cuddy Valley

Probably one of the most popular trails on the mountain, South Ridge is close to the Mt. Pinos and McGill campgrounds. The many small water crossings and cross-country ski jumps will excite riders who are looking for beauty, challenge and time to enjoy camp life.

Getting There: Park just outside Mt. Pinos Campground, about 2.5 miles up the road from McGill Camp (see McJeff Trail Warm-up for directions).

Ride into the camp and go left at the cross-country ski trail sign. The trail is a fairly wide cross-country route with numerous jumps of different sizes. Small spring seepages cross the trail as you descend. At 1.7 miles the trail appears to fork. The right trail follows the creek for 100 feet and then fades out. Go left and at 2.0 miles you return to the Mt. Pinos highway. Turn left again and ride up the pavement 0.7 mile to Mt. Pinos Camp.

56 North Ridge/McGill Trail

Distance: 5.9 miles one way, 13.9 miles round trip
Difficulty: Moderate to strenuous—includes jumps and a long return
Elevation: Start/high point 8,360'; low point 6,203'; 2,157' loss/gain
Ride Type: Trail, fire road, pavement return (shuttle or loop)
Season: Late April to November
Topo Map: Cuddy Valley

This is one of two routes from the end of the Mt. Pinos Road at Chula Vista Camp to the bottom of the mountain. Although not as well known as the Harvest/South Ridge Trail descent, the dense pine forest and distance from the highway and campgrounds create a more tranquil and unique experience. You can also do it as a one-way shuttle.

Getting There: From I-5, exit at Frazier Park and head west up the mountain to the end of the pavement. Park at the Chula Vista parking lot near Mt. Pinos' summit. If you do this as a shuttle, leave a vehicle at the McGill Trailhead at the bottom of the mountain.

Ride up the Condor Peak Road 0.1 mile to a gate. Go past the gate 50 feet and take the old road to your right. This is North Ridge Trail. A sign at 0.2 mile marks Meadow Trail to the left. Continue northeast on North Ridge Trail, straight ahead. It is wide and descends gradually. The trail becomes a singletrack at 0.8 mile and descends steeply down a rocky gully. Use necessary caution here. You reach a junction at 1.0 mile. Stay to the right on the singletrack. The trail drops left to join a Jeffrey Pine Flat (JPF) road at 1.2 miles.

Follow this JPF road east, dropping again. Roots and occasional water bars make great jumps. Ride to the junction at 2.0 miles and go left onto the McJeff Trail. The start of this is marked by a small jump. McJeff is liberally dotted with large jumps, so

exercise restraint. At 2.5 miles, turn left (north) onto the unmarked McGill Trail. Continue to ride north on McGill to the junction with the Whitehorn Nature Trail at 2.6 miles. Turn left again on the McGill Trail.

Please use caution and control your speed since this trail is heavily used by hikers and equestrians. McGill Trail drops down the lower slopes to the bottom of Mt. Pinos. On the trip down, you encounter switchbacks, occasional rocks, whitehorn booby traps, and even a fallen tree with a narrow opening cut in it. Have fun, but be careful. You reach Mt. Pinos Road at 5.9 miles.

If you left a car at the bottom, you can shuttle back to Chula Vista Campground up the road. Otherwise, ride the 8 miles up Mt. Pinos Road to return.

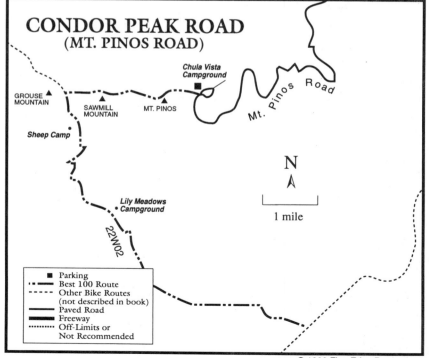

© 1993 Fine Edge Productions

57 Condor Peak Road

Distance: 3 miles
Difficulty: Moderate, strenuous
Elevation: High point 8,831'; low point/start 8,360'; 471' gain/loss
Ride Type: Fire road, in and out
Season: Late April to November
Topo Maps: Sawmill Mountain, Cuddy Valley

This is a relatively rugged, though short, fire road climb to the summit of Mt. Pinos. The view from the summit is well worth the effort, and for an added bonus you can occasionally spot California condor. Please note that all trails from the summit enter wilderness (no bicycles allowed), so you must return the way you came.

Getting There: Park at the Chula Vista Camp parking lot (see directions for the previous ride).

The road leaves the parking lot near its entrance on the left (west) side. At first the road is fairly smooth and the climbing relatively easy. But soon it steepens and becomes rocky. At 0.9 mile you cross a small meadow and the going becomes easier. Three small spurs join the main road: one at 0.9 mile, another at 1.2 miles, and the last at 1.4 miles. Each spur is 0.1 to 0.2 mile long and ends at a vista point. If you explore any of the spurs, return to the main road the way you came. Continue up the road, passing a microwave facility on your right at 1.4 miles, and you reach the summit lookout at 1.5 miles.

There are several benches here where you can relax and take in the magnificent view. To the north, San Joaquin Valley stretches out to the horizon, and the city of Bakersfield can be discerned at the south end of the valley. To the northeast, if the air is clear, the southern ramparts of the Sierra Nevada can be seen. Toward the east, Antelope Valley and the high desert stretch to the horizon. In springtime the desert explodes with color as the California poppies bloom. The rugged Dick Smith and Sespe Wilderness Areas stretch from west to south. These areas are home to the recently reintroduced California condor. These rare and majestic birds are sometimes spotted soaring over Mt. Pinos in their search for food.

Enjoy the view, and when you are ready, return to Chula Vista parking lot the way you came.

For additional rides in this area, please refer to *Mountain Biking The Coast Range, Guide 8, The Saugus District of Angeles National Forest with Mt. Pinos* by Mike Troy and Kevin Woten, ISBN 0-938665-09-X (see p. 304).

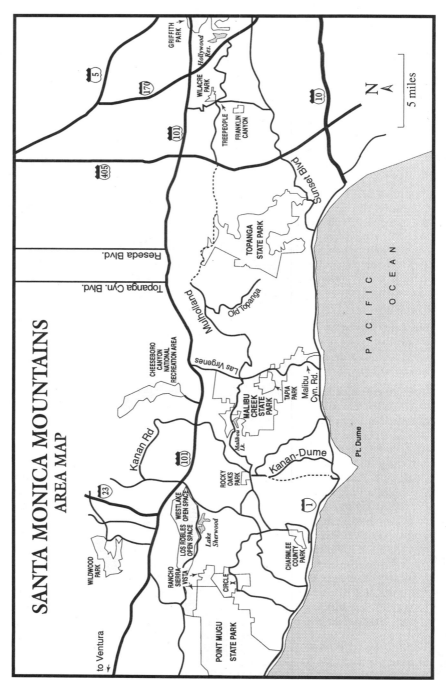

SANTA MONICA MOUNTAINS
AREA MAP

N
5 miles

PACIFIC OCEAN

GRIFFITH PARK
Hollywood Res.
WILACRE PARK
TREEPEOPLE
FRANKLIN CANYON
Sunset Blvd.
TOPANGA STATE PARK
Old Topanga
Mulholland
Reseda Blvd.
Topanga Cyn. Blvd.
CHEESEBORO CANYON NATIONAL RECREATION AREA
Las Virgenes
MALIBU CREEK STATE PARK
TAPIA PARK
Malibu Cyn. Rd.
Malibu Lk.
Kanan Rd.
Kanan-Dume
Pt. Dume
ROCKY OAKS PARK
WESTLAKE OPEN SPACE
LOS ROBLES OPEN SPACE
Lake Sherwood
WILDWOOD PARK
RANCHO SIERRA VISTA
CIRCLE X
CHARMLEE COUNTY PARK
POINT MUGU STATE PARK
to Ventura

5
170
10
101
405
23
1

CHAPTER 7

Santa Monica Mountains

By Jim Hasenauer and Mark Langton

Within minutes of Los Angeles, one of the largest urban centers in the country, the mountain bicyclist enters a world more natural, more rugged and in striking contrast to the sprawling city and suburbs below. This is the Santa Monica Mountains National Recreation Area, with more miles of more varied mountain bike riding than any other urban park in the United States. Wildlife and natural vegetation abound; deer and bobcat are occasionally seen within yards of residential developments.

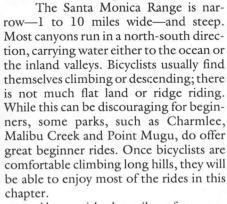

The Santa Monica Range is narrow—1 to 10 miles wide—and steep. Most canyons run in a north-south direction, carrying water either to the ocean or the inland valleys. Bicyclists usually find themselves climbing or descending; there is not much flat land or ridge riding. While this can be discouraging for beginners, some parks, such as Charmlee, Malibu Creek and Point Mugu, do offer great beginner rides. Once bicyclists are comfortable climbing long hills, they will be able to enjoy most of the rides in this chapter.

Along with the miles of tremendous riding opportunities in the Santa Monicas come certain responsibilities and restrictions. Mountain bicyclists must be aware of current land management policies and honor all regulations; they must minimize impact on the land and be cognizant of the safety and enjoyment of other users. At press time, all the rides in this chapter are legally open to bicyclists, but regulations are in flux and changes occur regularly. For up-to-date information contact the appropriate land managers.

We hope you will join the rest of the responsible mountain bikers in the Santa Monica Mountains National Recreation Area to spread the message of conscientious, courteous mountain biking throughout the Santa Monica Mountains and continue to make mountain biking safe and fun for all users.

Topanga State Park

Getting There: The best access to this state park is from Trippet Ranch. From the San Fernando Valley, go south on Topanga Canyon Boulevard. From the top of Topanga, turn left on Entrada and proceed uphill to Topanga State Park. Stay on Entrada, passing two lower lots. At the junction, bear left on Entrada, left into the parking area, and pay a $5 day-use fee. At the fire road entrance on the southeast end of the parking lot a sign reads: *2 miles to Eagle Rock, 2.2 to Waterfall Santa Inez Trail* (closed to bikes), *4.8 to Mulholland* (fire road #30), *8 miles to Temescal Conference Grounds, 8.7 miles to Will Rogers* (closed to bikes), *3 miles to Parker Mesa Overlook* (south), *4.8 Pacific Palisades* (Paseo Miramar).

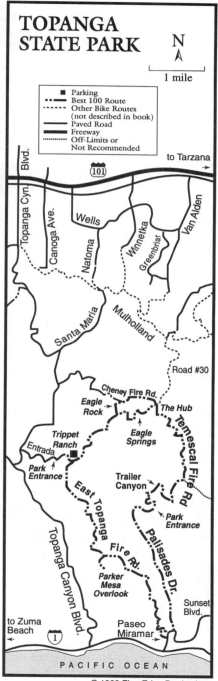

© 1993 Fine Edge Productions

58 Trippet Ranch/ East Topanga Loop

Distance: 19.5 miles
Difficulty: Very strenuous, nontechnical
Elevation: 3,500' gain (approximate)
Ride Type: Loop on fire road
Season: Year round

This 19.5-mile ride has plenty of climbing for intermediate to expert cyclists. Leaving the parking lot at Trippet Ranch, ride uphill to a T and go left. At 1.3 miles there is a three-way fork. (No bikes allowed on the left fork, Musch Trail.) Trippet Ranch Trail on the middle fork climbs to Eagle Rock. For this ride, however, take the right fork, descending to Eagle Springs and climbing to the Hub at mile 3.3. Head right (south) on East Temescal fire road.

At mile 6.3, go through the fire gate and on to the junction of Temescal and Trailer Canyons (left is Temescal, and the trail is closed to bikes farther down). Turn right on Trailer Canyon, a long, steep, rutted downhill. *Control your speed.* At 7.9 miles go through a closed fire gate and continue descending to mile 8.7. Go through another closed fire gate

and leave the dirt. This is a short cul-de-sac at Michael Drive; the sign reads *Topanga State Park, Trailer Canyon Entrance.*

Turn right on Michael Drive and left at the T intersection at Vereda de la Montura. Go half a block and turn right on Palisades Drive (deli with restrooms and water). Descend to mile 11.8; turn right on Sunset Boulevard. At mile 12.0 turn right on Paseo Miramar. Dig in, it's a climb! Follow the yellow lines in the road to the fire road entrance at 13.3 miles. Continue climbing. The junction with Parker Mesa Overlook fire road is at 15.5 miles. For a short out and back with nice views, turn left and go 0.5 mile to a dead-end overlook. At mile 16.5 you're back heading north on East Topanga fire road. It returns you to the Trippet Ranch parking lot at mile 19.5.

59 Eagle Springs/ Eagle Rock Loop

Distance: 6.4 miles
Difficulty: Moderate to difficult (steep climbs depending on direction), nontechnical
Elevation: 1,000' gain (approximate)
Ride Type: Loop on fire road
Season: Year round

This relatively short loop has great vistas and overlooks. It branches off from the Trippet Ranch/East

Topanga Loop at the Hub. If you go in a counter clockwise direction once you get to the Eagle Springs/Eagle

Rock Y, the ride is moderate, as you will avoid the steep climb up to Eagle Rock. However, be careful coming back from the Hub as the descents are fast and rocky, and there is frequently heavy traffic coming up.

Beginning at Trippet Ranch, set your odometer at 0.0. Exit at the back of the parking lot past the picnic tables. Stay on the main fire road, bearing uphill, and you come to a T intersection. Take the fire road left (north) towards the Hub and Eagle Rock. You climb a fair amount, with Topanga Canyon on your left. Continue to 1.3 miles and a three-way intersection. (This loop brings you back out on the middle road, but the singletrack to the far left is off-limits to bikes.) Go right at the intersection, heading downhill. Continue on this fire road to the Hub at 3.3 miles (port-a-potty and info kiosk).

Once at the Hub, there are two left alternatives and one right. Right goes down Temescal fire road to Sunset Boulevard. The left that leads downhill is fire road #30 to Mulholland. For this ride, however, take the other left, which switches back uphill towards Eagle Rock. Continue on the rolling fire road, watching for hikers on the descents! At 4.4 miles you come to Eagle Rock, which is a good place to park the bikes and walk out onto the rock and explore the caves on the south side of the formation. The fire road you can see on the far ridge to the northwest is East Topanga fire road that leads down to Paseo Miramar.

Continuing down from Eagle Rock, you make a steep descent back down to Eagle Springs/Eagle Rock Y intersection. Continue straight to return to Trippet Ranch.

Malibu Creek State Park

Malibu Creek State Park, one of the three large state parks in the Santa Monica Mountains, offers connecting trails from the coast to the south and west. The variety of terrain and natural features enables bicyclists to enjoy a diversity of riding experiences. There are suitable rides in this area for mountain bicyclists of all levels.

Traveling south on Las Virgenes Road from Freeway 101, you can imagine what were once unspoiled views of the mountains. The land adjacent

to the road was slated to be acquired for park land, but when funds were not available, much of it was developed as high density housing. This is a clear example of the "condominimization" of the mountains, a pattern that now threatens the north slopes of the Santa Monicas along the 101 corridor from Calabasas to Point Mugu.

The Visitor's Center at Malibu Creek State Park has fascinating exhibits that document past uses of the park land, an area rich in history. A year-round stream that cuts through Malibu Gorge has always supported a bountiful plant and wildlife population. Human habitation dates back at least 5,000 years. The Chumash Indians had their largest Santa Monica Mountains settlement near here. Later the valleys and grasslands were used for cattle grazing in the Mexican rancho days. An old adobe ranch house from this period is currently being restored just east of the park.

The property was later developed as the Crags Country Club, a private hunting and fishing club. Century Lake was built in 1901 for the members, some of whom built small houses here as weekend retreats. The ruins of one home, the John Mott adobe, can still be seen. The area was then acquired as the 20th Century Movie Ranch. Dozens of films were made here, since the variety of terrain and plant life allowed filmmakers to recreate settings from around the world. In addition to many westerns, the 20th Century Ranch simulated Africa in several Tarzan movies. Perhaps its most famous set was for the television series "M*A*S*H." Some of you may remember an episode in which the 4077th returned to the smoldering remains of their camp. The episode was filmed after a terrible brush fire swept the park in 1982. Now all that remains of the "M*A*S*H" site are a couple of burned out jeeps.

Today, Malibu Creek State Park is used by bicyclists, hikers, equestrians, fishermen, picnickers and, most recently, campers who come to enjoy its rugged character. The Grotto and Century Lake are rich with bass. This much water is rare in the Santa Monicas, so unusual plant and animal life abound. The trails on the floor of the park are generally flat, inviting users of all levels, but the trails that climb to Castro Crest are steep and demanding. Because the park is so heavily used, bicyclists should always use extra caution.

Getting There: Park entrance is at Mulholland and Las Virgines. Take Freeway 101 to Las Virgines-Malibu Canyon. Go south 3 miles, cross Mulholland, and continue 0.3 mile to the park entrance on the right ($5 day-use fee). There is parking outside the entrance, too. You can also access Malibu Creek State Park via the Liberty Canyon and Grasslands Trails. For the Liberty Canyon Trail, travel north on 101 past Las Virgenes Road/Malibu Canyon Road to Liberty Canyon Road, and then go south (left) approximately a mile to the intersection of Liberty Canyon and Park Vista. There is a black wrought iron fence with a walk-through that passes between some houses and horse stables. The Grasslands Trail crosses Mulholland Drive about a quarter mile north of Las Virgenes Road. You can park along Mulholland and access the park from here—the trail starts with a horse walkover next to a private driveway. There is also access to Malibu Creek on Crags Drive: From Lake Vista Drive off Mulholland Highway, turn on Crags Drive to the park boundary. Within 0.8 mile you come to a parking area. A sign at the park gate reads *Bulldog Motorway.*

60 Crags Road/Bulldog Loop/ Lakeside Lateral Loop

Distance: 6.8 miles / 18 miles / 8.6 miles
Difficulty: Varies from easy to difficult, depending on options taken
Elevation: 300' gain/3,500' gain/1,000' gain (all approximate)
Ride Type: Out and back/loop/out and back with loop—all on fire roads.
Season: Year round

At the last parking lot by the restrooms just off Malibu Canyon Road, set your odometer to 0.0. Take the road signed *Authorized Vehicles Only*, cross a little bridge, and begin Crags Road, which here in the park is dirt. At mile 1.71 cross another bridge and continue on the main trail. At mile 2.41 Lost Cabin Trail on the left is marked by an Indian mortar rock. (Lost Cabin goes 0.7 mile to a dead end). At mile 2.42 you're riding through a burned out set of the television series "M*A*S*H." You'll recognize the mountains as those in helicopter scenes in the opening credits of the series.

At mile 2.71 go right at the fork (left is Bulldog Motorway, marked by a sign that reads *Park Boundary*

4.3 Miles, Castro Peak Motorway 3.4 miles). Within 0.39 mile you come to another fork. Go left here, and continue another 0.27 mile to Crags Drive at the park boundary, mile 3.4. (A right takes you 0.29 mile to a dead end at another park boundary and the waterfall end of Malibu Lake. The lake is private and not accessible.) Retrace your route to the parking lot for a 6.8-mile out and back.

For a tougher ride, try the climb up Bulldog. From the fork at 2.71 miles, head up Bulldog to the ridge of Castro Crest and Mesa Peak. At 0.3 mile past the fork you come to a closed gate. Lift your bike over the railroad ties and reset your odometer to 0.0 mile. Continue straight at mile 0.84. The road to the right is a dead

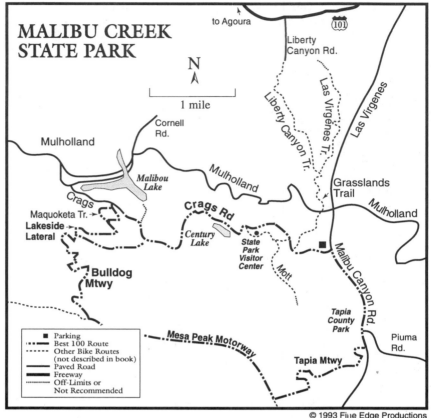

© 1993 Fine Edge Productions

end. At mile 1.11 bear left. (To the right begins the Lakeside Lateral fire road/Lookout Loop, described at the end of this ride.)

At 1.16 there is a false summit—a cool, shady saddle with a little downhill. Enjoy it, that's all you get! Mile 3.35: Closed gate. Mile 3.40 marks the top of Bulldog and the junction with Castro Crest Motorway. Turn left. (Right goes to antenna towers on Castro Peak and descends via Newton or Brewster Motorways to Latigo Canyon.)

After the left turn, descend to mile 4.23 and the Corral Canyon parking lot, continuing through the parking lot and out onto the pave-

ment. Watch for a fire road on the left at mile 4.58. There is a wooden fence where telephone wires cross the road. Turn left on the fire road (Mesa Peak Motorway), which has several good climbs and descends to a fork at 7.2 miles with Puerco Canyon on the right. Go left at the fork.

In a short distance, Mesa Peak fire road comes in from the right. Bear left, descending. At mile 9.07 (you are now on Tapia Motorway) there is a hairpin right turn at a chain link fence, and the trail forks. Bear right up a little hill. At mile 9.77 the fire road ends at Malibu Canyon Road just south of Tapia County Park. A sign by the fire road reads *Tractors only*. Watch for cars, cross the street, and then turn left back to Malibu Creek State Park, passing the Hindu Temple on the right. Turn left into the state park, and at 11.98 miles you're back at the parking lot where you started.

For the Lakeside Lateral/ Lookout Loop, take the Lakeside Lateral fire road at the junction 1.11 miles from the beginning of Bulldog Loop. Climb the short hill and turn right at the top. This takes you over to Lookout Road, which descends back to paved Crags Road and the park entrance. It is a good alternate route if you want to add a little distance to the Crags Road Malibu Creek

route or don't want to do the entire Bulldog Loop. Be careful as you descend after rolling for about 3/4 mile. The fire road gets very steep and, depending on the time of year, can either be extremely rutted, loose, rocky, or all of the above.

At mile 1.91 you come to the park boundary and the pavement. You can either make a right on Lookout and follow it all the way down to Crags Road, or continue down on Maquoketah Trail (paved), which winds over to Lookout where you turn left to Crags. Turn right on Crags to the park entrance. Total distance of Lakeside Lateral/Lookout Loop from Bulldog is 3.2 miles.

61 *Cheeseboro Canyon:* Sulphur Springs Trail

Distance: 12.5 miles
Difficulty: Moderate, somewhat technical
Elevation: 500' gain (approximate)
Ride Type: Out and back on dirt road and singletrack
Season: Year round

Technically, Cheeseboro Canyon National Recreation Area is not part of the Santa Monica Mountains. It is, however, the major National Park Service (NPS) holding in the Santa Monica Mountains National Recreation Area, and it is the major wildlife corridor for animals traveling from the Angeles Forest and Santa Susanna Mountains to the Santa Monicas. It's one of the few parks with open singletracks. The NPS is very good about signing trails for approved travel. Please obey signs that indicate approved use. Part of an old cattle ranch, the area resembles Marin County— rolling hills, coastal

oaks, sea breezes on the ridges and enough horse and cow plop to remind you that this is the West. Wildlife includes golden eagles, deer, bobcat, hawks, coyotes and the usual assortment of reptiles. *Caution: There are many rattlesnakes here.*

Cheeseboro Canyon has been a hotbed of political activity since it borders China Flats and Palo Camado Canyon, areas that have been sought for development for years. China Flats and Palo Camado Canyon are owned by actor/comedian Bob Hope, and it was his dream to build a championship golf course in Palo Camado Canyon. Because this area is a major

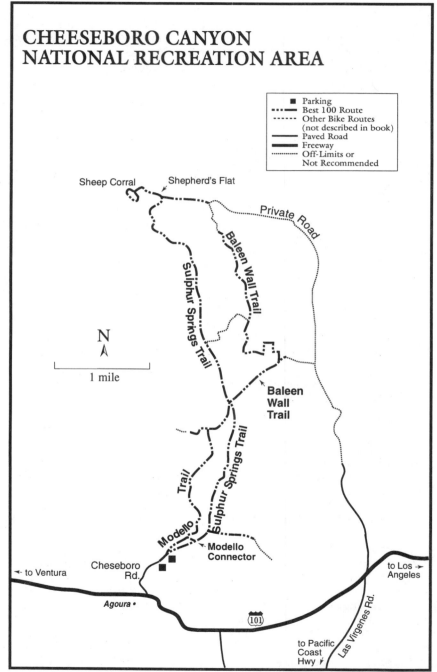

CHEESEBORO CANYON NATIONAL RECREATION AREA

■ Parking
Best 100 Route
Other Bike Routes
(not described in book)
Paved Road
Freeway
Off-Limits or
Not Recommended

Sheep Corral   Shepherd's Flat

Private Road

Baleen Wall Trail

Sulphur Springs Trail

N

1 mile

Baleen
Wall
Trail

Trail

Sulphur Springs Trail

Modello

Modello
Connector

Cheseboro
Rd.

← to Ventura

to Los →
Angeles

Agoura •

101

Las Virgenes Rd.

to Pacific
Coast
Hwy ↓

© 1993 Fine Edge Productions

wildlife corridor, environmentalists feel that no development should take place on surrounding undeveloped acreage. These environmentalists effectively blocked the development in Palo Camado, and a new deal was structured to combine that development with another proposed residential community development east of the park boundary.

At the time of this guide's printing, the viability of that community was still being studied. Such a development would include dedicating approximately 3,000 acres of open space that would be annexed onto Cheeseboro Canyon directly to the east (Malibu Canyon) and north, much of it open and usable for mountain biking. Another 7,300 acres of open space would also be turned over to public holdings in the Santa Monica and Santa Susanna mountains should the deal go through. Currently the property to the east and north of Cheeseboro Canyon remains accessible via park roads, yet it is technically private and you are subject to

any enforcement deemed appropriate by law.

The main Sulphur Springs trail is a 6.25-mile dead-end route with three offshoots. Riders on the main trail can explore the canyon bottomland, which rolls through grasslands and coastal oak groves into dense chaparral. The side trails that climb to the ridges above the park afford bird's-eye views of the canyon below.

Getting There: Take Freeway 101 to the Cheseboro exit (2.7 miles west of Las Virgines Road or 2.4 miles east of Kanan-Dume Road). Head north and make a quick right on Cheseboro Road. Follow the narrow street 1 mile to a right turn just before the sign: *Agoura Hills City Limit*. You can park here or continue up the gravel road 1/4 mile to another parking lot.

Begin at the outer gate off Cheseboro Road, and proceed 1/4 mile to the other parking lot and the Sulphur Springs trail entrance. There is a bulletin board information center

where you can study maps and read about the Cheeseboro Recreation Area's natural history. There are port-a-potties here, but no water is available. At mile 0.81 go past the south entrance to Modello Trail on the left. At mile 0.96 you pass the junction with Canyon Overlook Trail on the right. At 1.3 miles the area to the side of the trail is signed *Research Area*. (Stay out; do not leave the main trail. The Park Service is trying to restore native grasslands and to study the impact of fire and other phenomena on the oak and native flora.)

At 1.5 miles bear left past the Y with Baleen Wall Trail on the right. At 1.6 miles go straight at the junction with Modello Trail (on the left), and at mile 4.1 you pass a hiking trail headed toward the Baleen Wall posted *No bikes*. (It is illegal to take your bike on this trail.) At mile 4.4 the road

turns to singletrack and crosses a stream. On the left, just after you cross the stream, you can see a rock with some interesting fossils.

The singletrack follows the sometimes sandy stream bed up the canyon. There are short, steep dips and climbs and plenty of rocks on the trail. At mile 5.75 the trail comes to a T-junction with both right and left forks going approximately 1/4 mile to dead-end turnarounds. In spring the area around these forks has plenty of wildflowers. Return to the trailhead from the T, watching for Modello Trail on the right. Take it (see Modello Trail below), or continue straight to the main parking lot at mile 12.5.

From the Sulphur Springs Trail, you have several optional trails to explore. **Canyon Overlook Trail** leaves Sulphur Springs Trail 0.96 mile from the park entrance. Turn right for a non-technical 0.7-mile, 500-foot climb (east and then south) to a hill overlooking some of the canyons and ridges of Cheeseboro Park. When the mustard is blooming in the spring this area is carpeted in yellow. The road is quite rutted so *watch your steep downhill return* to the Sulphur Springs Trail.

Baleen Wall Trail offers 5.4 miles of moderate dirt road with a 2-mile service road option. You gain 2,000 feet in elevation on this out and back ride. At 1.5 miles on the Sulphur Springs Trail turn right onto the Baleen Wall Trail. Reset your odometer to 0.0 mile. Bear left past the service road at mile 0.7 on the right. (It climbs for a mile up to electric towers and great views of the canyon.) The trail climbs steeply. At 1.26 miles you pass a water tank on the left and head back to the north. At 2.5 miles the road forks again; follow the main road. The hiking trail to the left is just that: *iIlegal for bikes*. The road dead-ends at the last electric tower at mile 2.72 in high grass. From here, you can see the top of the Baleen Wall rock formations. Return down the long descent to Sulphur Springs Trail.

Modello Trail, an easy to moderate doubletrack and dirt road combination, is a good optional return route to the parking area. There is a 1,000-foot elevation gain and some exposure. At 0.81 mile on the Sulphur Springs Trail you pass the south entrance to the Modello Trail on the left. Farther up Sulphur Springs at 1.6 miles is the north entrance of Modello on the left. You will probably want to ride the rest of Sulphur Springs Trail and/or Balleen Wall Trail before returning to this point. When you are ready, reset your odometer to 0.0 at the north entrance to Modello Trail. Climb 0.3 mile (west) to a left turn onto doubletrack. (The right dead-ends at a fence.) Continue climbing to the junction at mile 1.0 and turn right to descend 0.3 mile to the parking lots. (The left descends to the south junction with Sulphur Springs Trail.)

Point Mugu State Park

Point Mugu State Park is one of the most popular bicycling areas in the Santa Monicas. It has spectacular scenery and several loop options for bicyclists. The main trail—actually an old fire road—is relatively flat and connects Newbury Park with the beach, where there is camping at Sycamore Canyon Campground.

The park offers five miles of ocean shoreline, two long rides in canyon bottomland, and a long ridge ride overlooking both the canyon and ocean. La Jolla Valley *(currently closed to bikes)* has one of the finest displays of native grasslands left in California. Bluffs near the ocean are among the few places in the world with giant coreopsis, a small tree-like shrub with bright yellow spring flowers. Silvery sycamores, thriving on deep underground water, mark the canyon floor and put on a wild display of color in the fall.

The park is inhabited by several large animals including at least two mountain lions (one is called Big Tail). In winter, thousands of Monarch butterflies come through during their migration south from colder climes. And because Point Mugu is located on the northwest tip of Santa Monica Bay, it provides an excellent viewing point for the California gray whale migrations in winter and spring.

Four miles northwest of Sycamore Cove, an observation platform on the west side of Pacific Coast Highway overlooks the saltwater Mugu Lagoon. There is a picnic table here, and it's a good place to watch for birds. Point Mugu Rock, a popular bouldering area for climbers, is located one mile to the southeast. From the observation platform you can see several rare or endangered birds, including the brown pelican, light footed clapper rail, Belding savannah sparrow, California least tern and marsh sandpiper. To the east of the lagoon grows the giant coreopsis. Do not disturb these birds or plants; they are protected species. *Note:* The property behind the fence belongs to the government. Unauthorized persons must stay out.

Many archeological sites from the Chumash culture have been discovered at Point Mugu State Park. Ranching began during the Spanish period when the area was known as the Guadalasca Land Grant. Most recently it was the Danielson family ranch. The Danielsons sold the land to the state to be preserved as a park. This was a critical event in the development of the Santa Monica Mountains National Recreation Area, since there were plans to develop a hotel and golf course on the Point Mugu park land. Local environmentalists joined efforts, and eventually this western cornerstone to the Santa Monicas was acquired for public use.

Sycamore Canyon in Point Mugu State Park draws big crowds. Use extra caution if you ride here, especially on summer weekends. For a more pleasant ride, we suggest cycling during the week or in winter.

Getting There: The best access is from the beach at Sycamore Canyon Campground, 5 miles north of Leo Carrillo State Beach on Pacific Coast Highway. A $5 entry fee is required for campground day use. If you're coming from Newbury Park, take 101 Freeway north and exit on Wendy 10.8 miles past Kanan-Dume, turning left (south) toward the mountains. In 3.2 miles Wendy ends at Potrero Road. Turn right. At the junction with Reino, bear left on Potrero Road, then turn left on Pinehill (at the stop sign) onto a dirt road. Follow the dirt road to the parking lot. Ride your bike around the locked fire gate to enter the park.

62 Big Sycamore Canyon Fire Road

Distance: 16.4 miles
Difficulty: Generally easy with a steep climb on the north end, nontechnical
Elevation: 1,000' gain (500' in last 3/4 mile at north end)
Ride Type: Out and back with several loop possibilities
Season: Year round

Big Sycamore Canyon fire road (also known as Big Sycamore Canyon Trail) begins at the north end of the Sycamore Canyon Campground. It winds along the bottom of deep, enclosed Sycamore Canyon through sycamore and oak groves near a seasonal stream.

Entrance to the fire road is at the far end of the campground. At 2.04 miles, you pass a picnic bench under a huge overhanging oak tree. At mile 3.9 is the entrance to the newly completed Wood Canyon View Trail. It is currently a multi-use trail, the only true singletrack in this park that is open to mountain bikes. Please use extra caution since it is certainly being looked at under a microscope to determine its ultimate existence as a true multi-use trail. (See Sycamore Canyon/Overlook Trail Loop for trail description and mileage.)

Keep right at the Wood Canyon Junction, mile 4.0. At mile 4.42 is the fire road cutoff to Ranch Center Road on the left. Keep right. At mile 4.72 is a junction with a paved road. Stay left on the pavement and watch for occasional cars. (Right leads to Danielson Multi-Use Area.) At 5.15 miles you will find water and port-a-potties. At 5.56 keep right at the fork. Ranch Center Road (paved) goes left. At 6.57 miles there is water and a California Wilderness Area trailhead signed *Closed to bikes*. Begin a steep hill. Climb to the top of the hill at a water tower at mile 7.2. The road drops down to Satwiwa Nature Center at 8.18 miles and out the Newbury Park exit.

63 Sycamore/Wood Canyon Loop with Guadalasca Trail

Distance: 11.4 or 13.5 miles (plus 2.64 miles for Guadalasca)
Difficulty: Easy to moderate with one difficult climb; Guadalasca is moderate, technical.
Elevation: 1,750' gain (including Guadalasca)
Ride Type: Loop on dirt and pavement
Season: Year round

Wood Canyon is a beautiful, shaded, stream-side environment with abundant wildlife. This wonderful ride offers two options: an 11.4-mile loop is almost all on dirt, while the 13.5-mile trip climbs the paved but seldom used Ranch Center Road. (At Ranch Center you can see the old ranch

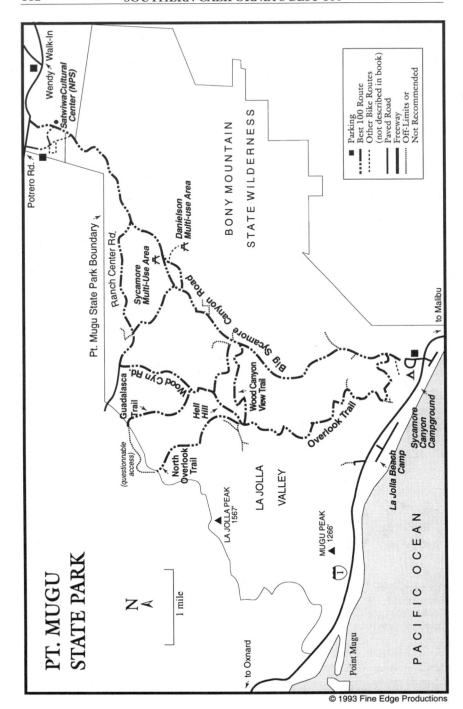

PT. MUGU
STATE PARK

N

1 mile

to Oxnard

Point Mugu

PACIFIC OCEAN

MUGU PEAK
1266'

LA JOLLA PEAK
1567'

LA JOLLA
VALLEY

North Overlook Trail

(questionable access)

Guadalasca Trail

Hell Hill

Wood Cyn Rd.

Wood Canyon View Trail

Overlook Trail

La Jolla Beach Camp

Sycamore Canyon Campground

Big Sycamore Canyon Road

Ranch Center Rd.

Pt. Mugu State Park Boundary

Sycamore Multi-Use Area

Danielson Multi-use Area

BONY MOUNTAIN

STATE WILDERNESS

to Malibu

Potrero Rd.

Wendy Walk-In

Satwiwa Cultural Center (NPS)

Parking
Best 100 Route
Other Bike Routes
(not described in book)
Paved Road
Freeway
Off-Limits or
Not Recommended

© 1993 Fine Edge Productions

house, which now houses park employees.) Both rides start on Big Sycamore Canyon fire road at Pacific Coast Highway, climb to a water tower overlooking the Ranch Center, then follow the fire road through lush, rolling Wood Canyon.

The entrance to Big Sycamore Canyon fire road is at the end of the campground. At mile 0.45 you pass Sycamore/Overlook Junction and at 2.04 there's a picnic table and an overhanging oak. Mile 4.0 marks the junction of Sycamore and Wood Canyons. Bear right. Turn left at 4.42 miles onto a fire road cutoff to Ranch Center Road. This is a steep climb to a water tower at 5.43 miles and the crest of Ranch Center Road. Turn left and descend a paved, steep downhill. *Caution: There are off-camber turns, occasional cars and trucks, and loose gravel.* At the bottom of the hill, turn left through the Ranch Center parking lot at 5.87 miles (phone and port-a-potty available). Turn left again on Wood Canyon Road, which takes you through some exciting whoop-de-doos. *Caution: Control your speed and watch for other users. There are several blind corners here.*

At mile 7.14 you come to the Guadalasca Trail, which used to be a ranch road. It has overgrown and deteriorated into a singletrack that climbs to the park boundary at 1.32 miles from Wood Canyon. You start out along a creek bed in a beautifully wooded canyon, then climb along the east side of a narrow valley to the ridge overlooking Camarillo Valley. You can go past the gate to the ridge another tenth of a mile, but doing so is at your own risk. This boundary is the focal point of yet another ambiguous and politically charged situation. Even though the land beyond

the fence is state park property, the state has granted an easement to the private property owner for access and other considerations. The private property owner is very tenacious regarding the easement. Guadalasca has for years been used to travel outside the park and up to the North Overlook Trail. It has just recently been opened to multi-use, and the possibility of gaining access onto the easement is still eminent.

Back at the entrance to Guadalasca Trail, continue down Wood Canyon. At mile 7.52 you come to Deer Camp Junction (water). Go left at the fork. (Hell Hill rises at the right fork and climbs to Overlook Trail). At mile 8.3 you rejoin Big Sycamore Canyon fire road. Turn right and return to Big Sycamore Canyon Campground to exit at mile 11.4.

For a slightly longer loop with more paved road, try the one used by the Hollywood YMCA Adventure Trails Program when it took inner city kids mountain biking in Sycamore Canyon. If you wish to do this version, stay right on Big Sycamore Canyon fire road at the 4.42 mile junction. Continue on the main trail to 4.72 miles and the junction with a paved road. Go left on the paved road (right is the Danielson Multi-Use Area). At 5.15 miles you'll find water and a port-a-potty. At 5.56 miles turn left at the fork with Ranch Center Road (paved) and climb two hills to the water tower at mile 7.5. From here the ride is identical to the one described above. Mile 7.94: to Ranch Center. Mile 9.59: Deer Camp Junction; bear left. Mile 10.37: junction with Big Sycamore Canyon fire road. Turn right toward the campground. At mile 13.47 the fire road exits at the campground.

64 Sycamore Canyon/ Overlook Trail Loop

Distance: 9.8 miles
Difficulty: Moderate with one very steep hill, nontechnical
Elevation: 2,500' gain
Ride Type: Loop on dirt roads and singletrack
Season: Year round

This ride climbs to Overlook Trail and can be done in either direction. If you ride counter-clockwise you have a shorter, steeper climb with a longer descent and better ocean views. Prior to the opening of Wood Canyon View Trail (part of the Backbone Trail), you had to climb Hell Hill at the base of Deer Camp Junction. Now you have the option of climbing the 1.82-mile-long Wood Canyon View Trail, a wonderfully winding singletrack with canyon and ocean views. It's a little longer, but it is much easier and more fun than climbing Hell Hill. While there is fair to good line-of-sight most of the way, there are still several blind corners. *Watch for bikes coming down, and be extra careful of hikers and equestrians if you are traveling downhill on Wood Canyon View Trail.*

The entrance to Big Sycamore Canyon fire road is at the end of the campground. At mile 0.45 you pass Sycamore/Overlook Junction. (If you wish to do this ride clockwise, turn left here and reverse the following directions.) At mile 2.04 pass the picnic tables at an overhanging oak. Turn left at 3.9 miles onto Wood Canyon View Trail and climb 1.82 miles to Overlook Trail. Or you can stay on Sycamore Canyon one tenth of a mile farther to Wood Canyon Junction on the left at 4.0 miles. Continue to Deer Camp Junction at 4.8 miles.

At Deer Camp junction bear left and uphill at a fork to climb Hell Hill. Wood Canyon View Trail meets the Overlook Trail just a few yards west of the four-way intersection of Hell Hill, La Jolla Valley Trail and North Overlook Trail at 5.72 miles (5.62 if you took Wood Canyon and Hell Hill). Turn left (west) on Overlook, which follows ridges down to Big Sycamore Canyon. (To the right —northeast, away from ocean—is the North Overlook Trail, which climbs moderately 1 mile and then descends 0.3 mile to the park boundary, affording beautiful views of the canyon below, as well as some higher elevation ocean vistas.)

There are great views of Sycamore Canyon, La Jolla Valley and the ocean as you make your final descent along Overlook Trail. (Going straight leads to La Jolla Valley, which is *currently closed to bikes.*) Caution: When descending Overlook Trail towards the ocean, watch for hikers coming uphill. At mile 9.34 Overlook Trail rejoins Big Sycamore Canyon fire road. Go right into the campground and exit at mile 9.79.

Westlake Open Space:

65 Conejo Crest/White Horse/ Triunfo Park

Distance: 6.82 miles, with shorter loops available
Difficulty: Moderate to difficult, with some advanced technical singletrack skills required
Elevation: 1,500' gain (approximate)
Ride Type: Loop on dirt roads and singletrack
Season: Year round

Getting There: There are several access points to the Westlake Open Space. From the east side you can enter at Fairview off the 101 at Hampshire, or across the street from the equestrian center off Potrero Road in Westlake Village. From the west, you can access the upper plateau before the Los Robles Ridge Trail by taking Moorpark Road off the 101, going south to Los Padres, left to Hillsborough, and right to the top of the hill. Access is on the right. However, the majority of the trail network is off Hampshire to the east.

For Hampshire trail access, go north on Freeway 101 to Thousand Oaks, exit Hampshire Road, go south towards Westlake to Willow Lane (the first street after you go under the freeway from the San Fernando Valley/Agoura or after turning right off the freeway coming from Ventura). Turn right on Willow to Fairview Road, then left on Fairview. Fairview ends at Foothill Road. Straight ahead you see a dirt road going between some houses. You can drive up this road to a locked gate, but the road is not well suited to vehicular travel.

At Foothill and Fairview, set your odometer to 0.0. Continue up the fire road to a pump house on the left and a locked gate at mile 0.33. Go over the gate and turn right on the fire road. At mile 0.98 you come to a three-way intersection. Straight ahead you can see the fire road as it dips down into a saddle and then reappears under a row of wire towers. Left takes you back towards Westlake and houses; to the right is a steep climb that leads to a very technical singletrack that ends up back down at Freeway 101 and Rancho Road.

Continue straight, descending quickly and then climbing steeply to another intersection at mile 1.19. To the right you can see a fire road descent, which is the Los Robles Canyon Trail over to the Los Robles Ridge Trail. Just behind you back down the steep climb is the entrance to Triunfo Park Trail. This is a very technical singletrack of 0.9 mile that goes down to Triunfo Park in Westlake. For the Conejo Crest and White Horse Canyon Trail, turn left uphill at this intersection onto the narrow, rocky doubletrack.

Continue climbing until the hill tops out at a T. Here you have a beautiful view of the Santa Monicas to the west. The road winding up behind the rocky knob hill across the valley is Decker Road. To the left you can see part of Westlake Lake, and above that and to the right is Westlake Reservoir. Go right from the T intersection to continue on Conejo Crest (left drops quickly to houses).

You will be on a ridge trail that is known as The Cobbles because of the rocky surface of the trail. At mile 1.86 you come to a descent that is very steep and loose. *Please use caution.* At the bottom of the steep descent (mile 1.96) there is a trail to the

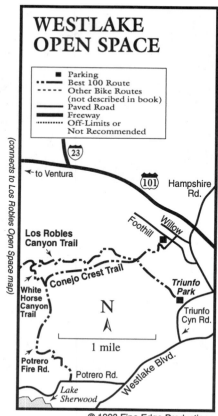

© 1993 Fine Edge Productions

right that takes you directly into White Horse Canyon. Continue straight on this fun, rolling doubletrack to mile 2.17 and a fire road T. Going right takes you into White Horse Canyon; left goes to the beginning of the White Horse Canyon Trail.

Continue to the left downhill and then up and over another rise. At 2.39 miles there is a sign on the right for the White Horse Canyon Loop. The Equestrian Alternative Trail to the left is a fun route down to the houses below. Continuing on the fire road straight ahead will take you to Potrero Road and the equestrian center. Turn right onto the White Horse Canyon Trail for a short but extremely fun singletrack that takes you over to the main fire road at 2.7 miles into White Horse Canyon. Turn left downhill and follow to mile 3.42, and the main Los Robles Canyon fire road. Left takes you to the upper plateau and Hillsborough trailhead (and Los Robles Ridge Trail); right takes you back to your vehicle.

Continue right on the fire road to a fun descent and then a series of moderate switchback climbs. To your left is the Conejo Valley and Freeway 101. At 4.61 miles you arrive back at the three-way intersection and the entrance to Triunfo Park Trail. From here you can go back to where you started, or descend Triunfo Park Trail.

If you choose to take the Triunfo Park Trail, you come to the end of the trail at a locked gate. To the left is a trail that takes you around a sand volleyball court towards a steep walk-up. Continuing uphill, it flattens out a bit and then gets very steep again. At the top of this second steep section you can turn left and follow the fire road up to the first three-way intersection you came to when you began your ride (mile 0.98). From this point, turn right and continue back down to the locked gate and pump house on your left (Fairview).

For a less strenuous loop, instead of following the fire road up after climbing up the two steep sections, go left downhill about 50 yards from the knoll you're on and then turn right at the bottom onto a narrow doubletrack. Just a short way down is a motorcycle trail on the left going straight down into a small valley. On the other side you can see another fire road, which is what you want to access. Drop down the motorcycle trail and follow it up the other side of the valley to a trail that merges you into the fire road. Stay on the main fire road, bearing right past the first Y in about 50 yards, then left at another Y, mile 1.63. Continue to a locked gate and pump station (mile 1.87), then turn right to go back down to Fairview.

66 Los Robles Canyon Open Space:
Los Robles Trail

Distance: 10 miles one way
Difficulty: Moderate with some difficult, technical singletrack sections
Elevation: 2,500' gain (approximate)
Ride Type: One way on dirt roads and singletrack
Season: Year round

Administered by COSCA, Los Robles Canyon Open Space offers several miles of interconnected singletracks and fire roads with a variety of terrain and vegetation. Because Los Robles is surrounded by residential areas, you never feel completely free of the city. You see houses, the freeway or construction almost everywhere you ride here. Still, the rides are challenging, and there are many wildflowers in season. *Caution: The area is heavily used by equestrians, especially on weekends.*

The main Los Robles Ridge Trail runs 10 miles west to east between Newbury Park and Westlake Village. (Hidden Valley and Rancho

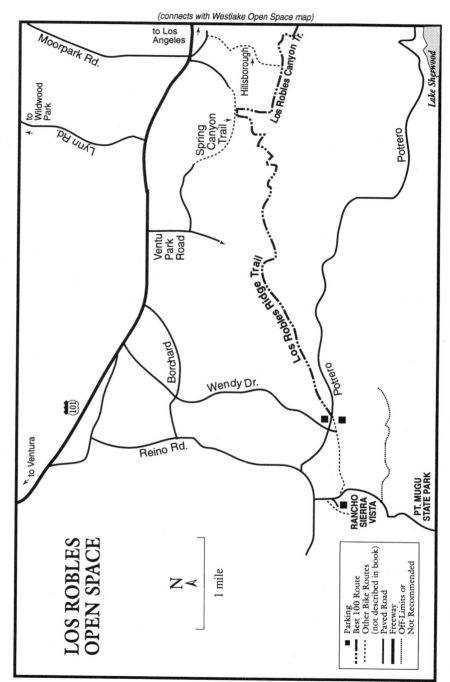

(connects with Westlake Open Space map)

to Los Angeles

Moorpark Rd.

to Wildwood Park

Lynn Rd.

Hillsborough

Los Robles Canyon Tr.

Lake Sherwood

Spring Canyon Trail

Potrero

Ventu Park Road

Los Robles Ridge Trail

Borchard

Wendy Dr.

Potrero

101

Reino Rd.

Potrero

to Ventura

RANCHO SIERRA VISTA

PT. MUGU STATE PARK

LOS ROBLES OPEN SPACE

N

1 mile

■	Parking
·····	Best 100 Route
- - -	Other Bike Routes (not described in book)
——	Paved Road
≡≡	Freeway
········	Off-Limits or Not Recommended

© 1993 Fine Edge Productions

Sierra Vista are to the south.) There are several connectors coming in from the north and south along the way. At the east end, the main trail forks to three different trailheads: Fairview, Triunfo Park and Lake Sherwood (see Westlake Open Space). The trail description below goes from west to east, but you can ride it in either direction.

Getting There: From the 101, exit at Wendy and go left (toward the coast). When Wendy ends at Potrero, go left 0.5 mile to gravel parking lot on left. There's water and trail information at the trailhead. Other access: Moorpark Road/Fairview Road/Triunfo Park/ Lake Sherwood.

Begin Los Robles Trail at the gravel parking lot and take a short climb up to and across a paved road. At mile 1.1 there is a sign: *Lake Sherwood 9 miles, Triunfo Park 8 miles, Cultural Center 4 miles.* The trail rolls along the north hillside above a residential area. Soon you cross two metal bars on the trail and begin a steep climb. The trail abuts private property and a fence on the north. At 2.0 miles, begin a steep descent. At mile 2.33 cross another bar and continue straight on the main trail. Go left at the fork at 2.63. (Right leads to private property by a barn on the hill.)

Here the trail becomes a singletrack. At mile 2.93 cross Ventu Park Road and continue the singletrack climb to 4.0 miles. There's a fork at mile 4.38, but you continue straight on Los Robles Trail. (The right fork is a 1-mile climb on the Scenic Vista trail to a dead end.) Begin a mile-long descent on switchbacks. This area has been damaged by skidding bicycles, and there are deep ruts in the center of most of

the turns. At the bottom, there is much horse damage as well. *Use caution through this entire section. Control your speed. Don't skid.*

At mile 5.56 cross another metal bar, bear right and climb to a fork. Go right at the top of the hill, following signs to Lake Sherwood and Triunfo Park (left goes to Moorpark Road). Climb the steep hill. At 6.17 miles, you pass a picnic table in an oak grove where you go left at a junction just past the sign: *Los Padres Road .5 miles, Fairview Road 4 miles, Lake Sherwood*

Road 4 miles. Climb the steep hill, cross a dirt road and then go through the center of Upper Meadow (upper plateau).

You come to an intersection with a gate on the right. To the left is Hillsborough Street, which leads down to Moorpark Road. Climb past a metal gate at mile 7.57. The trail forks at 7.8 miles. To the right is the White Horse Canyon Trail. To ride the rest of the Los Robles Trail, continue straight on the main fire road. (See Westlake Open Space trail descriptions for routes and distances in this area and from this point on Los Robles Trail.)

There are several options once you get to the Westlake Open Space. You can turn around and go back the same way, which in itself is a very different ride from the direction you just came. Many people take Potrero Road through Hidden Valley back to their cars in Newbury Park. If you choose to do this, turn right back at the White Horse Canyon Trail. If you make no turns off the main trail, you eventually come to Potrero Road and the equestrian center. (See White Horse Canyon and Conejo Crest trail descriptions.) Once you are on Potrero Road, turn right and continue all the way through Hidden Valley. You pass by cattle and horse ranches, climb up out of the valley, and then descend a half mile to the entrance to Los Robles Ridge Trail on Potrero and the Wendy Walk-In.

You can also take Hampshire Road to Thousand Oaks Boulevard and surface streets back to Newbury Park. Once you have exited Westlake Open Space at Fairview (see Westlake Open Space trail descriptions), turn left on Hampshire under Freeway 101 to Thousand Oaks Boulevard. Turn left, proceed to Moorpark Road, then turn right. Go up to Hillcrest Drive, turn left and follow all the way to the intersection of Lynn and Hillcrest. The Oaks Mall will be on your left. Turn right on Hillcrest and continue until it runs into Camino Dos Rios. Turn left and continue over the freeway, with Camino Dos Rios turning into Wendy Drive. Follow Wendy back to Potrero and turn left; parking is located a half mile up Potrero.

For additional rides in this area, please refer to *Mountain Biking the Coast Range, Guide 7, The Santa Monica Mountains,* second edition, by Jim Hasenauer and Mark Langton, ISBN 0-938665-10-3 (see p. 304).

CHAPTER 8

Ventura County
and the Sespe

By Mickey McTigue

Ventura County is located on the Southern California coast, adjacent to and directly west of Los Angeles County. A small county by California standards, it's only 45 miles east to west by 60 miles north to south. Almost all the population is located in the southern half on the coastal plains and river valleys. The Los Padres National Forest takes up most of the mountainous northern half. The many miles of trails and dirt roads in the forest combined with a mild climate make mountain bicycling an exciting year-round sport here.

The inland resort town of Ojai is surrounded by mountains with many miles of scenic roads and trails, some easy, others challenging to expert riders. Concerts, plays, tennis tournaments, golf, fishing and other recreation activities will complement your mountain bicycling trip to Ojai. Riding is possible all year except during heavy winter rains.

Pine Mountain summit is north of Ojai in rugged mountainous terrain near the center of the southern part of the Los Padres National Forest. Here near the 5,000 foot level you can really get away from it all on shorter trips into Chorro Grande Canyon or skirt the headwaters of the Sespe on the

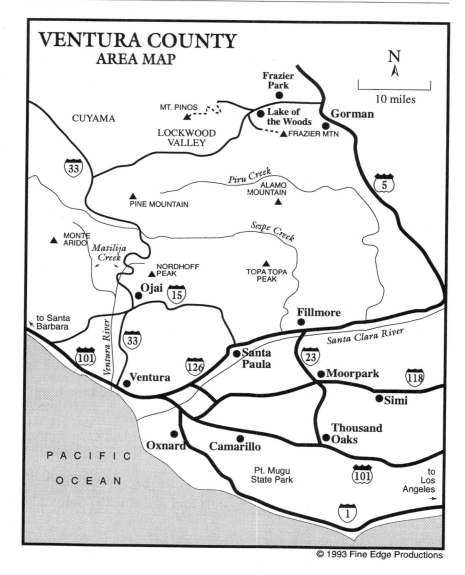

VENTURA COUNTY
AREA MAP

N

10 miles

Frazier
Park

MT. PINOS

CUYAMA

Lake of
the Woods   Gorman

LOCKWOOD
VALLEY   FRAZIER MTN

33

Piru Creek

ALAMO
MOUNTAIN

PINE MOUNTAIN

Sespe Creek

MONTE
ARIDO   Matilija
          Creek

NORDHOFF
PEAK   TOPA TOPA
                PEAK

Ojai   15

Fillmore

to Santa
Barbara

Ventura River

33

Santa Clara River

101   126   Santa
                  Paula   23

Ventura   Moorpark   118

                                Simi

                        Thousand
Oxnard   Camarillo   Oaks

PACIFIC
                Pt. Mugu   101   to
OCEAN   State Park   Los
                                             Angeles

                                1

5

© 1993 Fine Edge Productions

remote Monte Arido Road. Late spring, summer, and fall are best; expect snow and mud in winter.

Alamo and Frazier Mountains are in the northeastern part of the county and accessible from Interstate 5. These 7,000-foot and 8,000-foot mountains have good roads near their summits. You ride through pine forests with amazing clear-day views of the San Joaquin and Antelope Valleys and even across the county to the ocean. Visit during the summer and fall as there's heavy snow here in winter.

Ojai Valley

The Ojai Valley gets much of its beauty from the surrounding mountains. The many diverse trails along those steep slopes enable mountain bicyclists to enjoy that beauty from many different angles and perspectives. The valley has retained its image as a village in a rural setting by preserving the native oak and sycamore trees and by the cultivation of extensive orange groves. Farming was the first major activity here, but the mild climate and serene panorama soon attracted many winter visitors, creating a resort industry.

A great variety of places to stay are now available—from the usual motels and bed and breakfasts to full-service hotels that feature activities like diet and exercise regimens, tennis, swimming, golf, etc. Family and friends of hard core mountain bicyclists will be able to find many alternative activities here. The oldest tennis tournament in the country, started in 1899, attracts the nation's best interscholastic players. It is held every year in late April and uses every court in the valley for a week. The rest of the year there are enough courts for all.

A world acclaimed music festival held every year since 1946 is played outdoors in Ojai's Libby Bowl the last weekend in May. A parade that seems to involve most of the people of the valley is held every Fourth of July, and around mid-September the Mexican Fiesta does the same with plenty of special Mexican foods. There are also specialty shops, an unusual bookstore, plays, a Sunday sidewalk art display, camping, and fishing for state record bass at Lake Casitas.

You can get to Ojai Valley from U.S. Highway 101 on the coast in Ventura by taking State Highway 33 north. In 11.2 miles State Highway 150 joins in from the west. Stay on 150 to the east when 33 branches northwest 2 miles farther. Another mile puts you in downtown Ojai with its famed arched arcade sidewalk cover. Highway 33 passes through the valley and continues north into the Los Padres National Forest. More excellent mountain bicycling is located there, and you may want to try those areas while staying in the Ojai Valley.

Winter rainstorms are often very heavy, causing flooded streams and muddy trails. The shale on the mountains drains fast and most trails are passable again soon. The valley floor, at 800 feet, seldom has snow although frost is common. Summer days can be very hot and dry, and riding early in the morning is advised. Unless you are used to extreme heat, don't ride in the noon sun. Always carry plenty of water.

Strong endurance riders will find bicycle transportation enough to get to and from the rides listed in this chapter. Most riders will want a vehicle to get to the trailheads. On some

routes where you come out at a second trailhead another vehicle is needed to retrieve the first one. A simpler method is to have someone drop you off at the remote trailhead and then you ride back to town or wherever you are staying.

All the rides described in this section have exceptional scenic vistas overlooking Ojai Valley. Shelf Road is a short easy ride on the north edge of town. Sulphur Mountain Road steadily climbs 2,300 feet on 9 miles of good dirt road. This mountain is directly south of the valley and is usually ridden up and back but can be part of a loop ride. Upper Ojai to Ojai over Nordhoff Ridge is a much more difficult 24-mile ride up to and along the main mountain ridge north of the valley. You ride the Gridley Trail singletrack back down off the mountain. Rose Valley to Ojai over Nordhoff Ridge starts from Rose Valley, 18 miles by paved road north of Ojai. You climb steeply up onto Nordhoff Ridge and can either return to Ojai via Sisar Road (moderate difficulty) or the Gridley Trail singletrack (shorter and more technical).

For the latest safety and trail information, call the USFS Ranger Station in Ojai at (805) 646-4348.

67 Shelf Road

Distance: 1.75 miles one way
Difficulty: Easy, nontechnical
Elevation: 1,000'
Ride Type: Out and back or loop on dirt road
Season: Spring, summer, fall

A short, easy dirt road that's 1.75 miles long, Shelf Road is a public route closed to motor traffic and gated at each end. It runs east and west at the north edge of town between Signal Street and Gridley Road. Signal Street crosses Ojai Avenue at the main traffic light in downtown Ojai where the Post Office is located.

Getting There: Park along Signal Street, Grand Avenue, or near your favorite restaurant or ice cream shop. Take plenty of water since none is available en route. Riding in summer is best done in early morning or late afternoon.

This delightful road climbs and descends less than 200 feet, keeping most of the time around the 1,000

foot elevation contour. Take Signal Street north and uphill about 1.25 miles to its end, bearing slightly right past a white gate. Stay on the main dirt road and watch for walkers, runners and horseback riders. You have views of the east end of Ojai, and the steep slopes put you right above some residences. An excellent way to start the day is a sunrise ride before breakfast or brunch. You can make this a loop ride by taking Gridley Road downhill from the east end of Shelf Road. Where Gridley crosses Grand Avenue, turn right and return to Signal Street. One way on Shelf Road takes about 30 minutes with enough time to look at the scenery. Meditative riders will take much longer, but it's time well spent.

68 Sulphur Mountain Road

Distance: 9 miles one way
Difficulty: Moderate, nontechnical
Elevation: 300' to 2,600'; 2,300' difference
Ride Type: Out and back or loop on dirt road
Season: Spring, summer, fall

Sulphur Mountain Road is a county road, graded dirt and gravel, and is closed to motor vehicles, except property owners along the road, the Edison Company and Ventura County vehicles. It's open to walkers, bicycles, and horses. This ride is good all year except just after a rainstorm, when it usually is muddy. There is no drinking water available; bring plenty, it can be a hot ride. The views are exceptional mountain vistas to the north and Lake Casitas to the west.

Getting There: Turn east off Highway 33, between Casitas Springs and San Antonio Creek Bridge, 6.5 miles south of Ojai and 7.4 miles north of Highway 101 in Ventura. Travel east on the paved road past the Girl Scout Camp on the left to a locked gate. Park at the turnout on Sulphur Mountain Road and Highway 33 (mile marker 7.40). Do not block the locked gate. Past the gate all the land on both sides of the road is private and posted "No Trespassing." You must stay on the road. The side roads are also private and posted. Only the main road is public property and open to bicyclists. This is a very popular bicycle route and you should be alert for other riders going the opposite way, and especially for hikers and horse riders.

Past the gate you will be climbing and turning to the north. About 100 yards up the dirt road you will encounter heavy black oil on the right side of the road; a little farther up you will see the source. It is a natural oil spring that has been running for years, maybe centuries. Sometimes it runs out on the road and the mess is hard to avoid.

The first mile is a steep but rideable climb up through oak forest and the shade is welcome. After a short level section the climbing resumes at an easier grade and this is typical for most of this route. You climb to the east along the ridge of this mountain, first on the south side toward the ocean, and at other times on the north. There your view is of the whole Ojai Valley with the rugged mountains beyond that ring the valley.

The earth here is covered mainly with grasses, live oaks, and scattered sage. It's quite green in early spring with lots of flowers, later becoming very dry and brown. Those who travel silently and watch carefully may see wildlife. I have seen several coyotes, some bobcats, deer, quail, hawks, snakes and lots of small birds. Tarantulas, those large (6-inch diameter), black, hairy, scary-looking spiders, are sometimes common on the road in late afternoon in the fall. Just steer around them and you shouldn't have any trouble.

Often there are cattle on the road, including large bulls. Slow travel and patience are the best ways to get

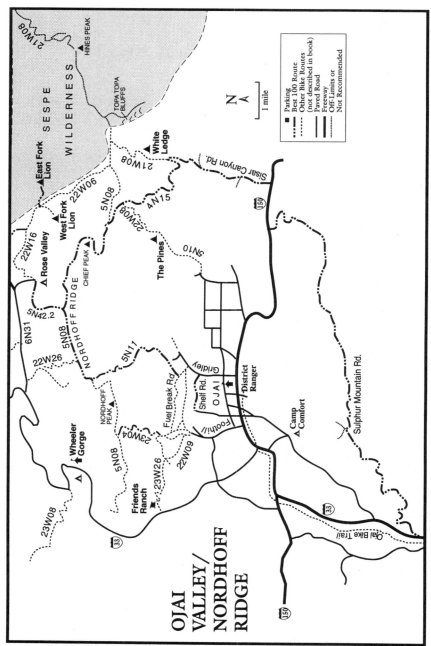

OJAI VALLEY/ NORDHOFF RIDGE

Legend:
- ■ Parking
- Best 100 Route
- Other Bike Routes (not described in book)
- Paved Road
- Freeway
- Off-Limits or Not Recommended

N
1 mile

© 1993 Fine Edge Productions

past them. Give them time and they'll usually get off the road. Don't run or chase them, just move slowly past. Close all gates you open.

As the road goes on and up to the top, you have views of Topa Topa Bluff, Sisar Canyon, and Santa Paula Peak. The southern view, after your initial climb out of Ventura River Canyon, looks across Cañada Larga to Ventura, Oxnard and the Pacific Ocean. On clear days, you can see several of the coastal islands: Anacapa, Santa Cruz, and Santa Rosa. There are occasional days of Santa Ana northeast winds when you can see all seven of the islands, including Catalina, Santa Barbara, San Nicolas and San Miguel.

You can turn around anywhere and return, or continue on to the top and beyond. After 9 miles, the road is paved and you may loop on through to Upper Ojai and Highway 150. Turn left (west) onto Highway 150 and it's 6 miles back to Ojai.

69 Upper Ojai to Ojai over Nordhoff Ridge

Distance: 24 miles (33 miles if you ride from downtown Ojai)
Difficulty: Difficult, occasionally technical
Elevation: 1,600' to 5,200' to 800' (a 3,400' climb)
Ride Type: One way on dirt roads and singletrack (the longer version is a loop)
Season: Spring, summer, fall

This 24-mile off-highway route along the Ojai Front Range is difficult due to the elevation gain, the long distance and the descent along the Gridley Trail singletrack. Start early and plan for an all-day ride. You should not attempt this ride if you dislike narrow trails or have little or no experience on singletrack. The route links Sisar Canyon Road in Upper Ojai to Gridley Trail, which leads toward downtown Ojai. You may ride in the reverse order if you prefer or just part way and return.

Getting There: First, you have to get to Sisar Road, 9 miles east of Ojai on Highway 150. Park along 150 next to Summit School. Very strong riders might just ride out from Ojai, but be aware of the 850-foot climb. If you have two cars, leave one in Ojai and one at Sisar Road to be picked up later, or maybe someone can drop you off and take the car back to Ojai.

From Highway 150 just east of Summit School, Sisar Road heads north, climbing 3,400 feet in about 8 miles. It has an almost continuous grade and is usually in good condition, although in winter snow occurs at upper elevations and in summer it can be very hot. Start at dawn and ride up in the shade on the southwest slopes to avoid the worst heat.

As you leave Highway 150, Sisar Road passes homes on both sides of the road. Past the last house, the road turns slightly right and you need to stay on the main road by keeping to the right, avoiding left forks until you reach the Forest Service locked gate. Beyond this gate there is one more right fork, a private road to a remote ranch—keep out.

The road soon switchbacks up Sisar Canyon and at 3 miles you are at the junction of Trail 21W08. (White Ledge Trail Camp, located about 1 mile up the trail, is a pleasant spot shaded by pungent scented bay trees. The spring there runs all year at considerable volume.) Past this junction, Sisar Road leaves the canyon and crosses a ridge out to the west of Sisar Canyon. Along the right side of the road at the 7-mile point, water is piped to a water trough from Wilsie Spring just above the road.

Near the top of Sisar Road, Horn Canyon Trail (22W08) crosses the road. This steep rough trail is not recommended for bicycle use. Just another 0.5 mile and Sisar Road ends at the top of the ridge and meets Road 5N08. From this ridge you get your first view to the north, looking out over the Sespe Canyon, past the Piedra Blanca Sandstone formation to the cliffs of Reyes, Haddock and Thorn Point Peaks.

This marks the end of 8-mile Sisar Road section of this ride. It's a good turnaround point if you just want a 16-mile out and back.

Continuing on to Nordhoff Ridge, the next section is more moderate riding with some steep downhills and a net elevation loss of 1,600 feet in 7.75 miles. Turn left (west) onto Road 5N08 at its junction with Sisar Road. You quickly get a break, descending 250 feet in a mile on the north side of the ridge. At a low point on the ridge you start a long climb around the east and north sides of Chief Peak, regaining the altitude you just lost. It's not very steep and the scenery makes up for it. On the northwest side of Chief Peak the road travels on Nordhoff Ridge and drops and climbs very steeply for about a half mile. Some hills can be climbed with the momentum gained coming down the previous hill. This is also the highest elevation of the trip. There are places along the ridge where you look right down to Ojai Valley.

At 13 miles, Chief Peak Road descends to the right past a cattleguard and gate. Continue on the ridge ahead to the west, easily descending 500 feet in 1.5 miles to the junction with Howard Canyon Trail (22W26). When you look west over Nordhoff Ridge you can see Nordhoff Peak, at the same elevation as you are. It once housed a lookout, and the steel tower is still standing. Now the road begins a much steeper descent of 900 feet in 1.25 miles to Gridley Saddle. At the saddle you will have ridden 16 miles from Upper Ojai. Gridley Trail, the third and last leg of this ride, is to your left (south) at the saddle.

Gridley Trail (5N11) hugs the side of the canyon and winds down into the valley with many switchbacks. Most of it isn't very steep (you go from 3,600 feet to 1,600 feet in 6 miles), but it is considered technical because of the huge dropoffs over the edge. Go slowly, or if you're not sure of your skill get off and walk—and live to ride another day. About half-way down, the trail widens where it

used to be a road. Water is available about a half mile down at Gridley Spring, a former camp that washed out. A plastic pipe carries water to a horse water trough; your water (treat it!)is from the stream above the trail.

After a break you continue down on the west side of the canyon and soon are passing avocado groves. Take the right (west) fork at the saddle and you are now on a road. Go down this road 0.3 mile and at the out-bend take the marked trail on your left steeply downhill. You need to walk the first part of this short connector trail, and might as well walk all of it due to rocks.

Now at 22 miles you are on paved Gridley Road, and it's a smooth ride back to town. Watch your speed down this steep twisty road until you get to the straight part. Turn right at Grand Avenue and ride to town. A left turn onto Montgomery Street will take you back to Ojai Avenue.

70 Rose Valley to Ojai Valley

Distance: 24.5 miles or 13.5 miles
Difficulty: Very difficult, extremely steep in places
Elevation: 3,400' to 5,000' to 800' (1,600' gain)
Ride Type: Depends on options taken, part of longer loop
Season: Spring, summer, fall

If you use two cars or have someone drive you up and return the car, this ride will let you explore the same areas as the previous route with much less climbing. Strong riders can ride this as a loop by riding back up Highway 33 to Rose Valley. There are two versions of this ride, both starting out the same.

Getting There: Head west on Highway 150 to Highway 33 by Vons.

Take Highway 33 north, up past Wheeler Gorge. This is a scenic mountain highway and there are no services, so be sure to check your vehicle and have plenty of gas. As you drive up the mountain you see vertical white signs along the roadside that mark the road edge and hazards like culverts. Many have the mileage from Ventura marked on them. At mile marker 25.84 take the signed Rose Valley Road east 3.5 miles. When you see a small lake on the left, take the signed road right to Rose Valley Falls and Campground. Park beside the upper lake below the campground.

Ride through the campground and take the gated road to the right (west). Although this road (5N42.2) is so steep in places it is hard to even walk, it is still the easiest way up to Nordhoff Ridge. This is because you climb only 1,600 feet to reach the high point of the ride instead of climbing 3,400 feet up Sisar Road.

When you get to the top of Nordhoff Ridge you have two options. The first option takes you left (east) on Road 5N08 around Chief Peak to Sisar Road, down to High-

way 150, and west 9 miles on pavement back to town for a total ride of 24.5 miles. (Just reverse the directions for the Upper Ojai to Ojai ride starting at "At 13 miles....") Although longer, this route is easier because it is all on roads and the last 9 miles on the highway is almost all downhill.

For the second, harder option, you turn right (west) on Road 5N08 and connect with Gridley Trail to Ojai for a total ride of 13.5 miles. This way is more difficult due to the steep descent to Gridley Saddle and the narrow trail in Gridley Canyon. For this option, follow the directions for the Upper Ojai to Ojai ride starting at "At 13 miles Chief Peak Road...."

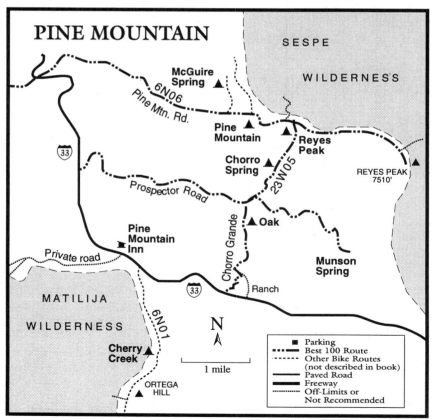

PINE MOUNTAIN

SESPE

WILDERNESS

McGuire Spring

6N06

Pine Mtn. Rd.

Pine Mountain

Reyes Peak

Chorro Spring

23W05

REYES PEAK 7510'

Prospector Road

Chorro Grande

Oak

Pine Mountain Inn

Munson Spring

Private road

33

Ranch

MATILIJA

WILDERNESS

6N01

N

1 mile

Cherry Creek

ORTEGA HILL

■ Parking
▪▪▪ Best 100 Route
---- Other Bike Routes (not described in book)
— Paved Road
▬ Freeway
⋯⋯ Off-Limits or Not Recommended

Pine Mountain

Looking north from Ventura, the highest, most distant mountain you can see is Pine Mountain, 30 miles away. Winter snow is visible from Ventura, but the pine forest above 6,000 feet is not readily apparent from this distance.

From Pine Mountain Summit on Highway 33 (mile 42.7), drive east on the paved ridge road for great car camping areas. You'll find campsites among the tall pines and near large sandstone outcroppings. (Caution: Bring all your own water—none is available on the ridge top.) The daytime views both north and south are special, and clear nights offer outstanding views of city lights at the beach and masses of stars in the sky.

The pavement ends just past the last developed campsite near the point where Chorro Grande Trail comes in. Mountain biking on the unpaved ridge road to Reyes Peak is fairly easy. Chorro Grande Trail descends steeply to the south past two trail camps—the upper one next to a spring—and ends at Highway 33. An 8-mile dirt road traverses the south slopes, crossing Chorro Grande Trail.

Monte Arido Road heads west from Pine Mountain Summit across the highway from Pine Mountain Road. The locked gate at the highway restricts access on this dirt road to ranches along the road and 4WD vehicles with a day permit available at the Forest Service Ojai Ranger District Office. This book describes a one-way, shuttle-assisted ride that takes you out via Murietta Canyon; however, riding part of Monte Arido Road also makes for a good out-and-back ride, and the route can also be incorporated into overnight rides. There is a small store/cafe at Pine Mountain Inn; no phone, no gas. The nearest phones for emergency service are at the U.S. Forest Service Ozena Station, or in Ventucopa to the north, and Wheeler Gorge Station to the south.

71 Pine Mountain Road

Distance: 7.5 miles
Difficulty: Easy, nontechnical (high altitude 2,020' climb on paved part)
Elevation: 5,080' to 7,100'; 2,020' difference
Ride Type: Paved and dirt road
Season: Spring, summer, fall

Getting There: Park at the turnout off Highway 33 at mile 42.7, or at campground parking areas and roadside parking on Pine Mountain Road. There are several campgrounds along the paved road, but no developed sites on the dirt portion that goes out to Reyes Peak.

You can begin riding paved Pine Mountain Road (6N06) at the junction of Highway 33 or from any of the camps along the way. The riding is fairly easy, but remember, you are climbing at high altitude. The height of the mountain provides extensive views of portions of the backcountry.

The dirt section of this road is graded, in good repair and fairly level. Although open to motor vehicles, there's not much traffic here. The road connects to Chorro Grande Trail (23W05, see below). At the end of the dirt part of the road at the wilder-ness boundary is Reyes Peak Trail (23W04), closed to bicycles. Be sure to bring plenty of water; there is none available on the mountain top and it is a mile down to Raspberry Spring on the north and 0.8 mile down to Chorro Spring on the south.

72 Chorro Grande Trail

Distance: 5.4 miles one way (17.5-mile loop option)
Difficulty: Very difficult above Prospector Road, moderate below
Elevation: 4,050' to 7,100'; 3,050' difference
Ride Type: One way on paved road and singletrack (stronger riders can do a loop)
Season: Spring, summer, fall

This trail passes through three zones with sudden, dramatic terrain and vegetation changes. From the top at 7,100 feet you ride down 600 feet in 1 mile, passing through scattered pine and fir forest where most of the yearly precipitation is snowfall. Melting snow causes very little erosion here. The middle 2 miles drop steeply (1,000 feet) on a ridge through low-growing chaparral and areas with severe erosion. These two upper zones are too steep to ride up. The lowest zone can be accessed from Highway 33 and is a canyon and streamside environment. Here are 2 miles of trail with only a 400 foot net gain, large sandstone formations and Oak Trail Camp under spreading shade trees.

Getting There: Parking at the lower end is at the turnout at mile 36.6, off Highway 33. At the upper end, park your shuttle vehicle near the pavement/dirt junction, just past the last campsite on Pine Mountain Road (6N06). Park off to the side, out of traffic. Car campsites are available along Road 6N06; Chorro Spring and Oak trail camps are on 23W05.

Pine Mountain Road pavement ends at a gate (seasonal closure during wet weather). Here a sign directs you to Chorro Grande Trail, which appears to plunge down the south side of the mountain. By looking carefully you should be able to see the switchbacks that others have cut across. Past these short switchbacks the trail traverses east along the slopes through mixed forest. At 0.45 mile you pass through an open, flattish area before descending more steep rocky sections. Suddenly at 0.8 mile Chorro Camp and spring appear.

This excellent trail camp is in a little hollow filled with large trees. The spring is under a huge boulder and forms a pool in a small cave before running down the canyon. One campsite is right next to the spring and another is about 75 feet uphill next to a 4-foot diameter fir tree. A third, less-used site is located just east of the lower trail sign.

Riding out of this little canyon, you suddenly leave the tall trees behind and enter low chaparral on steep slopes. Here at 1 mile you can view Sespe Creek below and clear to its headwaters at the Potrero Seco grassland to the west. For the next 2 miles the trail descends a ridge into Chorro Grande Canyon. Slow travel is required along rocky sections and areas of sharp switchbacks. Wildflowers are abundant all along this ridge and in the canyon below. At 2.9 miles the trail widens when it joins an old cat road by the stream. Soon at 3.0 miles you cross Prospector Road. Be sure to cross the stream here in late spring to see a meadow filled with Matilija poppies—five inches across— blooming white and yellow.

The trail is much easier to ride below Prospector Road. The catway roads here are part of an extensive mineral prospect across the south side of Pine Mountain. Looking east near mile 3.3, a large open cut with tailings is evident. At the bottom of a short, steep, rocky hill at 3.6 miles is a flat with Oak Camp beside the trail. It has three sites well apart from each other under shady oak trees. The creek beside this camp dries out

sometimes, but water can generally be found upstream within a half mile.

After traveling over some low hills on your way down the canyon, you come to a trail junction. The trail you need turns right abruptly and can be missed. (The trail straight ahead passes onto private land and is used by horse riders from the pack station below.) Continuing down the right fork on Chorro Grande Trail, you encounter a very large sandstone formation at 4.4 miles. The trail then crosses two creeks and a small wash, dropping and climbing steeply at each until at 4.75 miles you reach a high point. Then it's downhill on a good singletrack to the highway at 5.4 miles.

If you're a strong rider get an early start, park at the lower trailhead, mile 36.6, and ride up Highway 33 to the summit pass, mile 42.7. Turn right and go 6 miles up Pine Mountain Road (6N06) to Chorro Grande Trail. Take this singletrack 5.4 miles back down to your starting point for a 17.5-mile loop.

73 Prospector Road

Distance: 4.6 miles one way to Chorro Grande Trail; 8 miles total
Difficulty: Moderate, nontechnical
Elevation: 4,500' to 5,200'; many ups and down
Ride Type: Depends on options taken
Season: Spring, summer, fall

This hidden road winds its way east for 8 miles, roughly parallel to and about a mile north of Highway 33. It dips in and out of canyons that drain the south side of Pine Mountain ridge. The first 2 miles, shown on topo and Forest Service maps, are very old. The other 6 miles, along with many spur roads, were built by prospectors looking for gypsum

deposits here in the late 1960s. They staked mineral claims and still maintain the road but do not have title to the land, which is open for recreation. The end of the original 2.1-mile road passes through private property for about 3/4 mile. Please respect this property, which is currently not posted.

I especially like this road because the hills are short with only a minor elevation change of 600 feet. The varied terrain keeps my interest with new views and conditions every mile. This is a ride I want to share with my friends as a day ride and also for overnight trips.

A special hazard here is a tenacious glue-like adobe soil that, if wet from rain or snow melt, sticks to everything it touches.

Getting There: Park at Highway 33 turnouts at mile 40.5, at Chorro Grande Trailhead (mile 36.6), or at Pine Mountain Inn (mile 38.9). You can camp at Oak Trail Camp, 0.5 mile down Chorro Grande Trail. There's possible car-camping at Pine Mountain Inn, but a fee is required.

For a short ride up and back, park in the Highway 33 turnout just up the hill from the roadhead at the 40.5 milepost, or park by Pine Mountain Inn and ride up the highway 1.6 miles to the roadhead.

A longer loop ride is best done by parking at Pine Mountain Inn, riding up the highway, doing Prospector Road to Chorro Grande Trail, going down the trail to Highway 33, and riding the highway back to the start at Pine Mountain Inn. This totals 10.5 miles with 3.9 miles on the highway and 2 miles downhill on singletrack. (If you park at Pine Mountain Inn, let them know where

you are going and be sure not to block their drive.)

The highway climbs steadily to the northwest from the Inn through a pine-forested canyon, which narrows noticeably near Prospector Road, 1.6 miles from the Inn at milepost 40.5. Prospector Road is on the right past a locked gate at the highway. Ride down and cross Adobe Creek, then turn right and enter a narrow canyon. Some short steep climbs and creek crossings at 0.5 and 0.7 mile take you past the narrow part of the canyon where many varieties of trees grow (oak, pine, fir, willow, bay, etc.).

At 0.8 mile the canyon opens up and the road turns to the east, switchbacking and then climbing out of the canyon. This hill starts out steep but gets easier near the top, where, at 1.3 miles, you have a good view of the grassy hillsides ahead. A short spur road to the right ends at a guzzler. This is a fiberglass water catcher and cistern that provides water for wildlife.

Next you have some level riding before a sharp right turn and a steady climb across a grassy hill. For the next 3/4 mile the road crosses private property. Keep to the main route and avoid the spur roads in this area. When you reach the upper end of the grassland—at 2.1 miles with a spur road to the left and a large pine on the right—you are on the high point of this road at 5,200 feet.

From here, Prospector Road is rougher and drops steeply into a small canyon, but it comes out the other side with an easy grade. There is an open gate just before you get to another ridge at 2.5 miles, where a deeper canyon can be seen ahead. This is the west fork of Godwin Canyon, and for the next 2 miles you get

a high point, and you can look into the east branch of Chorro Grande Canyon. It's a steep, rocky descent to the bottom at 1.1 miles from Chorro Grande Trail. You have a substantial climb out the other side of this canyon, starting with an easy grade and ending with 100 yards of walking to the top at 1.6 miles. Here, in a saddle at 5,000 feet, a spur road climbs to the south and then descends and climbs on a ridge a quarter mile away.

to know the other two forks by descending into and climbing out of them. The climbs are not as bad as they look. The scenery is wild and the ridges between the canyons offer good views and possible camping or lunch opportunities.

Soon, at 4.4 miles, you are looking down into Chorro Grande Canyon with the road below crossing a meadow of Matilija poppies. You can also see Chorro Grande Trail descending with switchbacks and then crossing Prospector Road just east of the creek. There is usually water in the creeks. There at 4.6 miles you can head down Chorro Grande Trail 2 miles to Highway 33 (see previous ride) and back north 2.3 miles to Pine Mountain Inn. Or you can choose to go on to Munson Canyon and return, 3.4 miles one way by a rougher, steeper road.

To continue to Munson Canyon, cross Chorro Canyon Trail on Prospector Road, which curves north with a steep climb for 0.3 mile. On top it is suddenly flat with oak trees in level clearings in the brush. A spur road runs out the ridge to the south and ends on a small peak. Cross the flat, go into a dip and short climb to

Prospector Road then winds down into Burro Canyon and crosses the creek at 2.2 miles. Then it heads down the canyon with an easy grade on the east side of the creek where, at 2.4 miles, there is a sweeping 180° turn to the left. You end up heading north again and climbing steeply back up to another saddle. Here at 2.8 miles you finally see into Munson Canyon. First you have a short, steep descent, then some level road until on the west side of the canyon the road gives out and it is a very steep descent to the canyon bottom. Across the canyon, just up from the bottom, is Munson Spring. It gushes out of the hillside under a tangle of vegetation that includes stinging nettle. (Beware, it is very painful! Use aloe or mugwort for relief.) Miners dug a pond on the hillside here, and it is jammed with cattails.

From the end of the road you must backtrack to Chorro Grande Trail to get back to the highway. (The trail seen heading almost straight up the south side of Reyes Peak here is old, heavily eroded and not used anymore.)

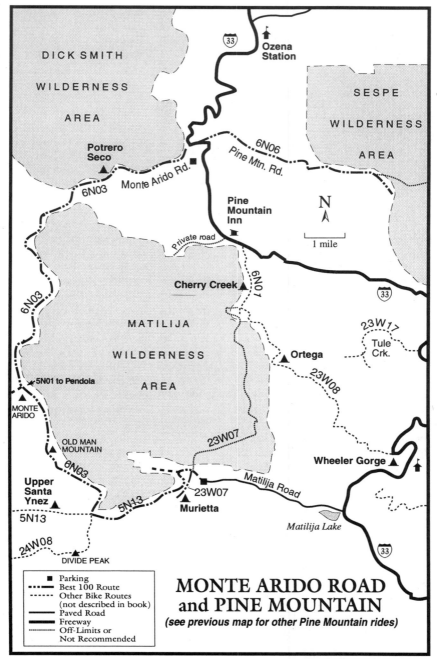

MONTE ARIDO ROAD
and PINE MOUNTAIN
(see previous map for other Pine Mountain rides)

■   Parking
▪▪▪▪ Best 100 Route
- - - - Other Bike Routes
       (not described in book)
——— Paved Road
▬▬▬ Freeway
········· Off-Limits or
       Not Recommended

© 1993 Fine Edge Productions

74 Monte Arido Road/ Murietta Canyon

Distance: 25 miles
Difficulty: Moderate to Potrero Seco; more difficult to Monte Arido; very difficult near Old Man Mountain; many steep hills, long distance
Elevation: 5,080' to 6,000' to 3,400'
Ride Type: One-way with shuttle on dirt roads
Season: Spring, summer, fall

This ridge-top road provides exceptional views of wilderness landscapes with few human alterations. Most of those are historic ranches at the northern end of the road, between Highway 33 and Potrero Seco. In this area, the road runs near the border of the Dick Smith Wilderness, and from many high points you can look out over most of the wilderness to the northwest. The southern 15 miles of the ride takes you along the border of the Matilija Wilderness to the east, with excellent views down into remote, steep, narrow canyons. Following the ridge, the road climbs and drops many times.

Excellent day rides can be enjoyed by parking at the upper roadhead and traveling into Potrero Seco, returning the way you came in. Three miles one way takes less than an hour with only a net descent of 150 feet. A more strenuous effort will take you farther out to the Three Sisters Rocks, 7 miles and 2 hours one way. (These times include a lot of sightseeing. Fast riders can do it in half the time.) Bring a map, compass, and binoculars to locate distant landmarks; by remembering them you will be able to tell where you are. Riding past the Three Sisters puts you farther into the mountains on a ridge that gets tougher the farther you go. Somewhere about the 10-

mile mark you need to decide to go back or continue past the point where turning back is not a good option.

Getting There: Park on Highway 33 at Pine Mountain Summit Pass (milepost 42.7). Leave a second vehicle at the parking area at the locked gate end of Matilija Road, just before Murietta Camp. Bring plenty of water since none is available. Nearest services are in Ojai. Caution: Winter storms bring heavy snow, and the adobe mud is bad during spring thaw. Riding in on frozen roads in the morning can leave you stuck with a noon thaw miles from the highway.

Starting from Pine Mountain Summit Pass, head west on Monte Arido Road (6N03) past the locked gate. Watch out for occasional motor vehicle traffic operated here under special permit from the Forest Service. Right away you have a steep descent and climb to a saddle at 0.3 mile, where a good road branches to the south, climbing slightly for 0.2 mile to a locked gate posted *No Trespassing.* Continuing west on Road 6N03 from the saddle, you climb a little more easily to the ridge.

Riding close to the ridge top you can see a deep canyon to the south; past that you cross a cattleguard (0.8 mile). A spur road branches southwest here to the Dent Ranch, and the main road passes between pine trees to the west. There is more easy riding and you start passing the first large grass slopes; then at the top of a grade (1.6 miles) you can see down across the Potrero Seco and the headwaters of the Sespe. Two ranches are situated alongside the creek among

the cottonwood trees. The descent to the ranches has two downhill runs separated by a slight climb over a saddle. As you approach the ranches keep right, cross a cattleguard (2.25 miles), and climb toward the west across a gently sloping field.

Just before a large green tank, take a road on the right 100 yards to Potrero Seco Trail Camp, 3 miles from the start. The camp is set in a hollow with hills on three sides, open to the east. There are three tables and fireplaces shaded by oak and pine trees, but no water. Just northeast is the abandoned site of the old Potrero Seco Guard Station.

Going farther south on Monte Arido Road (6N03), you first climb moderately for a mile, and then on the right pass the Loma Victor Road

(7N05) that descends on a ridge along the Dick Smith Wilderness boundary to Mono Creek and Don Victor Valley. Past this junction you climb a little more and make a steep descent to a saddle, where there is a short side road south to a dam and pond. On this saddle at 6.2 miles the Three Sisters Rocks can be seen ahead. A short steep climb gets you to these surprisingly large, isolated sandstone boulders at 6.8 miles. Shade and wind protection is available here, making it a good rest stop.

Hildreth Jeepway (6N17) starts here past a locked gate on the north side of the rocks and can be seen along the ridge out to Hildreth Peak to the west. From Potrero Seco to these rocks, the road has been gradually turning to the south and now the rest of the way is generally south.

A gate at 7.0 miles is the start of a very fast section, slightly downhill on good graded road. The climb ahead is typical with some short, steep, walk-and-push hills mixed with rideable areas—you go over a peak, down a steep hill, and repeat it again. Another gate (locked) at 12.2 miles is next to a dam and pond on the west side of the road. Climb again to the northwest side of Monte Arido and at 12.45 miles pass the Pendola Jeepway (5N01), which heads down into an open saucer-shaped canyon before descending the ridge to Pendola Station at Agua Caliente Canyon. (Experienced mountain bicyclists seeking a tough, challenging ride can start at Juncal Camp and ride up past Murietta Divide, making the steep climb to Monte Arido and returning by the Pendola Jeepway.)

Monte Arido, 13.2 miles long and 6,003 foot elevation, is the highest point on Road 6N03. You can make the short walk to the summit, just west and a little above the road. The next 1.5 miles has the steepest descent, so use your brakes to keep control and lower your bicycle seat if possible. From another saddle on the north side of Old Man Mountain, the road climbs around on the west slopes of this double peak, giving you a good view looking down to Juncal Dam and Jameson Lake. When I am really tired of climbing, there are the two similar uphills where they shouldn't be on the south side of Old

Man Mountain. Finally you lose altitude, steeply, with many switchbacks across a barren-looking landscape.

That scene changes suddenly while you make a short climb past pine trees growing among large sandstone boulders. There is more steep descending across a boulder garden until at 19 miles a road to your right leads to a small lake, too improbable to be overlooked. One more mile and at 20 miles even you are at Murietta Divide, which is pleasantly level after so much downhill. Go left (east) on 5N13, and it is another 5 miles down Murietta Canyon to your shuttle vehicle.

75 Alamo Mountain:
Alamo Mountain Loop Road

Distance: 8 miles
Difficulty: Easy, but remember at 6,500' you won't have much air to breathe
Elevation: 6,500' to 7,000'; 500' difference
Ride Type: Loop
Season: Summer and fall best

Alamo Mountain is a massive peak with a somewhat rounded top. Its highest point is 7,450 feet, but the road never gets higher than 7,000 feet. At this elevation snow occurs every year and sometimes remains for a long time. The best riding is in summer and fall. If you plan to camp during these warmer months, you still need to be prepared for cold nights on the mountain. Except for the noise and speed of motorcycles, this area has great riding. You get spectacular views of seldom-seen canyons from the higher elevations. Alamo Mountain is covered with huge trees, while Hungry Valley to the

northeast is dry and desert-like.

There is much evidence of gold mining in some areas of the region. Located on the north slope of the mountain above Piru Creek, the Castaic Mine was the most extensive and successful one, with two tunnels totaling over 2,200 feet in length. Mining continued here into the 1930s. Originally powered by a water wheel, the 5-stamp mill from this mine can now be seen in a historical museum in Santa Barbara. Gold panning is still a popular pastime along nearby streams.

Services and supplies are available only in Gorman on I-5. Most of

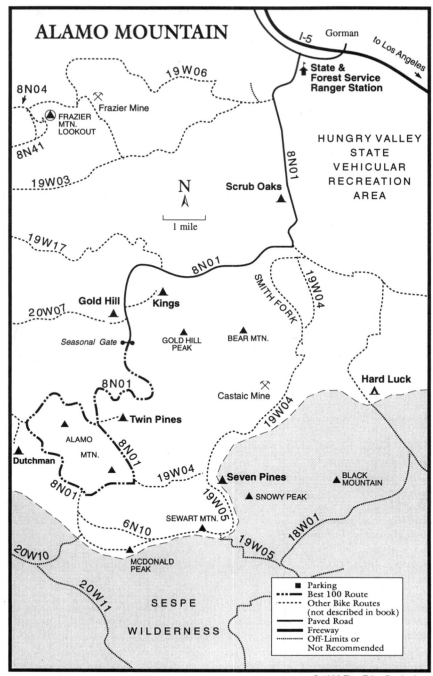

ALAMO MOUNTAIN

Gorman
to Los Angeles
I-5

State & Forest Service Ranger Station

8N04

19W06

Frazier Mine

FRAZIER MTN. LOOKOUT

8N41

HUNGRY VALLEY STATE VEHICULAR RECREATION AREA

19W03

8N01

N
1 mile

Scrub Oaks

19W17

8N01

SMITH FORK

19W04

Gold Hill

20W07

Kings

GOLD HILL PEAK

BEAR MTN.

Seasonal Gate

Hard Luck

Castaic Mine

8N01

19W04

Twin Pines

ALAMO

MTN.

8N01

Dutchman

8N01

19W04

Seven Pines

BLACK MOUNTAIN

19W05

SNOWY PEAK

6N10

SEWART MTN.

19W05

18W01

20W10

MCDONALD PEAK

20W11

SESPE

WILDERNESS

■ Parking
▪▪▪ Best 100 Route
---- Other Bike Routes
(not described in book)
— Paved Road
— Freeway
····· Off-Limits or
Not Recommended

© 1993 Fine Edge Productions

the roads and trails in this area are open to motorcycles and ATVs. Car camping with limited facilities is available at Kings Camp, Gold Hill Camp, Twin Pines and Dutchman camps on Alamo Mountain, and most sheltered spots in Hungry Valley (check with State Rangers).

Gold Hill Camp is located on a bluff above Piru Creek. The creek usually runs all year, although it's never very deep except during floods. Snow can occur here, but a lot of rain or snow is uncommon. Placer gold, washed downstream, is found along Piru Creek and in the bank under the bluff next to the camp. Panning and dredging are very popular along here.

Kings Camp, at the end of Road 8N01A, offers tables and fire pits in a grove of trees. To reach the camp, turn east from Gold Hill Road at mile 10.25 on to paved Road 8N01A and continue 0.5 mile. Water is not available at this camp.

You can ride your bike the 7 miles up Alamo Mountain Road on pavement, with a 2,500-foot elevation gain. Most riders, however, prefer to drive to the top and do the Alamo Mountain Loop Road. It circles Alamo Mountain between 6,500 feet and 7,000 feet for 8 miles of easy riding in mature pine forest. The views from all sides of Alamo Mountain are splendid. Although you may drive a vehicle around the mountain on this road, riding a bicycle puts you more in touch with the surroundings.

Getting There: Alamo Mountain is accessible by motor vehicle from Interstate 5 through the Hungry Valley State Vehicular Recreational Area (motorcycle and 4WD) on a generally paved road as far as the Gold Hill-Piru Creek crossing. Take Interstate

5 to Gorman (60 miles from Los Angeles, 40 miles from Bakersfield, and 70 miles from Ventura). Cross to the west side of I-5 opposite Gorman and go north on Peace Valley Road 1 mile. Turn left (west) at the SVRA Hungry Valley sign onto paved Gold Hill Road (8N01). A kiosk just ahead is run by the state to collect fees for SVRA use. No fee is required to pass through to the National Forest. Maps and current information are available from the State Ranger, and information is posted on large bulletin boards. Call ahead to check weather, closures, and special events scheduled here and in the National Forest: (805) 248-6447, P.O. Box 1360, Lebec, CA 93243-1360.

On Gold Hill Road at mile 5 there is an abrupt right turn. A dirt fork to the left is Hungry Valley Road, which leads to Snowy Creek Trail and farther on to Hard Luck Road. Go right and continue west on paved Gold Hill Road to the 10-mile mark at Piru Creek. A gate near the creek crossing is locked during stormy winter weather and when ice and snow are hazardous at higher elevations. Here, from the base of Alamo Mountain, Road 8N01 twists and turns up the mountain's north side. Above Piru Creek, Gold Hill Road (formerly graded dirt) was paved in the fall of 1992.

As you come up the mountain, a short spur road to the east leads steeply down to Twin Pines Camp, just a little before the Loop Road begins. Dutchman Camp, 2.5 miles west on the loop road, is spread over a larger area with more level ground. No water is available near Dutchman Camp, though. Park at the turnout near Twin Pines Camp.

The easiest way to do this loop is to ride counter-clockwise, starting toward the west. The 2.5-mile ride out to Dutchman Camp meanders along the slopes, passing through groves of pines. The 200-foot elevation gain isn't difficult, since it's done a little at a time. Where the road turns south, another lesser road heads farther east. This is the Miller Jeep Road (8N12) and it connects with the many doubletracks to the campsites next to the loop. The sites are spread out in this open place among a few scattered pines of good size.

On the 3-mile stretch from the camp out to the south point of the loop road, you travel fairly level the first mile. The next 2 miles climb 250 feet, descend into a small canyon, climb again and end at the same elevation as the camp. Rocks fall onto the road from the steeper slopes around the small canyon.

At the south point, Road 6N10 to McDonald Peak and Sewart Mountain descends steeply south. It's worthwhile to make the half-mile trip out to the ridge for the views down Alder Creek and out to the Sespe Narrows. Keep going south on the Loop Road without turning to the east or west. By going out this half mile you get most of the view afforded by doing a trip to Sewart Mountain. I highly recommend it if you have time while doing the loop.

The Loop Road is cut through the ridge here and turns sharply to the northeast. The view is into the upper parts of Snowy Creek Canyon, which starts from the south ridge of Alamo Mountain and curves around to the northeast. After riding northeast 0.7 mile from the south point on the Loop Road, you pass Snowy Creek Trail on the right. (Snowy Creek Trail is not recommended.) Continue on 1.8 miles, descending 300 feet, to complete your turn around the mountain and return to the starting point. The trees along this last section are a mixed forest of maples, oaks, and pines.

Frazier Mountain

Good dirt roads and thick pine forests create a tranquil, relaxed mood while you ride on the wide ridges of this high mountain. The trees muffle and block sound, so talking with hushed voices seems right here, like in a church or library. Broken tops on the largest trees attest to the power of wind, lightning and heavy snow, but on a bright summer day when the heat is tempered by the 7,500-foot elevation, this is a gentle wilderness. Most of the views through the trees are spectacular. The best view, of course, is from the fire lookout on the very top of the mountain at 8,013 feet—one of the few manned lookouts left in the southern forest. Visitors are welcome, but remember every day is a working day. Keep visits and distractions short.

Getting There: On Lockwood Valley Road, go west 0.9 mile from Lake of the Woods. Signs here direct you south to Frazier Mountain Road and Chuchupate Ranger Station. The station is near the highway and the best source of current information. Frazier Mountain Road is paved for 3 miles to over 7,000 feet. A good graded dirt road continues on to the fork at Overmeyer Flat, a good parking place. East Frazier Road to the left is 5.2 miles long. On the right, it's 1.6 miles to the lookout on the mountain top and 2 miles back by a loop road south of the lookout. West Frazier Road (8N41), also to the right, is 3.5 miles long and connects with the very steep and rough West Frazier Tie Road down the north side of the mountain.

Special Hazards: Spring and summer thunderstorms are common with possible heavy rain and the danger of lightning on high places. During storms, keep away from tall trees and metal structures like the lookout and nearby radio towers. Heavy winter snow occurs, and strong winds cause whiteouts and severe wind chill. In the shade at this high elevation, snow and ice can last a long time. Check conditions at the ranger station on the way up or call ahead.

76 Frazier Mountain Road

Distance: 7.4 miles
Difficulty: Moderate, nontechnical
Elevation: 5,200' to 8,013', 2913' difference
Ride Type: One way on pavement and dirt road
Season: Summer and fall best

Getting There: Go west 0.9 mile from Lake of the Woods on Lockwood Valley Road. Signs here direct you south to Frazier Mountain Road. If you park at the station and bicycle up the mountain, be sure to check at the desk for all day or long term parking. The parking in front of the office is for office visits only.

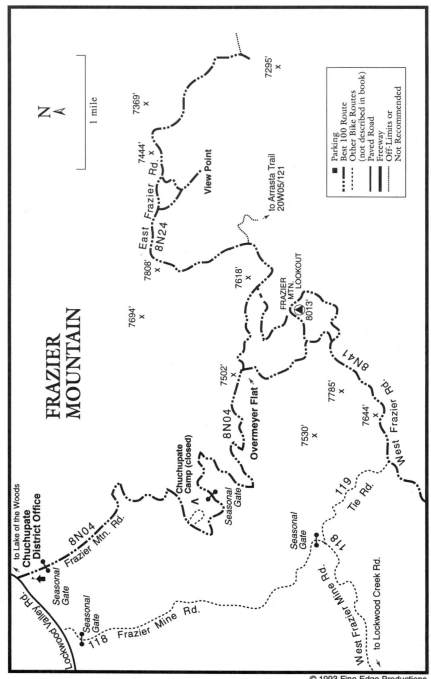

FRAZIER MOUNTAIN

N

1 mile

7295'
x

7369'
x

7444'
x

East Frazier Rd.

View Point

to Arrasta Trail
20W05/121

7808'
x

8N24

7618'
x

7694'
x

FRAZIER
MTN.
LOOKOUT
8013'

8N41

7502'
x

7785'
x

Overmeyer Flat

8N04

7644'
x

7530'
x

West Frazier Rd.

Chuchupate
Camp (closed)

Seasonal
Gate

119

Tie Rd.

118

Seasonal
Gate

to Lake of the Woods

Chuchupate
District Office

8N04

Frazier Mtn. Rd.

Seasonal
Gate

West Frazier Mine Rd.

Seasonal
Gate

118   Frazier Mine Rd.

Lockwood Valley Rd.

to Lockwood Creek Rd.

■ Parking
Best 100 Route
Other Bike Routes
(not described in book)
Paved Road
Freeway
Off-Limits or
Not Recommended

© 1993 Fine Edge Productions

As you do this ride up the mountain, be sure to stop and survey the distant terrain. Use a map and compass to become familiar with the features of the area and it will help you find your way.

For the first mile you climb steadily south on the road past chaparral and scattered pines. The road turns to the left a little and gets less steep at two houses — one stone, the other of logs. At 1.5 miles the first switchback turns to the right and cuts along the mountainside, which becomes much steeper. Camp buildings at 2.0 miles are on the left beyond a meadow full of grasses and wildflowers with water flowing out and across the road. Chuchupate Camp is at 2.5 miles, closed due to ground squirrels infested with fleas carrying bubonic plague.

Switchback again and turn left to double back above the camp, and at 3.0 miles the pavement ends at a seasonal closure gate. The dirt road past here is rocky but good. You keep heading southeast, and at 4.3 miles the road improves. Nearing the top, the trees are bigger and shade the road. At Overmeyer Flat, 5.8 miles, the road forks with East Frazier Road (8N24) branching left.

Keep to the right fork on Frazier Mountain Road for a nice half-mile ride to the lookout, which loops back to Overmeyer Flat with many scenic surprises. From Overmeyer Flat, it's 1.1 miles to the lookout junction. The left fork leads up 0.5 mile to the lookout, which is situated amid an amazing array of antennas on the mountain top. You may return to Overmeyer Flat by continuing past the lookout, heading south on a road that behaves itself, and traveling in a half circle to the west for 0.6 mile to West Frazier Road (8N41). Turn right, travel 0.3 mile and you will be back at the fork where you turned up to the lookout. Keep straight ahead, and 1.1 miles of riding will put you back at Overmeyer Flat.

77 West Frazier Road

Distance: 2.9 or 3.5 miles, depending on where you park
Difficulty: Moderate; steep, rough road last half mile
Elevation: 7,900' to 7,000'; 900' difference
Ride Type: One way on dirt roads
Season: Summer and fall best

Include the loop around the lookout when you ride out along the West Frazier Road. The view there is so spectacular, whereas the thick forest blocks almost all the views on the West Ridge Road. If you start from Overmeyer Flat, go past the roads to the lookout by keeping to the right.

Then on the way back, go up to the lookout on the road from the south, circling counter-clockwise. Ride the same counter-clockwise direction when parking near the lookout. The approach to the mountain top is easier from the south.

Getting There: Drive up Frazier Mountain Road and park at Overmeyer Flat (3.5-mile ride) or Frazier Mountain Lookout (2.9 mi.).

Starting from Overmeyer Flat, ride up the right fork at the nearby sign. The road turns southwest as it climbs along the slopes through pine forest. A spring at a stone water catchment is labeled as bad water. Here it's a good graded road, and at 1.1 miles you pass the main access road to the lookout. Signs at this left turn point the way, 0.5 mile up to the east. Keep riding straight ahead, and 0.3 mile farther another lesser traveled road also heads east to the lookout. (You take this one when you

return. It climbs in a 0.6-mile half circle up to the lookout.)

You descend toward the west along the ridge. Keep in mind that you have to come back up the same way and it will take longer. The ride is through thick forest with some small open areas. At 2.9 miles from Overmeyer Flat, or 2.3 miles from the lookout, West Frazier Tie Road branches off to the north. It's nearly level on the part you see, but it soon plunges down the mountain. Riding out on that level part is easier, however, than continuing west on West Frazier Road, which drops steeply and is rough the last 0.6 mile. No matter which way you go, you need to backtrack to return to the lookout.

78 East Frazier Road

Distance: 5.2 miles one way
Difficulty: Moderate, nontechnical
Elevation: 7,500' start; 7,800' high point; 7,350' end; 450' difference
Ride Type: One way on dirt roads
Season: Summer and fall best

This is a good ride for a hot summer day. It is usually cooler at this altitude and there is plenty of shade on the road, which travels along a broad ridge covered with pine forest. There are some less-traveled side roads and many clearings where you can get off the main road and enjoy the solitude. Bring a lunch, your camera, binoculars, a book, harmonica, or even a hammock. This is such a peaceful place that you should plan time for quiet, relaxing activities to experience the mood of the mountain. Most of the ride is easy, but there are a few short steep hills where you can expend some energy.

Getting There: Park along Frazier Mountain Road at Overmeyer Flat.

Ride up to the signed road fork and go left on East Frazier Road (8N24). You continue to climb moderately for 0.5 mile around the north side of the mountain. The upper end of a canyon is below to the east, and the road descends slightly toward the ridge at the head of this canyon. A water trough with water piped to it from a spring can be seen in the canyon below (water quality unknown). Near the bottom of this hill, at 0.9 mile, a rough, steep road heads up the northeast side of the mountain to the lookout. You descend to about 1.1 miles and then climb until you reach the Arrasta Trail (20W05/OHV 121) on the right (mile 1.5).

The road continues east on the ridge, dropping and climbing through thick forest. At 3.2 miles, a doubletrack to the right crosses the ridge for 0.45 mile to dead-end at an overlook viewpoint. From this promontory you can look west and see the microwave towers near the lookout. (On the way back, at 0.2 mile from the main road, another doubletrack heads east; at 3.5 miles a doubletrack on the right seems to head back up toward the road to the viewpoint. These two may connect, but I haven't tried it.) The main road crosses to the north side of the ridge so you can see out toward Bakersfield and down to Frazier Park. Just past that at 3.6 miles the road becomes divided while climbing a short hill.

Turning southeast and keeping on the ridge top, you pass the East Frazier Trail (19W06/OHV 120) at 5.1 miles. In this area there are many viewing places between the trees where you can see out across the Antelope Valley to Lancaster. The road descends more to the south and ends at a turn-around circle, 5.2 miles from Overmeyer Flat. For an easier trip, skip the last steep rocky descents and turn around at 5.0 miles.

If you want a more strenuous ride, go up to the lookout first on Road 8N04 rather than turning onto East Frazier Road. From the lookout, take the trail to the northwest, which heads down the mountain to the north, turns east, and then joins East Frazier Road 0.9 mile from its start at Frazier Mountain Road.

For additional rides in this area, please refer to *Mountain Biking the Coast Range, Guide 4, Ventura County and the Sespe,* third edition, by Mickey McTigue, ISBN 0-938665-18-9 (see p. 304).

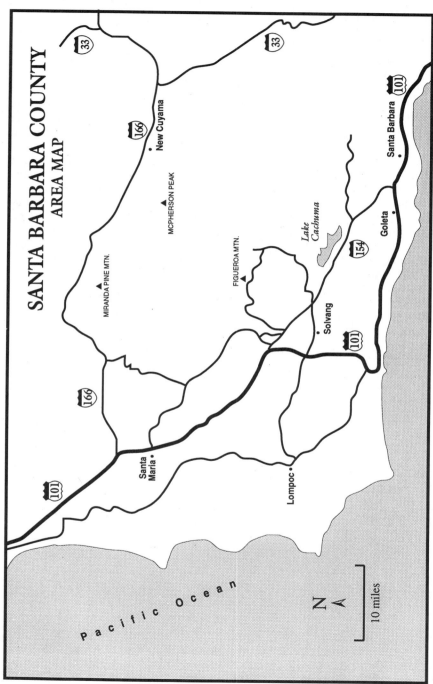

SANTA BARBARA COUNTY
AREA MAP

New Cuyama

McPHERSON PEAK

MIRANDA PINE MTN.

FIGUEROA MTN.

Lake Cachuma

Santa Barbara

Goleta

Solvang

Santa Maria

Lompoc

Pacific Ocean

N

10 miles

CHAPTER 9

Santa Barbara County

By Mickey McTigue and Don Douglass

Santa Barbara County, west of Los Angeles and Ventura counties, is the epitome of Southern California. Mountains tumble to a strip of palm-lined sand under almost perpetual sunshine. Ocean breezes keep temperatures down so you can enjoy a variety of recreational activities year round.

The Pacific Ocean borders on the south and west sides of this roughly rectangular county. Most of the population lives on a narrow strip between the mountains and the ocean on the south coast. The Los Padres National Forest takes up about one-third of the county, primarily in the east and northeast sections. Much of the west county is rural cattle and horse grazing land with more and more vineyards the past few years. The center of the county's forested area is taken up by large wilderness areas (off-limits to bikes), and the mountain bicycle routes are situated around their edges.

Figueroa Mountain is 25 miles northwest of Santa Barbara and overlooks the Santa Ynez Valley on the south and the San Rafael Wilderness to the north. The Wild Horse/Zaca Ridge Road that travels on a ridge from Figueroa Mountain 7.6 miles to the northwest surrounds you with spectacular scenery as you ride. Campgrounds on the mountain or on the east and north sides are available. The nearby town of Solvang can provide plenty of distractions for those tired of riding. Ride here in the spring, summer and fall. In winter, snow and mud are sometimes a problem.

The La Brea Canyon/Pine Canyon area is in the remote north central part of the county about 27 miles from Santa Maria over narrow paved and dirt roads. You should plan to day-ride here or stay at one of the campgrounds. This is a very good spot for those looking for less strenuous routes. Miles of nearly level road wind through canyons with meadows and oak and sycamore trees that beckon you on around the next bend. Although best in spring, the area is nice in fall. Summer, however, can be very hot. The road is closed to car traffic in wet weather, but if the road isn't muddy and the streams are not high, winter can be a fine time to ride here, too.

The 50-mile long Sierra Madre Ridge Road always takes me back in time. It gets me so far from civilization, and the more I explore the potreros—the large grasslands on the flattened mountaintops—the more mysterious they seem. How were they formed and what keeps the brush from growing in them? Strange rock formations, Native American rock art and soaring golden eagles add to the mystery. This is one of the more difficult places to get to, and only basic services are provided in the small, nearby town of New Cuyama, 55 miles east of Santa Maria. This area, too, is best in late spring. Summer and fall are fine, but winter snow and mud should be avoided.

Figueroa Mountain, La Brea Canyon and most of the Sierra Madre Road is in the Santa Lucia Ranger District. Information about trail conditions and fire permits is available by writing or calling the district office at 1616 Carlotti Drive, Santa Maria, CA 93454, (805) 925-9538.

79

Figueroa Mountain:

Wild Horse/
Zaca Ridge Road

Distance: 15.2 miles out and back; turn around anywhere for a shorter ride
Difficulty: Starts out easy and gradually becomes more difficult
Elevation: Start 3,450', climb to 4,200', descend to 3,600', end 3,650 at Wild Horse Peak
Ride Type: Out and back on dirt roads
Season: Spring, summer, fall

Figueroa Mountain sits on the north side of the Santa Ynez Valley. This wide pastoral valley with rolling, grass-covered hills and scattered oak trees is in sharp contrast to the steep, rugged mountains to the north. Several small communities provide services in the valley, and the Danish town of Solvang is a tourist favorite. The streets are crowded with visitors walking through this quaint village, visiting shops and sampling unusual foods in the many restaurants. An open air theater features plays in the evenings. To stay here make reservations in advance as it is usually booked up. If you are planning to camp, there are several campgrounds in the National Forest on and near Figueroa Mountain.

Figueroa Mountain, elevation 4,528 feet—a large mountain with several adjoining peaks—forms an east-west ridge from Cachuma Saddle, 7 miles west, to the forest boundary. With its steep meadows, scattered trees, and chaparral contrasting with large dark outcroppings of rock, the mountain presents a striking image from the south. Ranger Peak, at 4,652 feet, is one of the adjoining peaks of the Figueroa Mountain ridge.

Drive-in camps are at Cachuma (5 sites), east of the mountain; Davy Brown (13 sites) and Nira (11 sites), both north of the mountain; and Figueroa (33 sites), at 3,500 feet,

near the top on the south side. All sites are on a first come basis and fill up fast on long summer weekends.

Getting There: From Santa Barbara travel about 24 miles northwest on State Highway 154 over San Marcos Pass and past Lake Cachuma. Take Figueroa Mountain Road (7N07) north from Highway 154 at Los Olivos (3 miles east of Highway 101 on Highway 154). For 7 miles this narrow paved road passes ranches through rolling grasslands with large oak trees. It then climbs—sometimes steeply—6 miles to the Figueroa USFS station. Another half mile and you are at Wild Horse/Zaca Ridge Road. Park along the road here.

If you are planning to stay overnight, you can come in another way that brings you to several campgrounds. Take Highway 154 from Santa Barbara and pass Lake Cachuma. When you cross the Santa Ynez River, turn right (north) onto Armour Ranch Road and go 1.3 miles to Happy Canyon Road. Turn right (east) here and right again 1.1 miles farther where Baseline Road comes in, staying on Happy Canyon Road. Heading north through scenic Happy Canyon, the road keeps narrowing. Old oaks, barns and quiet pastoral scenery take you back in time—it's truly a lovely area. Nine miles from Highway 154 the road suddenly starts

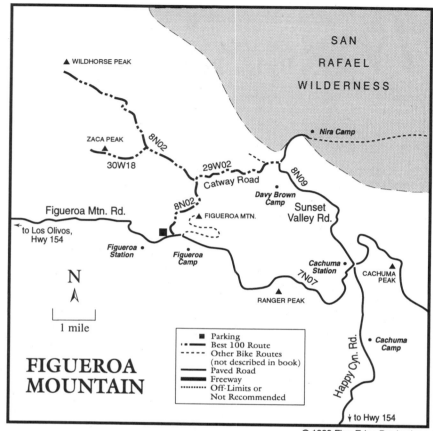

SAN
RAFAEL
WILDERNESS

▲ WILDHORSE PEAK

ZACA PEAK
▲

30W18

8N02

29W02
Catway Road

• Nira Camp

8N09

Davy Brown
Camp
Sunset
Valley Rd.

8N02

Figueroa Mtn. Rd.

▲ FIGUEROA MTN.

←to Los Olivos,
Hwy 154

Figueroa
Station •

Figueroa
Camp

Cachuma
Station •

CACHUMA
PEAK
▲

7N07

N
⋏

RANGER PEAK
▲

1 mile

Happy Cyn. Rd.

• Cachuma
Camp

FIGUEROA
MOUNTAIN

■   Parking
·▪·▪· Best 100 Route
‐ ‐ ‐ Other Bike Routes
       (not described in book)
       Paved Road
       Freeway
······· Off-Limits or
       Not Recommended

↟ to Hwy 154

© 1993 Fine Edge Productions

to climb through pine, oak and chaparral, and then you encounter more grasslands on the slopes before dropping into Cachuma Camp, next to a seasonal stream among sycamore, oak and pine. Two miles farther, at Cachuma Saddle, there is a USFS ranger station.

At the fork here, go left and proceed 6.8 miles to the start of this ride at the intersection fo Wild Horse/ Zaca Ridge Road (8N02). You pass Ranger Peak, Figueroa Camp, and the turn-off to Figueroa Mountain Lookout along the way. Other campgrounds can be reached if you

go straight ahead at the fork at the end of Happy Canyon Road. This is paved Sunset Valley Road (8N09), and it's 4 miles to Davy Brown Camp and 6.5 miles to Nira Camp.

This great 15-mile out-and-back ride has fantastic views of a large part of Santa Barbara County. It winds its way around the west side of Figueroa Mountain before heading west along the high ridge past Zaca Peak (4,341 feet) to Wild Horse Peak at the extreme west end of the ridge. The route could be called a Rim of the World Trail because of its outstanding views—the San Rafael Wilderness below you to the northeast, the Sisquoc River and the countless fertile valleys and wooded ridges all the way west to the ocean, and the Santa Ynez drainage and Solvang areas to the south. No water is available en route; prepare for plenty of sunshine!

To begin, look for an open gate on Road 8N02 with a sign that reads *Gate Temporarily Closed When the Road is Wet.* The dirt road heads north 0.4 mile—Catway Picnic Site on the left (west) has a picnic table and a good view across grassy meadows dotted with pine and oak trees. The pointed Zaca Peak appears to the northwest. At 2.2 miles there is a saddle with a doubletrack intersection. (The bottom of the saddle meets Catway OHV Route to Davy Brown Campground at 2.5 miles. *It is a steep, rough route.*) Continue uphill in a more westerly direction and pass through a white fence.

You come to a saddle with shade after 4.0 miles. At 4.4 miles a dirt road to the left leads downhill to 30W10 and 30W18 and then out to Zaca Peak, where you have wonderful views. *The road deteriorates west of here.* At 5.2 miles the road pitches into Cedros Saddle, a turn-around with parking for a dozen cars. From here, the Sulphur Springs Trail on the north side drops steeply downhill to Manzana Creek and the San Rafael Wilderness. The trail to the south side drops steeply down into Zaca Lake.

From this point, the road is rocky and loose and continues to undulate along the ridge. You pass directly above Zaca Lake until you reach the turn-around at Wild Horse Peak. You'll reach Wild Horse Peak at 7.6 miles. Although this area burned recently, it has outstanding views in all directions. From here, retrace your route to the appropriate trailhead.

If you camp in Sunset Valley at Davy Brown or Nira Camps, you can ride up the Catway OHV route to Wild Horse/Zaca Ridge Road on your bicycle and avoid a long trip around the mountain on paved roads 8N09 & 7N07.

To go west from Sunset Valley Road, at a small meadow turn west on an unmarked dirt road just north of Davy Brown (1.7 miles south of Nira Campground). At 0.0 mile pass a corral and you soon come to a fork. The road to the right, which is closed by a locked gate and signed as private property, follows the south side of the San Rafael Wilderness (bicycles not allowed). Take the left fork through a gate and over a steep berm. Continue steeply uphill. *Caution: Above the switchbacks poison oak crowds the trail.* At 2.6 miles you have the first level ground and a view back down to Davy Brown Campground. At 4.2 miles you come to Catway/Zaca Ridge Road. Turn left to Figueroa Mountain Road, 2.5 miles or turn right to Wild Horse Peak, 5.1 miles.

80 La Brea and Pine Canyons

Distance: 15.7 miles (one way) described; you can do any number of variations on the theme
Difficulty: Easy and nontechnical to moderate with some steep areas
Elevation: 980' to 2,500' to 1,230' to 1,400'
Ride Type: One way or out and back on dirt road
Season: Spring, summer, fall

Just 27 miles from Santa Maria, this pastoral canyon region, with five drive-in camps and good dirt roads, is an under-utilized area. Most of the year—except during the rainy season—the roads here are open and passable by passenger cars with reasonable ground clearance and careful drivers. *Remember—conditions can change quickly on remote mountain roads!* This beautiful area, with the wide, 7-mile La Brea Canyon Road, is one of the best for beginning riders. Oak and sycamore groves beside open grass fields and chaparral provide a varied landscape where it's a delight to ride. The nearly level road is easy to ride and fun to explore!

Pine Canyon is remote, but the two campgrounds and 3 miles of good dirt roads make the long drive over mountain dirt roads worth it.

Getting There: At Santa Maria take Betteravia Road east from Highway 101. Continue 8.4 miles to Santa Maria Mesa Road on your left. It crosses the Sisquoc River, and at 15.3 miles from Highway 101 connects with Tepusquet (Tip-es-kay) Road. Turn left, away from the river, and go up this beautiful canyon 4.5 miles, where you turn right (east) onto Colson Canyon Road.

Colson Canyon Road is the main access route to the La Brea-Pine Canyon areas for mining, ranching,

grazing and recreational activities. For 2.7 miles it passes private property before entering the federal forest at a large sign marked *Los Padres—Land of Many Uses.* The road follows the canyon bottom, crossing the usually dry stream bed many times. For most of its length, Colson Canyon is quite narrow with sheer sides. The road climbs steadily but there are some steep sections. Near Colson Camp the canyon widens with clusters of oaks growing here and there. Colson Camp, 4.1 miles from Tepusquet Road on the north side of Colson Canyon Road, has eight sites with shade oaks, piped water, tables, fire pits and pit toilets. *Please remember to pack out your own trash!*

Two-tenths of a mile farther up Colson Canyon Road, you pass the site of the former Colson USFS Station. All that remains are roads, building pads, pipes and telephone lines. Colson Saddle is located 0.5 mile above Colson Camp. Here you have the first view down into La Brea Canyon and over to the mountains and ridges beyond—an impressive sight. At the saddle a road north leads to some home sites and a very ugly strip-mining operation. To the south Alejandro Trail (31W15) takes off at a steel sign and switchbacks up the mountain. At the saddle there is a cattleguard and a gate for winter storm closure. Rattlesnake Canyon Road

(11N04) continues down to La Brea Canyon east of here.

Rattlesnake Canyon Road is open to motor vehicle traffic, except during wet winter weather when the gate at Colson Saddle is closed to all vehicles—except ranchers—in La Brea Canyon. When the seasonal gate is closed, you can cycle down Rattlesnake Canyon to La Brea Canyon and return. (The grade is fairly constant and all rideable uphill coming back.) From the top down, the road stays high up on the north side of the canyon for 1.5 miles and then starts into a series of switchbacks that descend the north ridge of Rattlesnake Canyon into La Brea Canyon. Rattlesnake Road crosses the usually dry La Brea Creek and ends at La Brea Road at a large sign with directions and distances.

Turning right and going downstream (south), it's 1.4 miles to Barrel Springs Camp. This is one of the best camps in the forest with piped-in water, pit toilets, 5 sites with

tables and fire pits. Park here or along La Brea Road. A large white locked gate with no trespassing signs 0.6 mile farther marks the boundary of private ranch lands and the end of the road for mountain bikes.

La Brea Canyon

Begin at the junction of Rattlesnake Canyon and La Brea Canyon Road. Traveling north (upstream) 5 miles from Rattlesnake Canyon Junction to Wagon Flat Camp, La Brea Road meanders across meadows and in and out of oak groves, crossing La Brea Creek several times as the canyon gradually narrows. Wagon Flat Camp is located on the east side of the road and overlooks the creek, which flows more here than farther downstream. The stream is the only water source. *Treat all water because of the cattle and up-canyon road crossings.* There are five sites with oak trees, tables, fire pits and pit toilets. (Just past Wagon Flat Camp a rough spur road branches east 0.75 mile to Lazy

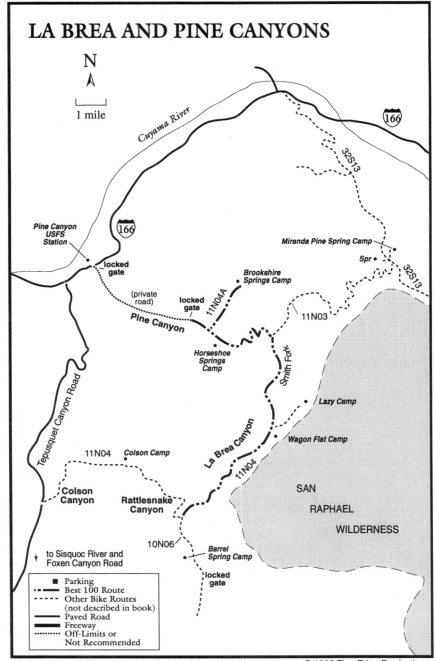

LA BREA AND PINE CANYONS

N

1 mile

Cuyama River

166

Pine Canyon
USFS
Station

locked
gate

166

Miranda Pine Spring Camp

Spr

32S13

32S13

(private
road)

locked
gate

11N04A

Brookshire
Springs Camp

11N03

Pine Canyon

Horseshoe
Springs
Camp

Smith Fork

Lazy Camp

La Brea Canyon

Wagon Flat Camp

Tepusquet Canyon Road

11N04   Colson Camp

11N04

SAN

Colson
Canyon

Rattlesnake
Canyon

RAPHAEL

WILDERNESS

10N06

to Sisquoc River and
Foxen Canyon Road

Barrel
Spring Camp

locked
gate

■ Parking
▬·▬ Best 100 Route
---- Other Bike Routes
        (not described in book)
▬ Paved Road
████ Freeway
········ Off-Limits or
        Not Recommended

Camp and the start of Kerry Canyon Trail, #30W02. Lazy Camp has two sites with tables and fire pits. This road is in very rough condition and is not suitable for cars.)

La Brea Canyon ends at the junction of Kerry and Smith Canyons, mile 7.0. The next section of La Brea Road takes off from the fork at Kerry Canyon Trail and goes to a ridge where it joins Horseshoe Canyon Road (11N04) and Miranda Pine Mountain Road (11N03).

Smith Canyon

When you enter Smith Canyon its narrow profile is apparent. The road passes a cattleguard and gate and climbs up the west side of the canyon for a short distance. The canyon opens up a little, the road levels out and then repeats its narrow, westside climb. At about 8.8 miles, the road crosses Smith Creek and passes a water trough fed by a pipe from the hillside. (As the sign warns, this water is unsafe to drink!)

Just past the water trough, the brush on the mountainsides changes suddenly, and you can see shrubs whose loose red bark hangs like shreds. [*Editor's Note:* Red bark chamiso, the dominant shrub in this one area only of the Los Padres National Forest, is uncommon in California. A native of northern Baja California, it grows in only one other area of California—the Santa Monica Mountains.]

At mile 9 the road crosses back to the west side of Smith Canyon. It then makes a serious climb out of the canyon onto the ridge. Buckhorn Ridge Road (32W01—a 4WD OHV route) starts south from La Brea Road just as it reaches the ridge top. La Brea Road follows this wide savannah-like ridge as it slopes up and north for one mile to join, at mile 10.7,

Horseshoe Canyon Road (11N04) and Miranda Pine Mountain Road (11N03). From this point you look down into Pine Canyon toward Cuyama Gorge.

Horseshoe Canyon

The road down Horseshoe Canyon twists steeply down the mountain in a westerly direction to Horseshoe Springs Camp. (The 2.5 miles of steep switchbacks seem much farther!) Horseshoe Springs Camp is located at 13.9 miles in a beautiful meadow with large shade oaks. An old stone wall with built-in stairs echoes tales of the past. Three sites with tables, fire pits and pit toilets are available. Water is piped to the camp.

Upper Pine Canyon

One-half mile west (downhill) from Horseshoe Springs Camp the road forks at an old oak tree. (The left fork is Pine Canyon Trail, #31W02, which continues up Pine Canyon.) Take the right fork (north), Road 11N04, into Upper Pine Canyon. This is a lesser traveled road, open to all vehicles. This part of the canyon appears to have a narrow dead-end. The canyon sides are steep and end in white cliffs with many small caves. The first mile follows the east side of the canyon. At 14.6 miles you come to a USFS gate. (Close this gate!) The road crosses the creek and passes a wire-fence corral, then crosses to the east side of the canyon again.

The road ends at Brookshire Springs Camp, 1.8 miles from Horseshoe Springs Camp and 15.7 miles from the beginning of La Brea Canyon Road. There are two sites—one next to the creek, the other under a large oak. Tables, fire pits and pit toilets are available. The water in the creek has been fouled by cattle, so be sure to treat it.

81 Sierra Madre Ridge Road

Distance: 56.2, 67.8 or 88.5 miles, depending on option taken
Difficulty: Easy to moderate, nontechnical, and long
Elevation: 1,500' to 5,700' to 4,500'
Ride Type: One way on dirt road
Season: Spring and fall best

Sierra Madre Road (32S13)— about 50 miles long—is the longest single dirt road in the Los Padres Forest. It is an excellent long-distance route, with superb views, good road surface and miles of easy grade. Nearest services are in New Cuyama or Santa Maria.

A lack of reliable water sources here is a real problem, but it can be overcome by proper planning. Since this is one of my favorite rides I have listed the solutions I use to ride the 44 miles east from Highway 166 to Salisbury Potrero, 8 miles down Newsome Canyon and 4.2 miles farther to New Cuyama. It is best done in the spring, second choice is the autumn. Avoid winter snow and mud or the extreme heat of summer.

You must be an experienced long distance bicyclist, bring a water filter, travel light and get an early start every day on these two-day rides.

Option 1: Self-contained, loaded bicycle camping, two-day tour of 88.5 miles. Park by the fire station in New Cuyama and tell the firefighters where you are going and when you will be back. Ride 26.4 miles west on the paved highway to where the river enters the gorge and turn left onto the signed Sierra Madre Road across from the Rock Front Ranch. The highway is fairly flat so you should be able to do this in 2.5 hours. You climb 3,400 in 10.5 miles to the east on the Sierra Madre Road to Timber Peak. Allow three hours for this long even grade. The next 12.8 miles to

Bates Canyon Road is much faster due to long gradual descents and climbs (1.5 hours). Go down Bates Canyon Road 2.8 miles to Cole Spring, 4.3 miles to Doc's Spring, or 5.8 miles to Bates Camp. Camp at one of the former trail camps or at Bates Camp.

The second day you climb back up to the ridge and continue east on Sierra Madre Road 10 miles to McPherson Peak. It's a fast ride to the peak and faster the next 8 miles down to Montgomery Potrero and Painted Rock Camp. Descend to Pine Corral Potrero and then climb a little on the 3.7 miles to Salisbury Potrero. There you turn left and descend the steep Bull Ridge Trail into Newsome Canyon to Perkins Road (8 miles). Take a very fast descent on paved Perkins Road 4.2 miles to New Cuyama.

Option 2: Lightweight touring, car camping. Have someone that likes to camp drive you to the start, drop you off, go to Bates Camp and set up camp while you ride the same route as the previous ride. Be very sure your driver knows where Bates Camp is! The second day you ride back up to the ridge and continue on over the potreros and down to New Cuyama. The driver has an easy day in camp, then packs up and meets you in New Cuyama. Total miles: 67.8

Option 3: Use two cars, one parked at each end of the ride, and pedal the whole trip, 56.2 miles, in one day. Carry water for the whole ride plus emergencies, start very early and keep moving. If things don't go as well as planned, go down Bates Canyon and take the highway back to New Cuyama.

Option 4: Sierra Madre Road is open most of the year to high clearance vehicles as far as McPherson

Peak and down Bates Canyon Road. You can have a vehicle sag for most of the ride, although this will take away some of the sense of discovery and adventure.

For convenience, this route description is divided into sections that give mileages, difficulty ratings and elevations.

Getting There: (Option 3) Park along Highway 166 at a large turnout at the top of a hill 0.2 miles toward New Cuyama from Sierra Madre Road. Park the second car in New Cuyama (see Option 1).

Sierra Madre Road to Miranda Pine Mountain

This 9-mile section of Sierra Madre Road has the most elevation change of the entire ride, but the 2,400-foot gain spread over 9 miles is not a difficult ride—just long. The road is in good shape and the view is terrific.

The lower section of the road passes through oak groves and grassland on the north side of the mountain for 4.5 miles. As you cross the ridge to the south side, there is a dramatic change in climate and vegetation—drier, warmer, more chaparral and almost no trees. For about one mile the road crosses the narrow ridge from north to south and back again, finally ending on the south side before the last 3 miles to Miranda Pine Mountain. One mile from Miranda Pine Mountain you can see a peak with white, flat-topped buildings and over a dozen microwave antennas. Charred branches and low new growth south of the road give evidence of a large wildfire in the late 1980s.

Just up the ridge from the "electronic" peak you enter a grove

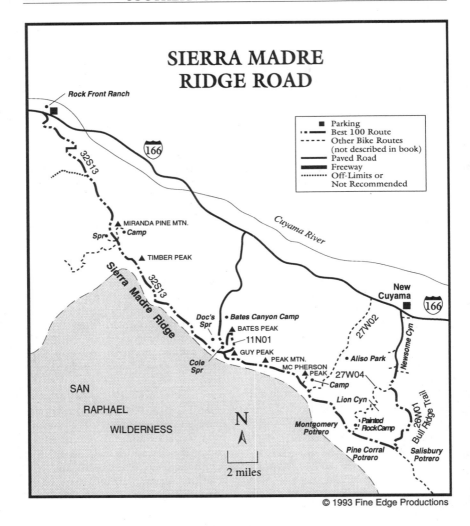

SIERRA MADRE
RIDGE ROAD

Rock Front Ranch

32S13

166

Legend:
- ■ Parking
- ·—·—· Best 100 Route
- - - - - Other Bike Routes
  (not described in book)
- —— Paved Road
- ▬▬▬ Freeway
- ·········· Off-Limits or
  Not Recommended

Cuyama River

▲ MIRANDA PINE MTN.
Spr • Camp

▲ TIMBER PEAK

Sierra Madre Ridge

32S13

New
Cuyama
■ 166

Doc's • Bates Canyon Camp
Spr   ▲ BATES PEAK
       11N01
Cole ▲ GUY PEAK
Spr   ▲ PEAK MTN.
         MC PHERSON
         ▲ PEAK   27W04
           • Camp

27W02

Newsome Cyn

• Aliso Park

SAN

RAPHAEL

WILDERNESS

N
Λ

Lion Cyn

Montgomery
Potrero

• Painted
  RockCamp

Bull Ridge Trail
26W01

Pine Corral   Salisbury
Potrero   Potrero

2 miles

© 1993 Fine Edge Productions

of pines south of Miranda Pine Mountain. At 4,061 feet, it gives some relief from the hot summer sun. Miranda Pines Camp is located among these pines on a high spot of the ridge, just east of the peak. It has shade, three sites with tables, fireplaces and one pit toilet, but no water. The daytime view is great and the nighttime sky is spectacular.

Farther east, Sierra Madre Road has a five-point intersection. A sharp left and a steep uphill 0.4 mile to the west takes you to Miranda Pines Camp. Straight ahead at the intersection, Sierra Madre Road heads east for 40 miles or more. A right turn to the south takes you on Miranda Pine Mountain Road, 3.5 miles to Pine Flat. A sharp right (southwest) at the intersection leads you on a short road that ends at a water tank below Miranda Pine Springs.

Miranda Pine Mountain to Bates Canyon Road

Although this section of Sierra Madre Road is the highest and most remote, it is the easiest riding, gaining 1,300 feet in 13.3 miles. While most other ridge routes follow a particular ridge, climbing up and down every peak, no matter how steep, this road was cut along the side of the ridge and around most of the steep peaks. This evened out the grade, making for a very enjoyable ride.

From Miranda Pine Mountain and the junction of roads 11N03 and 32S13 to Timber Peak, 2.5 miles east, there is a moderate climb of 800 feet with only a few steep sections. Just west of Timber Peak the road passes through an unusually deep, narrow cut across the ridge. The rocky and rutted road here contrasts with usually very good road conditions.

For 3.5 miles past Timber Peak the road climbs gradually south-southeast, remaining most of the way on the south side of the ridge, which drops off a little less steeply than the north side. Along the ridge near Spoor Mountain is a large reforestation area where the pines have grown to about 6 feet high.

At the 7-mile mark, the place noted on maps as *Pines Picnic Area* is just a wide spot along the road at this narrow saddle—no sign of any facilities. To the south are the headwaters of the south fork of La Brea and Horse Canyons which drain into the Sisquoc River.

The road continues southeast for mile after mile, near the 5,000 foot level—good riding and great views! At 11.3 miles there is a green water tank, near which a long ridge—between Horse and Water Canyons—leads south to the Sisquoc River.

At 12.9 miles there's a picnic site on a saddle. To the east, on a ridge north of Guy Peak, the road cutting down into Bates Canyon can be seen. From this point, you climb again, and at 13.3 miles (5,200 feet)—just west of Guy Mountain—you come to the junction with Bates Canyon Road (11N01).

Bates Canyon Road

Bates Canyon provides the best access to the 23 miles of Sierra Madre Road that lie between Miranda Pine Mountain and McPherson Peak. Bates Canyon Campground is located on the paved road just inside the National Forest at the mouth of the canyon. The six campsites have tables, fire pits and piped-in water, with two pit toilets and large white oak trees for shade. This is an excellent camp, not much used except during deer season.

Getting There: Follow these directions if you are driving to Bates Canyon Road rather than cycling from the beginning of the Sierra Madre Ridge Road. From Highway 101 in Santa Maria to Cottonwood Road on State Highway 166 it's a distance of 39.6 miles. Highway 166 is a good two lane highway, with some of the best scenery in the county. Going west on Highway 166 from the small town of Cuyama, it is 12.2 miles to Cottonwood Canyon Road. Large signs on both sides of the highway give directions to White Oak Station (not in use) and Bates Campground.

From Highway 166 the distance to Bates Canyon Campground is 6.6 miles through Cottonwood Canyon Road, on a narrow paved road. The road steadily climbs 1,200 feet through unfenced grazing land. In spring, visitors are in for a treat with the new green grass, scattered dark juniper and white oaks just breaking out in small pale leaves. And, if the timing is right, wildflowers perfume the air and dazzle you with color. Caution: The bees are also out in force!

Just below the campground to the west above the road is the White Oak Forest Service Station, now closed. Leave Bates Camp and go uphill (south) on the paved road 11N01. The pavement ends, and 0.2 mile from camp, there is a gate for seasonal closure to motor vehicles. The dirt road continues straight back

into the canyon staying west of the stream. The road is moderately steep but in good condition, except for a few rocky spots.

Bates Canyon Road leaves the Sierra Madre Road from a saddle that is below and to the west of Guy Peak (5,477 feet). You head east around the north side of Guy Peak until the road joins a ridge that connects Guy Peak to Bates Peak (4,422 feet). It descends on this ridge to just south of Bates Peak before doubling back to the west and into the east branch of Bates Canyon. In this deep canyon, thick with trees and undergrowth, you come to Cole Spring, 2.8 miles from the top.

This road continues to the west, descending steeply while crossing over

into the center branch of Bates Canyon. Here at 4.3 miles is the former site of Doc's Spring Trail Camp. The spring is a cool resting spot, 1.5 miles from Bates Camp. You cross to the west side of the canyon and descend to the south. After crossing the west branch you come to a seasonal gate and the paved part of the road 0.2 miles from Bates Camp.

Bates Canyon Road to McPherson Peak

Beginning at the junction with Bates Canyon Road at 5, 200 feet, this 10-mile segment of Sierra Madre Road passes around the south side of Guy Mountain, climbs past Hot Peak (5,587 feet), and then passes south of Peak Mountain at 5,843 feet, the high point of the Sierra Madre Ridge. Next you descend to a saddle at 5,400 feet and climb around the south side of McPherson Peak. Here, a road branches left and circles around the peak on the south and east sides, climbing to the top at 5,747 feet. This was once a lookout site, but it is now occupied by an Air Force microwave station with fuel tanks and generators. McPherson Camp is another 0.4 mile east at a rise on the ridge.

McPherson Peak to Salisbury Potrero

The last part of Sierra Madre Road is 11.7 miles long and mostly downhill, with a net elevation loss of 1,200 feet. Just east of McPherson Camp, you pass a locked gate and start a steep 1.5-mile descent to the junction with Hog Pen Spring Trail.

After an easy half-mile climb to pass by Hog Peak, you descend again on the rolling ridge road that has occasional small climbs. The road makes a final steep descent on a pair of switchbacks as you enter the potreros (meadows) of the Sierra Madre Ridge. As the road levels somewhat you pass the Jackson Trail to the right (south), which goes by a grazing lease cabin. Another 0.5 mile east, and at 8 miles from McPherson is the Painted Rock Trail Camp.

This camp, fenced to keep out range cattle, has three sites with tables, fire pits and an outhouse toilet. The camp is named for the many Chumash rock paintings in the caves here. These fragile paintings may be observed and photographed, but strict laws protect them in every way. Lion Canyon Trail starts to the east at the gate to the camp and turns south down into the canyon. It's a steep, rough, rocky trail, not recommended.

On the Sierra Madre Road you descend easily for 1.8 miles along the north side of the ridge across the head of Lion Canyon. The large sandstone outcroppings there have been eroded into shapes that are fascinating. At the low point on this part of the ridge you come to Pine Corral Potrero. This grass area has many large sandstone rocks that sometimes look like whales swimming through a field.

You climb 400 feet in 1.5 miles to 4,900 feet on the south side of Salisbury Mountain. Near a gate here the Sweetwater Trail can be seen crossing another potrero south and below the road. After a level 0.4 mile to the east you come to the head of the Newsome Canyon-Bull Ridge Trail, which takes you down Newsome Canyon to New Cuyama.

Newsome Canyon/ Bull Ridge Trail/Perkins Road

This last 12.2 miles takes you in to New Cuyama. When you leave Sierra Madre Road and turn to the north onto the signed Bull Ridge Trail (26W01), you first ride a short road down to a ranch on Salisbury Potrero. As you start down be sure to look ahead over the large meadow sloping to the east and take note of the far ridge line on the north side. The trail you want to follow crosses that ridge at a noticeable dip almost directly northeast of you and a little to the right of the ranch buildings (see photo below).

The road drops 170 feet in 0.4 mile to a low area in the huge meadow. Here the road turns right and descends to the buildings and corrals below. You need to keep on straight ahead on a much less-traveled track, climbing slightly across the hillside to regain 60 feet in 0.5 mile to the notch on the ridge.

Passing through the notch you leave the Sierra Madre potreros behind as suddenly as you entered them. For the next 2 miles you descend on an old road through mixed pines and chaparral. There is a wire fence gate across the road just above a saddle, where you climb a bit before resuming the descent. The trail gets narrower where it heads down across the grass-covered mountainside, with switchbacks at the steeper places. After more steep descending on the ridge to the canyon below, you are finally down on much more level ground in the canyon.

Turn right and head down the canyon. The trail gradually improves in the next mile, becoming a road where you pass another wire stock gate. (If you open a gate to pass through, be sure to properly close it behind you to prevent cattle from straying.) Another mile of easy descent and you are at the fork in the canyon with Lion Canyon on the left. Now it's a very easy mile to the locked gate with the parking area just beyond on the right.

The Johnston Ranch is to the left as you pass the corrals to head for the town of New Cuyama 4.2 miles ahead on paved Perkins Road. You also pass the Perez Ranch on your right and then an old Richfield refinery. Pass a road to the left (it goes to a landfill) and then descend through fenced range land to Highway 166 on the west side of town.

For additional rides in this area, please refer to Mountain *Biking the Coast Range, Guide 5, Santa Barbara County,* fourth edition, by Mickey McTigue and Don Douglass, ISBN 0-938665-25-1 (see p. 304).

CHAPTER 10

San Luis Obispo County

By Delaine Fragnoli and Mickey McTigue

Tucked between Santa Barbara County to the south and Monterey County to the north, San Luis Obispo County is best known for its lovely beaches. Part of what is known as the Central Coast, these beaches include famous Morro Bay and Pismo Beach. Farther north is San Simeon and Hearst Castle, the fantasy home of newspaper magnate William Randolph Hearst.

Although Los Padres National Forest continues into San Luis Obispo County from Santa Barbara County, much of it is wilderness (bikes prohibited). The best and most scenic riding is at the beach. At Montana De Oro State Park, just south of Morro Bay, you can mountain bike along dramatic cliffs, surf and sand below you. For a change of pace you can escape to the little-known and very different eastern side of the county. Here the Carrizo Plain, an oasis for birds and animals, calls to those who like exploring out-of-the-way places. To fully appreciate this dramatic landscape, plan on camping and spending a weekend.

San Luis Obispo's consistently mild cli-mate makes it bicycling-perfect year round. If you get tired of knobbies, it's gently rolling, chaparral-covered hills are ideal for road riding. Paso Robles, in the north central part of the county, is home to the annual Great Western Bike Rally, now in its 29th year. Held over Memorial Day weekend, the rally features road and off-road rides, a bicycle rodeo and other events. Write to P.O. Box 7000-617, Redondo Beach, CA 90277 for more information.

After riding, you may want to visit one of the area's wineries or poke around the town of San Luis Obispo, a good base for exploring the county. Be sure to see Mission San Luis Obispo De Tolosa. Often called the Prince of Missions, it was built in 1772. Today you can visit its museum and gardens.

Montana De Oro State Park

Located on the Pacific Ocean, Montana De Oro, or mountain of gold, is named not for the valuable metal, but for the brilliant gold color the landscape assumes in spring when it is covered by California poppies and other wildflowers. For mountain bikers, the park is a motherlode of singletrack riding.

At over 8,000 acres and with half a million visitors each year, this is one of California's largest and most popular state parks—and for good reason. Seven miles of shoreline offer spectacular views and cooling sea breezes. Tide pools and miles of sandy beaches add to the dramatic meeting of land and sea—a dynamic relationship that is still working its magic on the area.

The prevailing rock is mostly Monterey Shale. Formerly an ancient sea floor, it is made of mudstone deposited millions of years ago. Tiny fragments of once-living organisms drifted to the bottom of the sea, mixed with silt and sand, and solidified into thick layers. The grinding of tectonic plates in the earth's crust buckled and tilted the sedimentary layers, thrusting them out of the sea. Erosion and wave action turned them into a sloping beach. The level of the ocean also changed as ice ages came and went. This process has been repeated several times over the past 5 to 10 million years. You can see the successive marine terraces (former beaches) as you hike on the present bluff or climb the slopes of Valencia Peak.

Like much of Southern California, the area was occupied by the Chumash Indians until the Spanish forcibly moved them inland and unwittingly infected them with European diseases against which they had no immunity. Although the culture has all but vanished, Indian middens and village sites can still be seen in Montana De Oro State Park. Remember, it is against the law to tamper with or disturb any Indian sites. Look and ponder, but do not touch!

While you're exploring the park, you may also see the small brown coastal deer, wild fox and cottontail rabbits.

Today the park is popular with hikers and equestrians as well as mountain bikers. Eight trails, mostly singletracks, are open to cyclists: Rim Trail, Hazard Canyon Road, Manzanita Trail, Bloody Nose Trail, Ridge Trail, East Boundary Trail, Islay Creek Road and Bluff Trail. Many of these can be combined into a variety of loops, none of which is overly long or strenuous. Beginners and intermediates will feel comfortable here as they work on improving their singletracking skills. Elevations range from 50 feet to 1,650 feet. All trails in the park are open to hikers and all trails except the Bluff Trail are open to horses, so behave accordingly. Yield the trail!

Getting There: The park is about 12 miles west of San Luis Obispo and 7 miles south of Los Osos. These are the nearest services. From Highway 101 in San Luis Obispo, take the Los Osos/Baywood Park exit and go northwest on Los Osos Valley Road. After 12 miles it turns into Pecho Valley Road and leads into the park. From Highway 1 near Morro Bay, take the Los Osos/Baywood Park exit. Head south on South Bay Boulevard. At 5 miles you come to a T at Los Osos Valley Road. Go right and follow Los Osos Valley Road into Pecho Valley Road and the state park. Park headquarters and a campground are 2.7 miles past the park entrance sign.

As you enter the park, you will notice row upon row of eucalyptus trees. These were planted by Alexander S. Hazard in an ill-fated attempt to cash in on California's need for lumber. Hazard Canyon was a prospective timber farm, but eucalyptus proved unsatisfactory for commercial use. However, the trees do help with erosion control in this often windswept area.

Park headquarters are in the old Spooner Ranch House where you can pick up camping and park information. The Visitors Center is open on weekends and daily during summer months. There are picnic tables and barbecue stoves at Spooner's Cove. (Alden B. Spooner, Jr., and his sons were sheep and dairy farmers in the area in the late 19th and early 20th centuries.)

A primitive campground in the canyon behind the Spooner Ranch House has 50 campsites for tents, trailers or motorhomes. Tables, wood stoves, drinking water and primitive toilets are nearby, but there are no showers or dump stations. In addition, there are several more secluded walk-in environmental campsites. These are primitive sites that require a short hike to reach. You must carry in your water and other supplies. For all camping, bring your own firewood, since gathering wood is prohibited in California State Parks. For camping reservations (recommended during summer months), call MISTIX at 1-800-444-7275 inside California. Outside California, call 619-452-1950, or write P.O. Box 85705, San Diego, CA 92138-5705. Ranger headquarters can be reached at 805-528-0513. There is a telephone at the Visitors Center.

The Diablo Canyon Nuclear Power Plant is nearby and visitors are cautioned to tune their car radio to 920 or 1400 AM if they should hear steady sirens for 3 to 5 minutes— an early warning of a potential problem at the plant.

No sirens will alert you to the presence of poison oak, but be on the lookout—it grows throughout the park.

82 Bluff Trail

Distance: 4.2 miles
Difficulty: Easy, nontechnical
Ride Type: Dirt road, out and back
Elevation: Low point, 60'; high point, 100'
Season: Year round

This is a great warm-up ride with high marks for its scenic value. Maintain control and do not ride fast, because this is a popular trail. As the name implies, it follows bluffs (actually uplifted marine terrace), the ocean pounding below you, California poppies, lavender, and mustard plants blooming beside you. During winter months, gray whales migrate along the coast here.

Getting There: Park at the trailhead at the south end of the dirt parking area south of the park headquarters. The trailhead is marked on the west side of Pecho Valley Road, 2.7 miles beyond the park entrance sign.

Begin your ride by dropping to cross over a wooden foot bridge. Take the right fork, following the bluffs. Continue along the bluffs at 0.7 mile. You intersect a second wooden bridge that spans the creek. Go right, crossing the bridge. (If you go straight you'll end up back at Pecho Valley Road.) Just under a mile, overlooking Quarry Cove, there are restrooms and picnic tables—a nice stop for lunch or a snack.

At 1.7 miles turn left up the singletrack leading to Pecho Valley Road. You encounter the only mildly technical part of the ride here as the trail drops into a small ravine. You can see Grotto Rock, a good example of the eroding power of wind, sand, and surf.

After 2.1 miles of pedaling you are at a parking area and Coon Creek trailhead. Coon Creek Trail picks up on the other side of the road, but it is closed to bicycles. You can return to your starting point by heading up the paved Pecho Valley Road, or you can go back the way you came, which many cyclists prefer.

83 Islay/Ridge Loop

Distance: 7.8 miles
Difficulty: Moderate with some steep uphills and some technical sections
Elevation: Low point, 80'; high point 1,076'
Ride Type: Dirt road and singletrack loop
Season: Year round

Getting There: At park headquarters, find the gate on the east side, 200 feet from the parking area.

This wide fire road climbs along the north side of Islay Creek. Poison oak is plentiful on the roadsides. You may

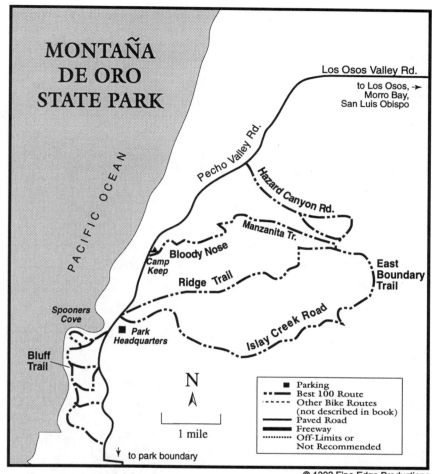

MONTAÑA
DE ORO
STATE PARK

Los Osos Valley Rd.

to Los Osos, →
Morro Bay,
San Luis Obispo

Pecho Valley Rd.

Hazard Canyon Rd.

Manzanita Tr.

Bloody Nose

Camp
Keep

Ridge Trail

East
Boundary
Trail

Spooners
Cove

Islay Creek Road

■ Park
Headquarters

Bluff
Trail

N
∧

1 mile

↓ to park boundary

■ Parking
Best 100 Route
Other Bike Routes
(not described in book)
Paved Road
Freeway
Off-Limits or
Not Recommended

© 1993 Fine Edge Productions

not see it because it is tangled with blackberry vines. Think twice about picking blackberries!

After a little less than 1.5 miles, the road descends through willow trees and past a waterfall on the left. Wildflowers thrive in this cool, wet, shady spot.

After three easy miles, you come to a trail junction. Turn left up East Boundary Trail, which skirts the park's eastern boundary. This narrow single-track runs through chaparral and native sage brush. Amid the few fun,

fast downhills, there are some uphill grunts—one of which you hit almost immediately.

Climb East Boundary to the ridge. Things get steeper as you follow the eastern boundary, but you soon level off as you head to a second ridge top. As you near the crest, a mile past the trail junction, look to your left for a singletrack that heads downhill. Wheeee! This is a sweet piece of trail—through a gulch and in and out of ground cover. You'll be using your technical skills here.

At 4.5 miles you climb again—this time past a stand of oak trees on the left. About 4.7 miles into your ride is a second trail junction. Take the left fork, Ridge Trail. It rolls west along the ridge line above Hazard Canyon with a few short steep uphills to keep you honest. You climb to Hazard Peak, at 1,076 feet, and then descend toward the ocean. Beautiful ocean views are yours as you pedal toward the surf.

The trail ends at Pecho Valley Road. A left and a short spin on pavement takes you back to park headquarters.

84 Hazard/Manzanita/ Bloody Nose Loop

Distance: 6.5 miles
Difficulty: Moderate with some technical sections
Elevation: Low point, 150'; high point, 800'
Ride Type: Dirt road and singletrack loop
Season: Year round

Getting There: When you enter Montana De Oro State Park, continue to the top of the hill. From here you can see Upper Hazard Canyon Road. A locked gate marks the entrance on the east side of Pecho Valley Road. Park across the road.

Head up Hazard Canyon Road past the horse camp. Continue past a second gate. Soon the road curves to the right, and at 1.0 mile you come to a junction with the Manzanita Trail off to the right. Climb this singletrack out of the canyon.

Manzanita Trail is a narrow singletrack that rises from the wet, wooded (willow and eucalyptus) creek bed to manzanita and sage. You need to be an ace of all terrains to handle the alternately sandy and shaley trail surface here.

At 2.3 miles East Boundary Trail intersects Manzanita. If you're pooped, you can go left back down to Hazard Canyon Road, but watch for railroad ties! To continue on Manzanita, go right. When you come to the next trail junction at 2.8 miles, stay on Manzanita, once again to your right.

In the next winding mile you fishtail and bounce through more sand and shale. At 3.8 miles Manzanita Trail ends at Bloody Nose Trail. Descend the trail to the left into the creek bottom. (Bloody Nose Trail also goes to the right, but the right fork is closed to bikes.)

Things get a little wilder along here as Bloody Nose Trail falls into and rises out of two creek beds. The ups and downs are short but steep. Throw in some ragged, jagged shale as well as some railroad ties and you've got yourself a challenge. With these obstacles, it's not hard to imagine a mountain biker with a bloody nose!

Just under 5 miles you visit the creek bottom again. A short climb over more railroad ties and you're at a picnic spot surrounded by the ubiquitous eucalyptus trees. From here you have about 0.3 mile to trail's end at Camp Keep and Pecho Valley Road. A right turn on Pecho Valley Road will take you back to your car, 1.5 miles away.

Another option would be to turn around and repeat the loop in reverse, although climbing back up Bloody Nose Trail would definitely be a challenge.

Carrizo Plain

The Carrizo Plain is an arid flat valley that lies in the remote southeast corner of San Luis Obispo County, midway between Bakersfield and Santa Maria. The valley floor is at an elevation of 2,000 feet and is bordered on the east by the 3,000 to 4,000 foot Temblor Range, so named because of the quakes from the San Andreas Fault that rip across the land on the east side of the valley at the base of the range. The Caliente Range (Caliente Peak—5,104 feet) is on the west side of the valley and angles into the Temblor Range at the valley's southeast end. You enter the narrow part of the valley here by climbing over this 2,800-foot hilly area.

The 85 miles of dirt roads and 15 miles of paved roads in the Carrizo Plain Natural Area are perfect for mountain bicycles. Much of the terrain is flat or rolling with short gentle climbs—no all-day climbs up some steep mountain at 3 miles per hour. Good roads and almost no traffic or buildings make it ideal for the bicycle traveler.

There are many interesting things to see in this land that at first glance appears empty. Great numbers of hawks, eagles, owls and meadow songbirds spend the winter on the plains while thousands of lesser sandhill cranes and migratory waterfowl are at Soda Lake (usually dry). Spring wildflower displays are often spectacular. The San Andreas Fault, the fault responsible for many of California's earthquakes, is visible along the east side where stream channels are offset hundreds of yards to the north. Tule elk and pronghorn antelope can sometimes be seen on the west side. Also on the west side at Painted Rock are Native American pictographs.

A yearly average of 8 to 10 inches of rainfall drains from these mountains out onto the valley floor and some makes its way to Soda Lake. The Carrizo Plain is a large depressed area with no outlet, so the water that drains into Soda Lake must leave by evaporation. The salts remain and the usually dry surface is a brilliant white. In winter this 3,000-acre lake bed receives enough water to attract large numbers of migratory birds.

Ongoing conversion of natural wildland in nearby San Joaquin Valley to farming and urban use is eliminating native plants and animals there. The Bureau of Land Management (BLM), which owns local mountain ranges and much of the Carrizo Plain, has since 1985 been working with wildlife and conservation agencies to create the Carrizo Natural Heritage Reserve. In cooperation with the Nature Conservancy, the BLM has been acquiring private land in the valley in order to provide coordinated management in the reserve for endangered plants and animals, and the protection of Native American rock art. The goal of public ownership in the reserve has almost been completed.

Specific management plans are still being developed, but the Nature

Conservancy has completed a visitor center that opens in the fall of 1993. Already open is a parking area and a three-quarter-mile walking trail to Painted Rock, the most elaborate Native American rock art site in North America. The BLM has reintroduced tule elk and up to 300 pronghorn antelope, which were native here only 75 years ago. Present plans are to protect and enhance the habitat for endangered species while encouraging public outdoor recreation. Mountain bicycling is favored due to low impact. These roads are open to motor vehicles, but the area is so remote and has so few residents that there is very little traffic. It's not unusual to meet only 3 or 4 cars and trucks in a day's ride.

The best time to ride here is in the spring when wildflowers are in bloom and the weather is moderate. Wildflower displays are variable and short lived so you could miss it and believe it's no big deal. However, if you keep trying there will be a day so brilliant you better have a camera to record it. Summer is just too hot unless you like full moon night rides. Autumn rides are okay but winter is variable and chancy. Because in many places the road is the lowest land, rain makes the roads impassable by creating ponds there. The soil then dries on top, and although it may look firm, it is treacherous. I have seen a car go down to the axles within 10 feet of firm ground.

Caution: This is a very remote area with little traffic. The weather can change fast in the winter, and rain could leave you stranded in mud. The summers are very hot and on these treeless plains there is almost no shade. There are no stores, no gas stations and no water available in the reserve. Bring all the water you need; it is far better to overestimate your needs than to underestimate them. Nearest Services are at the BLM Fire Station, Washburn Road; in an emergency, call 911 or 805-861-4119; for business, call 805-861-4110 or 861-4236. Other services are found in Maricopa or Taft.

85 Carrizo Plain Loop

Distance: 72.6 miles
Difficulty: Moderate in good weather; long distance, but good roads and no long, steep hills; nontechnical
Elevation: 3,000' to 1,917', 1,083' difference
Ride Type: Two-day ride on dirt roads and pavement
Season: Spring and fall best

The Carrizo Plain is a long narrow valley with Soda Lake Road running the length of it. To the east is the Elkhorn Plain at the base of the Temblor Range, separated from the Carrizo Plain by the low Panorama Hills and farther south by the Elkhorn Hills. The Elkhorn Road runs the length of this very narrow and parallel plain. Elkhorn Plain is higher than the Carrizo Plain and from several places along the road you can see out across the Carrizo Plain, especially on the northern half. These roads are not connected by cross roads except near each end, making for a long ride.

With a start/finish at Reyes Station the whole loop is 72.6 miles.

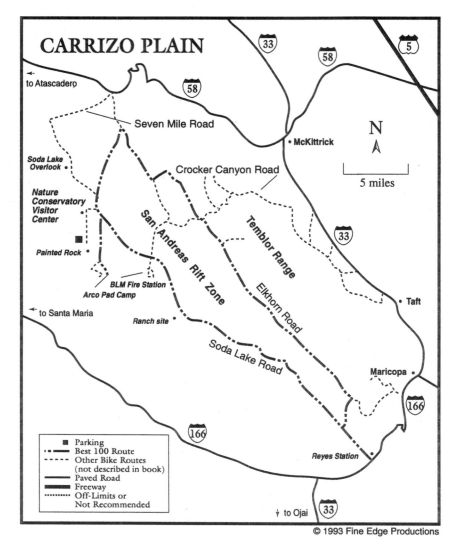

© 1993 Fine Edge Productions

If you ride the 5 miles up to the primitive camping area at the Selby-Arco pad and back to Soda Lake Road you have a total of 82.6 miles. Carrying all your camping gear and the necessary 3 or 4 gallons of water is more than most people are willing to do.

An alternative is to leave the second day's water and camping equipment in a vehicle parked at the Painted Rock Visitor Center. Park the second vehicle at Reyes Station, ride northwest through the Elkhorn Plain, south across the Carrizo Plain on Simmler Road to Soda Lake Road and the Visitor Center. First day mileage would be 42.6. Drive 5.8 miles to the camping area and the next morning drive back to the

Visitor Center. Park the car and ride 30 miles southeast on Soda Lake Road through the Carrizo Plain back to Reyes Station. For a one-day ride, just ride the part that interests you.

Getting There: From Highway 101, just north of Santa Maria, take State Highway 166 east 65 miles through the Cuyama Valley to the junction with State Highway 33. Continue east 4.7 miles to the signed Soda Lake Road on the left (north) at Reyes Station. This 76 gas station is the last one on your way to the reserve.

   . From Interstate 5 south of Bakersfield, take State Highway 166 24 miles west to Maricopa and then 9.3 miles southwest to Reyes Station and Soda Lake Road.

Park along Soda Lake Road near Reyes Station at Highway 166 or at Painted Rock Visitors Center on Soda Lake Road 30 miles northwest of Reyes Station. When you park at these places check with someone there to make sure your car is not in the way and let them know where you are going and when you will return. A good time to bring up parking arrangements is while making a purchase of gas or souvenirs, or making a donation. It's a small price to pay to have someone watching out for you.

Day 1—Reyes Station to Painted Rock Visitor Center

This is a 42.6-mile ride, based on parking a camping vehicle at the Visitor Center. Start from Reyes Station and ride northwest on paved Soda Lake Road passing treeless, grass covered, rolling hills. You descend and pass a salt rimmed sag pond formed where the land sinks into the San Andreas Fault. The road is built right next to the fault as you can see while you climb up from the sag pond, cross the county line and drop down to another sag pond. On the north end of this pond, at 3.5 miles, you turn right (east) onto the signed Elkhorn Road.

This graded dirt road climbs very steeply in places but only gains 250 feet in 1.1 miles to the high point of the ride at 3,000 feet. The descent east starts out steep but moderates when the road switchbacks twice and levels out where you circle around the south side of a large corral at 5.9 miles from Reyes Station. There is a good view northwest along this part of the Elkhorn Plain while you ride northeast 0.8 mile to the junction with Elkhorn Grade Road. Turn left.

The elevation at the junction is 2,406 feet. In the next 24 miles you go from 2,300 feet to 2,452 feet, and at the end of the plain you drop back to 2,354 feet. The scene is not a long, seemingly endless plain, but one that is broken up by low hills and washes that cross at right angles, breaking the ride into interesting segments. In each section the terrain changes slightly as do the plants. You pass many fences, cattle guards, water tanks and corrals, and after a while you may notice a pattern as about one set of each occurs every mile. There are many side tracks remaining from ranching operations, but you should keep to the main road that heads mostly northeast.

At 25.6 miles from Reyes Station you come to the signed Crocker Grade Road on the right that climbs 761 feet in 1.9 miles to Crocker Summit at 3,213 feet. Keep to the left and continue on Elkhorn Road across a deep gulch. On the other side is another junction. The road to the left (west) follows the water course you just crossed through the Panorama Hills down to the Carrizo

Plain. There it joins with the San Diego Creek Road, which heads straight south to Soda Lake Road just opposite Washburn Road.

Take Elkhorn Road on the right for another 5.1 miles, crossing more gulches and climbing over low hills before coming to the end of the Elkhorn Plain. Here at 31 miles from Reyes Station and at an elevation of 2,354 feet, you turn west and descend a narrow canyon to Carrizo Plain. At 32 miles the road turns north, where a lesser traveled road joins in from the south. You climb gradually, crossing several washes where trash has been strewn across the plain by flash floods, probably from a local dump. Go 0.4 mile past the power lines to the junction with Simmler Road at 36 miles. Highway 58 is 3 miles ahead to the north.

Turn sharp left and descend on Simmler Road back to the south, crossing under the power lines again. Simmler Road is less traveled and has some closed gates that you must re-close behind you. This road crosses the plain on a ridge that separates Soda Lake on the north from some smaller lakes to the south. The top of this ridge is fairly flat, but the sides have steep slopes down to the lakes on both side. This is a surprise since from a distance the area around the lake appears to be almost flat.

After 5.8 miles you come down off the ridge and Simmler Road ends at paved Soda Lake Road, 41.8 miles and at an elevation of 1,917 feet. Go south on Soda Lake Road 0.8 mile to the dirt road on the right; this leads to the Nature Conservancy's Painted Rock Visitor Center.

To get to the Selby Camping area, go southeast on Soda Lake Road, 0.7 mile from the Painted Rock Visitor Center drive. Take the dirt road

right (south) 4 miles to a fork and take the left fork 1 mile to the Arco oil exploration pad where you may camp.

Day 2—Painted Rock Visitor Center to Reyes Station

At 30 miles, this segment has shorter mileage. About a third of it is paved, too, making this day an easier ride except for the net elevation gain of 917 feet. About 300 feet of downhill that you have to make up again gives a total climb of around 1,200 feet. Almost all of it is gradual and not very difficult. The Carrizo Plain is much wider and flatter than the Elkhorn Plain.

Heading south on Soda Lake Road, at 5.8 miles from Painted Rock Road you cross a cattle guard at the intersection of Soda Lake Road and San Diego Creek Road on the north and Washburn Road to the south. The BLM fire station is 2.5 miles south on Washburn Road. The KCL ranch site, 5 miles farther southeast on Soda Lake Road, was to be a developed campground until it was found to be a significant archeological site.

The road stays on the west side of the plain where most of the farming and ranching activities took place. Over time I expect almost all of the buildings, water tanks and fences will be removed to restore the area to pre-settlement conditions.

After about 20 miles on the west side the road crosses the plain and starts climbing on the east side next to the Elkhorn hills. When you come to the paved part of the road there is one more short steep uphill and then a long steep downhill to where Elkhorn Road forks east. You pass the sag ponds and the county line, and climb the last hill to Reyes Station.

CHAPTER 11

Sierra Nevada & Inyo/White Mountains

by Don and Réanne Douglass

Side by side in Eastern California lie a desert valley of long summers and snow-capped mountains of long winters. Just east of the Sierra Nevada's bold alpine crest rises another mighty range almost as high, the Inyo-White Mountains. The Sierra is pale gray, its slopes angular, its peaks splintered. The Inyos are tawny, their slopes and crest rounded. The highest peaks of both, Mount Whitney and White Mountain Peak, stand well over fourteen thousand feet. Between these bulky ranges, only twenty miles separating their crests, lies a long narrow trough, Owens Valley. Running its length is the Owens River, fed by short streams which rise from Sierra glaciers and tumble down deep-slashed canyons.

Here is what Mary Austin called the Land of Little Rain. Pacific clouds billowing over the Sierra crest have already dropped most of their moisture on the Coast Ranges and the Sierra's west slope, nourishing dense forests of tall redwoods and yellow pine. East of the Sierra, in its rain shadow, little forest green softens the mountains' stark outlines. What trees there are—the twisted wind-stunted whitebark and bristlecone, widely spaced lodgepole and fir—only accentuate the land's severity. The grotesque Joshua, the sparse pinyon forests speckling the higher Inyo slopes emphasize its dryness. No carpet of grass cuts the sun's glare. All is grayed— tumbleweeds bleached straw color, gray-blue haze, dead-gray brush, pale gray boulders, gray-green pinyon, tan sand. In the arid climate, earth scars heal slowly. Hills ripped open by gold seekers, gullies torn by cloudbursts look as fresh and raw as they did a hundred years ago. The work of the land-shaping forces—earthquakes, volcanoes, water, ice—is on dramatic display. The intense desert sun is brutally honest, revealing austerity as well as majesty.

Excerpted from *Deepest Valley,* by Genny Smith

Just a three-hour drive from the Los Angeles Basin, Owens Valley, in the Southern Sierra, is a sparsely populated region with millions of acres of scenic public land offering endless possibilities for exploration by mountain bike.

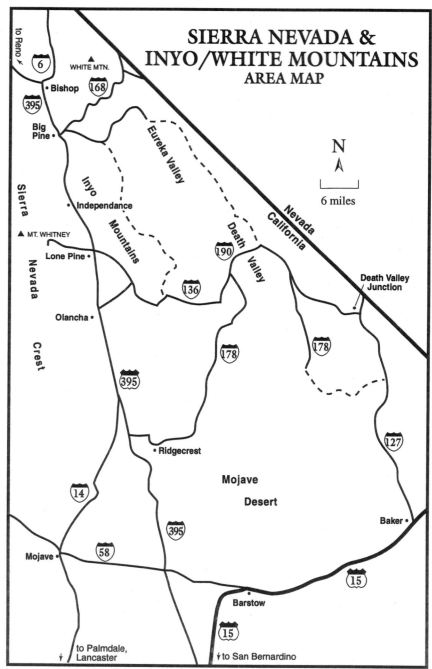

SIERRA NEVADA &
INYO/WHITE MOUNTAINS
AREA MAP

to Reno

6

WHITE MTN.

Bishop   168

395

Big
Pine

Eureka Valley

Inyo

Independance

Sierra

Mountains

MT. WHITNEY

Lone Pine

Nevada

Death

190

Valley

Nevada
California

N

6 miles

Death Valley
Junction

136

Olancha

178

178

Crest

395

127

Ridgecrest

Mojave

Desert

14

395

Baker

Mojave   58

15

Barstow

15

to Palmdale,
Lancaster

to San Bernardino

© 1993 Fine Edge Productions

The rides in this chapter have been chosen to introduce you to the Upper Mojave Desert, the southern Sierra Nevada and the Inyo and White Mountains, the regions that surround dramatic Owens Valley. The routes listed provide striking contrasts, sweeping panoramas, clean air and blue skies. If all this sounds good to you, we invite you to come and explore this vast exciting land!

The best source of topo maps in the area is Wilson's Eastside Sports (open seven days a week), 206 N. Main Street, Bishop, 619-873-7520.

Agencies:

Mt. Whitney Ranger District, Lone Pine, 619-876-5542

InterAgency Visitor Center, Lone Pine, 619-876-4252

White Mountain Ranger District, Bishop, 619-873-2500

Bureau of Land Management, Bishop, 619-872-4881

86 *Upper Mojave Desert:* Cactus Flat

Distance: 11 miles one way to the Jack Henry Mine, 15 miles to McCloud Flat
Difficulty: Easy to moderate
Elevation: Owens Valley 3,700'; Jack Henry Mine 4,800'; McCloud Flat 5,200'
Ride Type: Out and back on dirt roads with possible loops, or drive to mine site, camp and do numerous loops
Season: Late autumn, winter and early spring. In the spring, you may see wonderful displays of wildflowers, including cactus and Joshua trees.
Topo Map: Haiwee Reservoir

The dominating sight on Highway 395 as you approach Owens Valley from the south is Red Hill, a deep red cinder cone directly to the east of the highway. Although Red Hill is perhaps the most striking example of volcanic activity in this area, other cones, domes and lava flows abound here.

In spring the Upper Mojave Desert provides an outstanding display of wildflowers—brilliant yellow that carpets the valley for miles among sagebrush, creosote bushes and striking Joshua trees. Old mining roads crisscross Cactus Flat and McCloud Flat, providing access to a wonderful high desert environment. A moun-

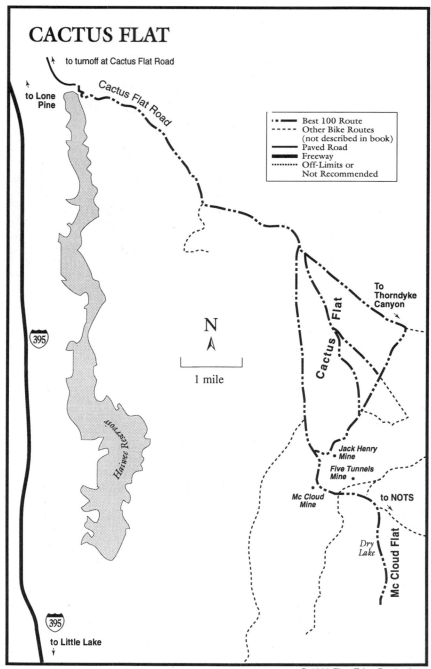

CACTUS FLAT

to turnoff at Cactus Flat Road

Cactus Flat Road

to Lone Pine

Best 100 Route
Other Bike Routes
(not described in book)
Paved Road
Freeway
Off-Limits or
Not Recommended

To Thorndyke Canyon

Cactus Flat

N

1 mile

Haiwee Reservoir

395

Jack Henry Mine

Five Tunnels Mine

Mc Cloud Mine

to NOTS

Dry Lake

Mc Cloud Flat

395

to Little Lake

© 1993 Fine Edge Productions

tain bike is the perfect way to appreciate the clean air, quietness and stark beauty of these largely unspoiled desert basins. Since they are remote, bring all the water you need for your trip. Nearest services are located at Coso Junction (gas, groceries and water) and Olancha (gas, groceries and cafe).

Getting There: Turn east off Highway 395 onto Cactus Flat Road (also known as Butterworth Ranch Road), located 21 miles south of Lone Pine, 3 miles south of Olancha, and about 17 miles north of Red Hill. Park well off the road. Set your odometer to 0.0 mile at the Olancha Highway Maintenance Yard.

As you continue east, the pavement ends at 1.4 miles, and at 2.6 miles you pass Haiwee Reservoir and start up a short steep hill to the junction of four corners. Continue straight, heading uphill southeast. At mile 6.6 you reach the top of a hill where you have a view of Cactus Flat. At 7.0 miles, a trail leads east to Thorndike Canyon, part of a loop trip that starts from Jack Henry Mine (this canyon is worth exploring if you want to do a side trip.) Continue due south on the main route among Joshua trees and cholla cactus.

Roads leading west go to a mine on the ridge at 9.0 miles, and a mile later you pass a side road that heads 3.5 miles up a box canyon to the southwest. At 10.3 miles, take the fork that goes due east to Jack Henry Mine. If you want to explore by bicycle or on foot, this spot makes a good primitive base camp. Notice the foundation and fireplace of an old mining cabin.

The main road to McCloud Flat continues southeast, but it is washed out at 10.6 miles, preventing

4WD passage. You have an excellent view of the high desert and Cactus Flat at this point, and just a half-mile walk or bike ride up the canyon takes you to McCloud Mine, where a rock cabin still stands. Be cautious around the shafts.

From the pass near McCloud Mine, you descend south toward McCloud Flat, and you can take a mining road due south into the hills or head northeast to the Five Tunnel Mine and then easterly up a beautiful draw. The main road itself continues east and down to a dry lake bed.

You can continue either due south to a large area of boulders or southeast through a draw to the boundary of the Naval Ordinance Training Stations (NOTS), where you must turn around since entry is prohibited. To return to your starting point, reverse your route.

Entirely surrounded by desert mountains, McCloud Flat is one of the most scenic high deserts in the region and is worth hours of exploration. In the past, extensive mining activity was carried out at the north end, but the setting now provides unusual solitude and serenity.

From the remains of the Jack Henry Mine cabin, you can make a loop trip leading directly northeast toward Thorndike Canyon. Choose any of three jeep trails that lead downhill to the northwest through Joshua trees and rejoin the main road at the 7.0 mile point described above.

Caution: Watch your step in this region and avoid all holes, caves, mines and structures.

Inyo Mountains

The Inyo Mountains form the southeastern boundary of Owens Valley and are the first of a series of north/south ridges that march across the Great Basin to the east. Although without water, the Inyos offer a cool alternative to the valley below. This was once a popular mining area, and history buffs will find many interesting sites to explore. Spectacular views of the Sierra Nevada to the west and Saline Valley to the east, along with the solitude of these mountains, make them one of the best kept secrets in the region.

87 Cerro Gordo/Swansea Loop (with Saline Valley Salt Tram)

Distance: 15 miles out and back to Cerro Gordo; 29.6 miles out and back to the Salt Tram; 33.4 miles as a loop
Difficulty: Strenuous on the uphill and technical because of steep, loose, rocky downhill
Elevation: Owens Valley 3,600' to Cerro Gordo 8,400'; 10,100' at Burgess Mine road
Ride Type: Out and back day trip; overnight loop on dirt roads
Season: All seasons depending upon weather; avoid unsettled weather
Topo Maps: Keeler; New York Butte (see also BLM Eureka/Saline Guide #1)

For an excellent introduction to the Inyo Mountains that includes interesting historical sites, outstanding views of Owens Dry Lake and the Southern Sierra (including Mt. Whitney), and some character-building climbs, give this loop a go. If you don't feel up to the entire 36-mile loop, you can do an out-and-back day trip of just over 26 miles from the floor of Owens Valley (3,600 feet) to Cerro Gordo (8,400 feet). Or you can drive to Cerro Gordo, leave a car, and bicycle out and back to the Saline Valley Salt Tram for a total of 15 miles. If you opt for the entire loop, which takes you 13 miles on a primitive wagon road along the spine of the Inyos (easier pedaling than the climb to Cerro Gordo), be prepared for a serious, waterless overnight expedition.

If you choose the day trip, be sure to turn around and start back early while you have sufficient strength and supplies. Since the area is subject to extremes in wind and temperature, you should be prepared for any kind of weather. (The authors experienced 60 mph sub-freezing winds at the top of Pleasant Peak one Memorial Day Weekend!)

In any case, plan to spend some time poking around Cerro Gordo—a bustling town in the 1870s whose mines yielded over 13 million dollars in silver bullion over a few short years. Visit the small museum and read about the town's history.

For the past several decades Cerro Gordo has been privately owned. Currently it is under lease to Phelps-Dodge for mining exploration. Special group tours of the old town may be arranged by telephoning the owner, Jodi Stewart, at 619-876-4154. If you drive to this point, check with the caretaker for instructions on where to park your vehicle .

Note: As we go to print, this area is under consideration for Wilderness classification. Please check with the BLM or Eastern Sierra InterAgency Visitor Center for current information before you head out on your excursion.

Getting There: From the junction of Highways 395 and 136 south of Lone Pine, head east on 136 along the north side of dry Owens Lake. Approximately 9 miles from the junction, look to the north of the highway, where you can see the remnants of the old Saline Valley Salt Tram. Completed in 1913, this electric marvel lifted salt from the east side of the Inyos at 1,059 feet in Saline Valley to the crest at 8,800 feet, then down again to Owens Valley, for a total of 14 miles and a 14,000-foot elevation gain and loss!

Continue another 2 miles on Highway 136 (about 11 miles from the junction of 395 and 136) for the turnoff to Cerro Gordo. Turn left on the dirt road and park your car to the side of the road.

The route up to Cerro Gordo from Highway 136 follows the Yellow Grade— a long hard grunt of 7.5 miles. Stay with it and eventually you'll make it to Cerro Gordo.

If you turn around at there, be aware that the ride downhill is steep. Guard against excessive speed and watch out for heavy trucks. Make frequent stops to enjoy the view and rest your brake hands.

If you are continuing the loop rather than returning down the Yellow Grade, or if you drove to Cerro Gordo and just want to ride the ridge to the Salt Tram, the next section takes you north along the west side of

the Inyo crest to the tram. From Cerro Gordo, head uphill (east) 200 yards and take a left on the dirt road. (Do not take the road that heads toward a radio tower.) Set your bike odometer to 0.0 mile as you pass the sign, *Private Property No Trespassing.* Fifty yards beyond that point, take the fainter dirt road to the west, which contours 0.2 mile to a wire rope gate and a worn BLM sign—*Swansea/ Cerro Gordo Road, Caution Dangerous Grades, 4WD only, do not disturb mining facilities, Salt Tram or cut any trees.* Unsnap the carabiner to let yourself through the gate, being sure to close it again.

From this point look back for a good view of the Cerro Gordo town site and mining operations. Continue contouring westerly around the hill for 0.5 mile, where you can see Owens Dry Lake and the southern part of Owens Valley. The colors of the dry lake, nearly a vertical mile below, change as salt concentrations vary; you may see anything from brilliant reds and purples to light blue and dazzling white. Continue to contour horizontally to the low saddle at 1.4 miles, riding cautiously across the shale and paying attention to the steep drop-off.

From the saddle, the main route goes steeply downhill, losing 500 feet or more in elevation before climbing steeply up a wash to another low saddle. The New York quadrangle map does not show the main route, but it does show a trail that contours horizontally northward from this saddle. The doubletrack that heads up to the right leads to the two metal mining buildings visible about 2 miles away and peters out at that point. (You can contour north on the old water line route, but the road is not in good condition.)

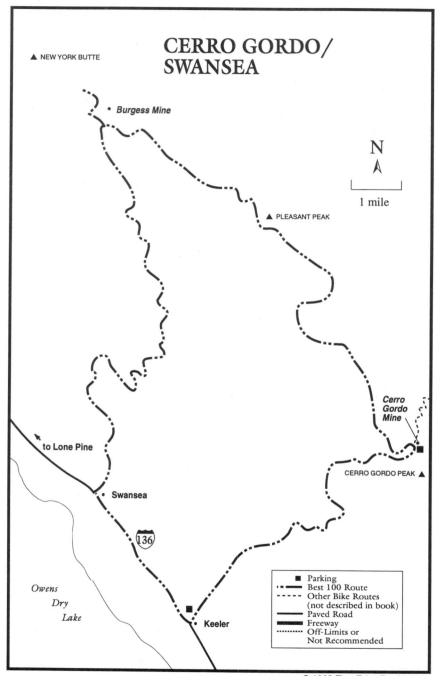

CERRO GORDO/ SWANSEA

▲ NEW YORK BUTTE

• Burgess Mine

N

1 mile

▲ PLEASANT PEAK

Cerro
Gordo
Mine

to Lone Pine

CERRO GORDO PEAK ▲

Swansea

136

Owens
Dry
Lake

Keeler

■   Parking
Best 100 Route
Other Bike Routes
(not described in book)
Paved Road
Freeway
Off-Limits or
Not Recommended

© 1993 Fine Edge Productions

At 2.3 miles you reach the bottom of the canyon, make a sharp right turn and start up a steep draw. (Push or carry your bike!) At 3.9 miles you come to a saddle where the road levels out and the route become rideable again. Just below here, the old and unused quadrangle contour trail joins this more traveled route. At 4.0 miles tracks to the left lead a quarter mile to a nice primitive campsite and fire ring in the pinyon trees. At 4.5 miles you cross to the east side of the ridge and can look directly down on Saline Dry Lake, 7,000 feet below you! From the west side of the ridge at 5.1 miles you have a good view of the ancient shoreline of Owens Dry Lake where Owens River flows into it.

You reach Pleasant Peak, 9,400 feet, at 5.5 miles. It's grassy and treeless, with a doubletrack that leads 200 yards to the summit. If the weather is agreeable, it's a good place for a picnic—the view in all directions is spectacular. From here the road contours downward to a knife-edge ridge at 7.0 miles with views of the dry lakes on both your right and left. You may feel like you're on a magic carpet with no one else in the world around you. From here, the route drops slowly down to the Salt Tram at 7.3 miles, where a low saddle affords another view of Saline Dry Lake and Owens Dry Lake.

This was the high point for the Salt Tram—8,800 feet—and the major transfer station between the ride up one side and down the other. The open wooden structure, 20 by 180 feet, is quite a work of art. Etched into the cement base near the main flywheel is the date September 2, 1912. The two load cables on which ore buckets ran are still in place, but the rougher pulling cables are strewn about. Examine the load cables that were made of square wire wound in such a way as to provide a smooth surface. Covered ore buckets rolled on two wheels on the load cables and were clamped onto the pulling cables with a locking device.

If mechanical things interest you, the transfer mechanisms—large flywheels, wooden-shoed brakes, seven-foot steel disc brakes, etc., should keep you poking around for a while. Truly a world-class project when it began rolling in 1915, it ran intermittently until the 1930s, when other sources of salt made operation unfeasible. Hundreds of supporting towers built on both sides of the ridge kept the buckets on course. These towers were constructed on very difficult terrain, and it's worth a hike to see the old buckets and equipment still in place. Please use extreme caution around this decaying equipment and do not disturb the tram in any way. Check out the old bunkhouse, made in tongue and groove fashion inside and out, located 50 yards to the southeast.

At this point—7.3 miles—if you're pooped you can turn around and head back to Cerro Gordo for a total of 14.6 miles.

If you're doing the full loop as an overnighter you might consider making primitive camp a tenth of a mile farther to the northwest. From there, it's only a short walk to view several towers and a transfer station.

Continuing northwest along the ridge as you head for Swansea, the trail contours downward to a small saddle at 7.9 miles. There's a junction at the foot of a peak at 9.8 miles. Follow the main route that veers right. (The left route goes over the peak.) At 10.1 miles, a road to the right goes out a mile to the head of Daisy Canyon. It's worth riding the extra mile to look down into the canyon through which the salt tram hauled salt up from Saline Valley. You'll appreciate the extraordinary man-made design when you view the sheerness of the canyon. (If you take this side trip, add the mileage on your odometer to those listed below.)

At 10.7 miles you are on a ridge again with excellent views. At 11.3 miles you come to a low spot on the saddle where there's a possible campsite. This is the 9,200-foot contour, and the road to Swansea starts down the ridge just to the south, heading in a southeasterly direction. If you want additional mileage and a side trip to Burgess Mine, take the road that heads northeast and climbs 700 feet in the next mile to the mine at 12.3 miles. The road dead-ends in 0.8 mile at 10,100 feet on the south side of New York Butte (10,688 feet). There are excellent campsites in this area and on a bluff a quarter mile to the west.

Returning to the Swansea Road at the 9,200-foot contour, reset your odometer to 0.0 miles. Caution: While the route below this point is nearly all downhill, it is steep, rocky and remote—considerably more difficult than the ridge route from Cerro Gordo. If you question your downhill skills, turn around at this point and retrace your route along the ridge and the Yellow Grade Road (not quite as steep) to the valley floor.

Swansea is 7 airline miles directly south and more than a mile below you. The 12.8 miles the authors recorded on their odometers seemed much too short for such an interesting descent.

To proceed down to Swansea, leave the Inyo Ridge and head south down the small ridge immediately to the west. Just 0.8 mile down you come to the first of several campsites among the pinyons. At 2.0 miles the road gets steep and rocky. At 2.8 miles the roadbed is washed out—detour. You drop into a creek bed at 3.9 miles and at 4.4 miles cross under the tramway. (Notice the six-story tram towers to the east at 5.6 miles.) You are now back in a wash with six-foot-high walls of alluvium.

At 6.8 miles you leave the wash, veer right and climb onto a better roadbed. You can't miss a big tram tower to the right at 7.3 miles. At the 6,600-foot contour (7.7 miles) there are faint tracks going a mile up to the right to a transfer station. (You can see Swansea from this station.) Just under 9 miles you drop down a very steep rocky canyon, then almost immediately go up a short, steep canyon. A half mile farther you cross under the tramway. About a third of a mile after that, the route follows a series of dry waterfalls. At 10.4 miles you pass under the tramway again as the canyon opens up.

Just when you thought you would never make it, there's Swansea and Highway 136 at mile 12.8! What is left of the foundation of the valley station can be found one mile north, just to the east of Highway 136. The ghost town of Keeler is 1 mile south on Highway 136.

88 Mazourka Canyon/ Santa Rita Flat

Distance: 18 miles one way, plus side trips
Difficulty: Moderate to strenuous; steep uphill, fast downhill
Elevation: 3,800' to 9,000'
Ride Type: Out and back on graded dirt roads and jeep trails
Season: Mazourka Canyon, all year, lower elevations; Badger Flat, summer, and early autumn; Santa Rita Flat, spring, summer, autumn; Snow Cap's Mine Road, autumn, winter and spring.
Topo Map: Independence

Rather than having a west to east orientation, Mazourka Canyon parallels the Inyo Crest in a north-south direction. Like much of the Inyos, the canyon is geologically composed of sedimentary deposits remaining from an ancient ocean. These have been folded and broken, and in many cases they stand on edge.

This area east of Independence was the first mining district established in Owens Valley, and during the early 1860s it supported two mining camps of more than 3,000 people. Gold, silver, copper, lead, zinc and talc were mined, but since production was limited, the mining towns soon disappeared.

Note: There are many mining claims in the vicinity; please respect all signs, gates and private property.

Getting There: Mazourka Canyon Road is located 0.4 mile south of Inyo County Courthouse in Independence. Park your car off the road.

Set your bicycle odometer to 0.0 mile and head due east. Just beyond the Los Angeles Aqueduct at 1.9 miles, the road drops down a 15-foot fault scarp, formed during the 1872 earthquake. You cross the Owens River at 3.8 miles, and at 4.4 miles the pavement becomes gravel.

Cross the old Carson & Colorado right-of-way where Kearsarge Station once stood. The route climbs an alluvial fan eastward, then heads north on a well-graded gravel road.

If you like to poke around mines, this area has plenty to keep you exploring for a season. Please remember to use caution at all times around any mine site.

At 5.8 miles Snow Cap's Mine Road to the left travels in a northerly direction for about 7 miles. Copper Queen Mine is located to the west at 7.2 miles. Lead Gulch road (with gate) heads east at 8.3 miles and winds for several miles to the Betty Jumbo Mine at the 7,500-foot level. We recommend exploring this area in cooler weather. Just short of 9 miles you enter Inyo National Forest.

At 9.3 miles you pass Squares Tunnel and two cabins east of the road. Paiute Monument (also called Winnedumah), an 8,369-foot granite monolith that can be seen clearly on the Inyo Crest from the valley floor, is 3 miles due east from here on the Inyo Ridge. You can read the legend of Winnedumah on a plaque in the lobby of the Winnedumah Inn in Independence.

At 11.7 miles you pass private property (several houses, trees, mining equipment, wrecked cars and a

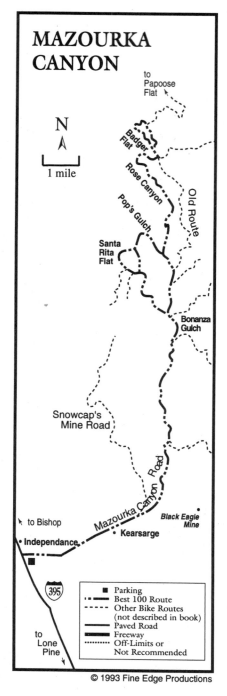

MAZOURKA CANYON

N

1 mile

to
Papoose
Flat

Badger
Flat

Rose Canyon

Pop's Gulch

Old Route

Santa
Rita
Flat

Bonanza
Gulch

Snowcap's
Mine Road

Mazourka Canyon Road

to Bishop

Black Eagle
Mine

Independence

Kearsarge

395

to
Lone
Pine

■   Parking
·-·-· Best 100 Route
------ Other Bike Routes
         (not described in book)
——— Paved Road
━━━ Freeway
········ Off-Limits or
         Not Recommended

© 1993 Fine Edge Productions

water tank on the hill). *Do not enter the property.* There is a cattle guard at 12.1 miles and just 0.2 mile later a sign: *Santa Rita Flat to the left. Badger Flat straight ahead.* At mile 12.8 Sunday Canyon enters from the west. At mile 13.6 a seldom-used jeep road leads up the narrow Mazourka Canyon to the right. Stay left on the main road, which enters Rose Canyon. From Pop's Gulch at 14.3 miles a good gravel road leads west to Santa Rita Flat. Beyond the 17-mile point, the road has northern exposure and is often under snow in winter or spring.

You come to Badger Flat, 18 miles, and are now in the heart of the Inyo Range where mining and hunting trails lead in all directions. The road west climbs to a ridge where you have an excellent view of the Sierra. Tamarack Canyon trail leads up the narrow opening 3 miles east to the north side of a prominent unnamed peak, elevation 10,724 feet. Proceed northwesterly from the eastern side of Badger Flats 1.5 miles to the Blue Bell Mine complex, where a trail leads first east, over a low saddle at the 9,600 foot level, then northwest for 4 miles down a treeless valley toward Papoose Flat.

In Badger Flat, a large bowl-shaped area of low brush and grass surrounded by tree-covered ridges, you can find numerous primitive camping opportunities. Following a winter of sufficient rain, the air is perfumed by many wildflowers here, and in this quiet place the charm of the Inyos will certainly grow on you.

From this point, you can retrace your route to your vehicle or you can descend to the 12.3-mile point to do the 6-mile Santa Rita Flat loop ride described next. As you descend, guard against heat buildup on your brakes and rims. (The road from

Badger Flat to Owens Valley descends nearly 5,000 feet in one swoop!)

Santa Rita Flat Loop: An unusually stark, quiet area with outstanding views of the Sierra, Santa Rita Flat cannot be seen from Owens Valley and comes as a surprise to the visitor. Small cattle and mining trails here provide hours of enjoyable exploration. The roads in this area are normally firm, but conditions change quickly with snow or rain. There are no trees along this four-mile flat, but it's gorgeous high-desert country.

Reset your odometer to 0.0 as you turn west off the main Mazourka Canyon Road onto the Santa Rita Flat road (signed), 12.3 miles from Highway 395. Follow the canyon up a gravel road. In about a mile from the turnoff, Santa Rita Flat (6,800 feet elevation) opens up to full view.

At 1.8 miles there's a corral and loading chute to the northeast of the road. Within about 300 yards, a road heads westerly to Santa Rita Spring, when you can make a primitive campsite near a rock outcropping. From Santa Rita Spring take the road across the valley to the east, making a loop to the south, or ride north over the ridge to Pop's Gulch, dropping into Al Rose Canyon (the 13.3-mile point mentioned in the ride above). At Pop's Gulch there is an interesting labyrinth of shallow, unreinforced tunnels and open pits in the alluvium. Be extremely cautious when you approach any of these tunnels—they could easily collapse or become sinkholes without warning. What appears as a trail on the topo map in Pop's Gulch is actually a gravel road, giving good loop possibilities from Santa Rita Springs.

Return to the main road, then back down to the valley floor. You have a long, fast, bumpy, high adrenaline ride. Solo travel is not recommended.

89 Andrews Mountain Loop

Distance: 25 miles round trip
Difficulty: Strenuous, long and very remote, must be self-sufficient
Elevation: 6,600' to 9,126'
Ride Type: Loop on dirt roads
Season: Spring through fall, weather permitting; avoid unsettled weather
Topo Map: Waucoba Mountain

This is a great trip for strong riders who are self-reliant and want a real wild-west backcountry challenge. The terrain resembles the Cerro Gordo area (second ride in this chapter) but with more vegetation. Unless you're a highly experienced backcountry cyclist, we recommend this trip be done with a 4WD support vehicle that can be left at a base camp or used as a sag wagon. Because you need to carry a great deal of water, it's critical to have a support vehicle if you wish to do a two-day trip.

In Owens Valley, you can camp at Inyo County Triangle Campground, junction of Highways 168 and 395 (closed in winter). Facilities include water and toilets. Along the route described you can find primi-

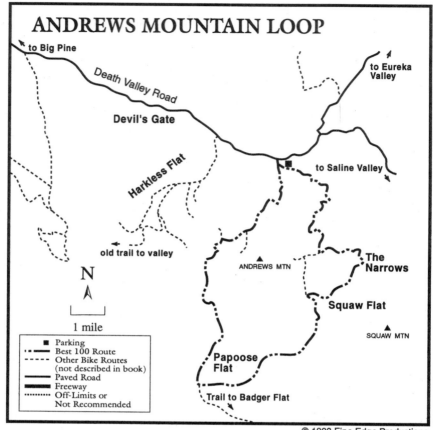

ANDREWS MOUNTAIN LOOP

to Big Pine

Death Valley Road

to Eureka Valley

Devil's Gate

Harkless Flat

to Saline Valley

old trail to valley

N

1 mile

ANDREWS MTN

The Narrows

Squaw Flat

SQUAW MTN

Papoose Flat

Trail to Badger Flat

- ■ Parking
- ▪-■- Best 100 Route
- --- Other Bike Routes (not described in book)
- ── Paved Road
- ▆▆ Freeway
- ⋯⋯ Off-Limits or Not Recommended

© 1993 Fine Edge Productions

tive campsites. Full services and accommodations are found in Big Pine.

Getting There: To begin the trip turn east off Highway 395 onto Highway 168 at the north end of Big Pine. Go 2.3 miles east to the Waucoba/Death Valley Road and turn right (south). The road is signed: *No accommodations or roadside service next 78 miles.* At 13.6 miles turn right (south) off Waucoba Road onto a dirt road (also shown as Hines Road on the topo map). You can leave your vehicle here, but be sure to park clear of the pavement or roadbed.

Set your odometer to 0.0 miles. The dirt road you take parallels the main road for several hundred yards before turning south. At 0.2 mile the road forks where a sign reads: *Papoose-Squaw Flat 4 x 4 advised.* Take the right (southerly) fork following a sand and gravel road. (Elevation at this point is about 7,000 feet.) You pass through a wide flat valley of sagebrush heading toward the treeline to the west of Andrews Mountain, the high peak directly ahead. At 1.5 miles the road makes a U-turn, dropping into a wash where pinyon and juniper trees begin to appear. Primitive campsites with trees are available at 2.5 miles. At 3.0 miles the canyon narrows, the shale road becomes deeply rutted and trees overhang the route. Ignore the road to the left at 3.2 miles. At approximately 8,000 feet mountain mahogany begins to appear.

At mile 4.1 you come to a draw and a fork in the road. Continue to the left, up the switchbacks. The summit, at 5.1 miles and 9,126 feet, has impressive panoramic views of the Inyo-White Mountain crest as well as the full Southern Sierra crest. Take a short walk along the crest to the northwest to observe the unusual vertical shale formations and to look directly across to Crater Mountain. The descent into Papoose Flat begins at 5.2 miles, passing through juniper and open sage. Take the left fork at 6.8 miles noticing the granite outcroppings covered with brightly colored lichen.

At 8.0 miles you cross a major drainage where the wash to the east flows into Squaw Flat. Climbing a shallow pass you come to a Y in the road at mile 9.0; take the left fork. (The right fork goes to Peak 9,093.) As you begin your steep descent, you have a good view of Papoose Flat and can see that, although the flat is open and covered with sagebrush, the ridges in all directions are covered with numerous small trees. The rocks along the fringe of the flat (at mile 10.3) offer good possibilities for base camp sites. If you do camp here, you need to obtain a campfire permit in advance. Please pack out all your trash and cover traces of your campsite. The area has remained primitive and clean because people who come here care deeply about it.

Just a short walk to the west gives you an outstanding view of Owens Valley and the Sierra Crest.

A word of warning: If you had any difficulty in getting to this point or if you're running low on water (two quarts or more for a day), return to the Death Valley Road by retracing your route; it's faster and far easier to return from this point.

The route to Squaw Flat becomes sandier and more difficult. There is no water available and the route is infrequently traveled.

To continue on the Andrews Mountain Loop, go 200 yards south to a major junction at mile 10.4 and take the east fork, which leads to Squaw Flat and the Andrews Mountain Loop. As you proceed east, you have an easy downhill ride initially. (Ignore a jeep road that comes in from the south at mile 11.5.) Continue down the middle of an easygoing wash, ignoring a jeep road from the south.

Use your imagination as you catch sight of a granite monolith to the left at mile 12.1. The wash widens at 12.7 miles, and you leave the granitic formations behind. Stay in the middle of the sandy wash, head toward Squaw Peak (10,358 feet) and contour across upper Squaw Flat. Waucoba Mountain (11,123 feet) comes into view on the ridge to the right of Squaw Peak. Continue following the wash down to mile 14.1, where it narrows before opening up again at the 8,000 foot contour.

After you cross a wash at 15.3 miles a major road joins from the south. Notice the route dead ahead that climbs steeply through a notch to the north, passing close to an unnamed red peak. This is a shortcut that avoids the narrows. At mile 16.4 you come to a three-way intersection. Ignore the left fork. Head straight to take the shortcut.

Take the right fork (east) if you want to continue the loop via Marble Canyon. The canyon narrows and you proceed east, where at mile 17.0 you drop into a sandy wash, due south of Peak 8,173. The road narrows slowly, and as the ramparts of Squaw Peak close in on you, there are interesting red lava flows along the way. You leave the wash temporarily at 17.8 miles and climb a short ridge on the east side. As the canyon walls get higher, the road gets bushier. At 18.6 miles you come to the narrows of Marble Canyon, where there are two old mining cabins. Leave your bike and proceed carefully on foot if you want to have a look into the narrows of Marble Canyon. The canyon descends steeply and is rarely visited, so keep this in mind and don't get carried away. Nobody would think to look for you in such a remote spot!

Continue up the canyon to the left (north) using the trail indicated on the topo map. Steep and rocky, the road bed itself is composed mostly of shale and gives poor traction. It is passable, regardless of what you are thinking now. (We call it Hell Canyon; you may call it what you wish.) Remember, we warned you when you were still fresh and had a chance to turn around!

With perseverance, you reach a small flat area on the north side of an unnamed peak at 20.5 miles. Turn northward, ignoring a set of weak tracks that lead west.

At mile 20.7 you intersect the main road that comes in from the southwest (the route of the shortcut). At 21.2 miles you gain the ridge

where you can find primitive campsites on the right. Ignore tracks heading left and right along the ridge. At this point, you can see White Mountain directly to the north, as well as the summit of the Death Valley Road below to the northeast. At 21.4 miles there are three tunnels to the left—use caution. At 22.7 miles the canyon narrows and becomes rockier. The trail splits at 23.0 miles and you can take either fork—both trails rejoin around the bend. Continue down a broad wash until you come back to the Papoose Flat sign (mile 24.8), the junction of the road where you began your route. Just beyond that, you return to the paved road to Big Pine.

White Mountains

On the rocky, windswept slopes of the White Mountains grow the oldest living trees in the world. Gnarled, twisted, and starkly beautiful, the bristlecone pines, with their stubby bottle-brush branches reaching for the sky, cling fiercely to the shallow and alkaline dolomite soil found on the higher slopes of the White Mountains. Bristlecones have adapted to this rude climate for over 4,000 years, growing often less than an inch in diameter during a century. Their exceptional age makes them of scientific value in studying climatic fluctuations that have occurred over the past 40 centuries. Plan to spend at least a full day visiting the Ancient Bristlecone Pine Forest, making the 4.5 mile Methuselah

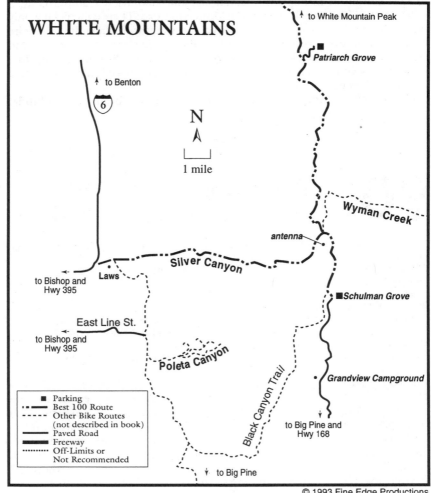

© 1993 Fine Edge Productions

Walk through Schulman Grove, then cycle 11 miles north to Patriarch Grove. Note: Since bicycles are not allowed on any of the trails within the Ancient Bristlecone Pine Area, you must stay on roads while cycling and leave your bicycles in the parking areas while walking on the footpaths.

If you are in good physical shape and want a climb with serious elevation gain, consider riding to the summit of White Mountain (14,242 feet), where you have unparalleled views of the entire 200-mile-long Sierra Nevada crest. The elevation at the peak, California's third highest mountain, is just 250 feet less than that of Mt. Whitney, visible to the southwest.

While camping is not allowed inside the Ancient Bristlecone Pine Forest, there are two campgrounds nearby: Cedar Flats is a group campground located on Highway 168 at the White Mountain Road turnoff (call the White Mountain Ranger Station in Bishop for reservations) and Grandview Campground, 5 miles north of Highway 168 on White Mountain Road. There is picnicking only at Schulman Grove and Patriarch Grove. No water is available in the White Mountains, so bring your own water in sufficient quantities for camping and cycling. Full services and accommodations are available in Bishop and Big Pine. If you're traveling by car be sure to fill your gas tank before you leave town; there are no services east of Big Pine.

The White Mountain crest is a place of unusual beauty and solitude. Please help keep it that way!

90 Schulman Grove/Patriarch Grove/White Mountain Peak

Distance: Schulman Grove to Patriarch Grove is 10.8 miles one way; Patriarch Grove to White Mountain Peak is 9 tough miles one way
Difficulty: Moderate to very strenuous due to high elevation; nontechnical
Elevation: Schulman Grove 10,100', Patriarch Grove 11,000', White Mountain Peak 14,242'
Ride Type: Out and back
Season: Late spring, summer and autumn; the Ancient Bristlecone Pine Forest is normally open between June 1 and October 30 (call ahead to White Mountain Ranger Station in Bishop, 619-873-2500, to verify that the road is open)
Topo Maps: White Mountain Peak, Blanco Mountain, Mount Barcroft, Bishop

Getting There: From Highway 395 at the north end of Big Pine, head east on Highway 168 for 12.9 miles and then turn north onto White Mountain Road at the sign marked *Bristlecone Pine Recreation Area,* just before Westgard Pass Summit. A mile beyond the USFS Entrance Station you pass the winter closure gate. As the road gains elevation it continues northward along the crest of the White Mountains, passing an ancient fossil site and Grandview Campground.

You can park at Schulman Grove and ride 12 miles to Patriarch Grove, or you can drive those 12 miles on well-graded dirt road.

At Schulman Grove, elevation 10,100 feet, the 3-mile Methuselah Loop Trail (hikers only) winds through the forest to the oldest known tree, Methuselah, dated at 4,600 years old and still going strong. A second and shorter trail leads to Pine Alpha, the first tree discovered to be over 4,000 years old. Information about the bristlecone pine is presented along the trail. *The Ancient Bristlecone Pine Forest is protected; please respect its fragile nature. Removal of living or dead plants is prohibited.*

As you head up to Patriarch Grove the terrain becomes more barren and rugged, the trees larger and more grotesque. Once at Patriarch, leave your bicycle in the parking area and proceed on foot to Patriarch Tree, located on a walking path just to the east. This tree has a circumference of 36 feet, 8 inches and is recognized as the world's largest bristlecone pine.

The University of California maintains Crooked Creek High Elevation Research Laboratory a few miles southeast of Patriarch, where experiments are performed on plants, animals and humans to determine the effects of high elevation. Because of the need for carefully controlled conditions, visitors are not permitted.

A 2-mile ride north beyond Patriarch Grove takes you close to the summit of Sheep Mountain at 12,497 feet. Here you can see White Mountain Peak (14,242 feet) in all its starkness and solitude. Even if you are acclimated to the high elevation you may find cycling slow-going. Don't be surprised if you feel like walking your bike much of the time. Breathe deeply and drink plenty of fluids, no matter whether you feel thirsty or not. The air is dry and thin and your system needs those fluids to keep going. Caution: This is certainly no place to be pushing hard if you have a weak ticker!

As the crest road continues to meander toward White Mountain, you drop down to a shallow saddle in the range and come to a locked gate (4.6 miles north of Patriarch Grove). Motor vehicles are not permitted beyond this point. While to date entry to this area has been open to foot traffic and mountain bikes, closure could occur at any time if adverse impact is found on the fragile slopes. Please respect the fragile environment and stay on the road at all times.

Before you begin the 7-mile climb to the summit of White Mountain Peak, remember that you must be totally self-sufficient here. While the jeep road passes the University of California's White Mountain Research Station a mile from the gate, no supplies are available there.

At the summit you can look across to the entire Sierra Nevada crest and see Bishop 10,000 feet directly below you, a fantastic panorama. If you study the construction of the research hut located on the summit you will notice its elaborate protection against lightning strikes. Does that tell you this is no place to be in a thunderstorm?

Retrace your route to Patriarch Grove/Schulman Grove once you've had your fill of this incredible view.

91 Silver Canyon— The Ultimate Kamikaze

Distance: 15 miles
Difficulty: Dangerous, strenuous, steep descent; don't attempt it solo or with children
Elevation: 10,800' to 4,000'
Ride Type: One way downhill on dirt road
Season: Summer
Topo Map: Bishop, Blanco Mtn.

Upper Silver Canyon is an exciting world-class downhill ride. Dangerous and extremely strenuous, this is not a family ride. Do not venture beyond the upper lip of Silver Canyon solo or without adequate experience and equipment—a strong, fully functional bicycle, hard helmet, gloves and coverings for your knees, elbows and shoulders.

Getting There: See the Schulman Grove ride above.

From Schulman Grove at the end of the paved road, ride north for 3 miles along the main dirt road, which climbs first to the west of the crest at 10,600 feet, then to the east before returning again to the west side at the Silver Canyon turnoff. Turn west on Silver Canyon Road, climbing several hundred yards over the Inyo crest, proper, passing a radio relay station located on Peak 10,842 to the north.

As you stand at the edge of Silver Canyon you have a wonderful view of the entire Sierra crest directly across Owens Valley and can see the paved road at Laws 7,000 feet below you. (Plan to visit Laws Railroad Museum at the bottom of Silver Canyon before you head in to Bishop.)

Silver Canyon Road is bladed and moderately well maintained since Southern California Edison uses it to service power lines that cross the White Mountains.

Danger: The Silver Canyon descent follows an extremely steep downhill grade that drops 3,000 feet in 3 miles. The slope averages 20% with stretches of 30% or more! Under such conditions, you need to maintain weight and traction on your back tire. There are four very sharp switchbacks, where if you lose control, you could become airborne. Maintain complete control of your bicycle at all times—the road bed has rocks, loose gravel and a short section of old crumbling asphalt, and it becomes quite rutted after rain or a snow melt.

Most Silver Canyon riders find it necessary to stop periodically to rest their hands and get blood back into their knuckles. Dismount and walk each switchback, if necessary, for a safe descent.

Three miles from the top you leave the ridge, drop into the canyon and approach the creek—your first watering spot. (Treat all water before drinking.) From here on, the road is nearly straight; there are no more switchbacks and the descent is fast! For the next 9 miles, you drop another 3,000 feet on your way to Laws. You cross about seven streams, some more than a foot deep, that run all year. Look ahead for thick vegetation that indicates water, and brake well before each crossing. If you take a stream at too high a speed you may come to a sudden and painful stop.

The road in the lower canyon is wide, well traveled and generally pleasant, although somewhat bumpy. As you emerge from the canyon, continue down the alluvial fan and enjoy the easy riding!

Note: This was the route of the original Plumline Outback Ultimate Kamikaze Race in the 1980s and was successfully ridden by experienced cyclists for several years. During the race, unusual safety precautions were taken with full communication and rescue teams in place.

The route is not to be taken lightly. If injuries or other nuisances occur, authorities may close this area to mountain bike use—make sure you are not the cause of such an unfortunate event. Do not practice downhill techniques in Silver Canyon, or in any location where you might be a threat or nuisance to other trail users. If you wish to practice your downhill skills, use the motorcycle trails in Poleta Canyon southeast of Bishop.

Southern Sierra Nevada

The alluvial fans and sub-ranges below the Sierra crest offer some easy, scenic riding and a good introduction to Owens Valley. Spring wildflowers give the dry desert fragrances not found in urban areas. Sierra peaks rise 10,000 feet above you to the west, reaching 14,495 feet atop Mt. Whitney, the highest peak in the continental United States.

92 Alabama Hills Loop

Distance: 18 miles round trip
Difficulty: Easy to moderate, nontechnical
Elevation: 3,700' to 4,800'
Ride Type: Out and back or loop on dirt roads and pavement
Season: All year, snow or heat permitting
Topo Maps: Lone Pine, Independence, Mt. Pinchot

Three miles west of Lone Pine lie the Alabama Hills Recreation Lands, a 30,000-acre jumble of gigantic boulders, rounded and weathered by time, where mountain bicyclists can find a myriad of possibilities for exploration on two wheels or on foot. Unique rock formations, spring wildflower displays, graded dirt roads and panoramic views make this an excellent area for families or cyclists who want more moderate practice fields. Camping facilities can be found at Boulder RV Park, Diaz Lake, Portagi Joe and Locust Grove County Parks; Tuttle Creek BLM Campground (closed in winter); and Lone Pine USFS campground. Nearest services are located in Lone Pine.

During the 1930s and '40s, Hollywood used the Alabama Hills as a locale for filming many classic Westerns, and the major north-south artery that cuts through the recreational area, Movie Road, is a reminder of those days. Confederate sympathizers named the area after the *Alabama,* which sank a Union ship during the Civil War.

Getting There: To make the 18 mile round trip, set your odometer to 0.0 at the junction of Highway 395 and Whitney Portal Road in Lone Pine.

Ride west up Whitney Portal Road. At mile 0.5 you pass Tuttle Creek Road—the county campgrounds are located to the south—and within a tenth of a mile you cross the Los Angeles Aqueduct. You can rest or picnic in the shade of cottonwood trees at 1.6 miles where Whitney Portal Road crosses Lone Pine Creek.

At mile 2.7 turn north onto Movie Flat Road (signed). The elevation at this point is 4,491 feet. Take time to explore the many rock formations and caves in this area. Of particular interest is a natural amphitheater where choral performances were given for a number of years. If you leave the main north-south road, be careful to keep your bearings. A road to the east at mile 3.7 leads into a badlands area where you can find other side roads leading to boulder-filled canyons. At the triangle at 4.2 miles, bear east on the main road.

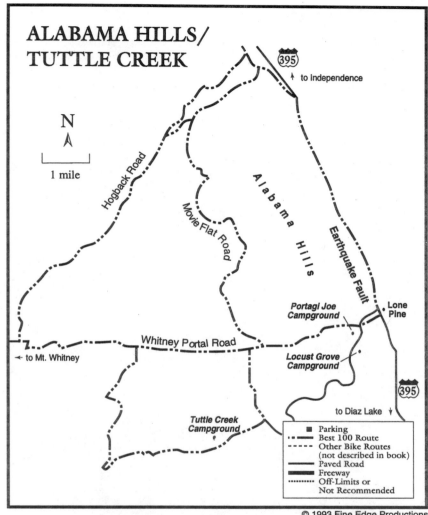

ALABAMA HILLS/ TUTTLE CREEK

N
∧

1 mile

Hogback Road

Movie Flat Road

Alabama Hills

Earthquake Fault

↑ to Independence

Portagi Joe Campground

Lone Pine

Whitney Portal Road

← to Mt. Whitney

Locust Grove Campground

to Diaz Lake ↓

Tuttle Creek Campground

■ Parking
▪—▪—▪ Best 100 Route
– – – Other Bike Routes (not described in book)
——— Paved Road
▬▬▬ Freeway
•••••••• Off-Limits or Not Recommended

© 1993 Fine Edge Productions

The west fork heads 0.5 mile to a major rock outcropping with overhanging caves.

At 4.6 miles you cross a steep wash (find shade under the willows downstream). In the springtime, this wash usually becomes a small creek. The road meanders along the western edge of the Alabama Hills for several more miles, and you have magnificent views of Mt. Whitney and the Sierra Crest the entire way. When you reach a Y at 7.9 miles, Movie Road bears left (northwest), but you can take either branch—they both feed into Hogback Road, where you turn right (east) and head downhill to Highway 395. When you cross Moffat Ranch Road just before Highway 395 the mileage is 9.2.

Hogback Creek flows into a Los Angeles Aqueduct catch basin at

11.7 miles. After you cross the Aqueduct and a cattle guard (12.1 miles) continue east to the stop sign at 12.2 miles—the junction with U.S. 395—and turn south for 6 miles to complete the 18-mile loop to Lone Pine.

Near the 16-mile point, take note of the uplifted boulders to the west of Highway 395, a fault scarp created by the 1872 earthquake that caused extensive damage and fatalities in Lone Pine. Land along this fault slipped from 12 to 20 feet vertically. A sign by the edge of the road points to a nearby cemetery where victims of the quake were buried.

To make a loop through the southern section of the Alabama Hills, proceed 4.5 miles south of Lone Pine on Highway 395, and turn west on Lubken Creek Road. After 4 more miles, turn north on Horseshoe Meadows Road and then east on Whitney Portal Road to return to Lone Pine. For a more picturesque loop, go west on Lubken for 3 miles, turn right (north) onto Tuttle Creek Road and follow it until it ends at Whitney Portal Road, where you turn east and head toward Lone Pine.

93 Tuttle Creek Loop

Distance: Short loop is about 5 miles; longer loop is 14.5 miles
Difficulty: Easy to moderate, nontechnical
Elevation: 5,100' to 6,400' to 5,100'
Ride Type: Loop on dirt roads and pavement
Season: Most of the year

Getting There: At the junction of Highway 395 and Mt. Whitney Road, turn west and head uphill 3.1 miles to Horseshoe Meadows Road. Turn south (left) and head two miles to the sign that indicates Tuttle Creek Campground. Turn west and uphill to the campground (5,100 feet).

Start at the campground. Cross to the south side of Tuttle Creek and follow the jeep road along Tuttle Creek up a moderately steep grade to the 6,400-foot elevation level. At this point, Tuttle Creek emerges from the canyon below Lone Pine Peak (12,944 feet), the mountain directly above you. Cross the wash on a foot path and continue up the jeep trail in a northerly direction until you arrive at Whitney Portal Road, where you turn right (east) and return to Tuttle Creek Campground, completing the short loop of 5 miles.

For a longer and even more scenic variation, turn left (west) on Mt. Whitney Road. You pass Lone Pine Campground (5,800 feet) and the Inyo National Forest boundary, 0.5 mile farther west at the 6,480-foot level. (You are now 8.2 miles from Lone Pine.) Just before the first major switchback starts up toward Whitney Portal, turn right (north) onto Hogback Road and reset your odometer to 0.0 miles. Hogback Road is not easily visible from Whitney Portal Road, so you need to watch carefully for it. There is about 200 yards of pavement before the road becomes dirt and turns abruptly downhill, becoming a wide, well-graded road.

Hogback Road drops 2,700 feet in the next 9 miles, so keep your speed under control. Sagebrush grows to gigantic proportions here, many bushes attaining more than five feet in height, and in the spring, desert dandelions, asters, lupine, and mallow cover the sandy floor.

At 1.9 miles (elevation 5,696 feet) a short road that goes west uphill 1.8 miles and dead-ends at Hogback Creek. For most of the descent to the valley floor (except for a short distance where the road heads east toward the Alabama Hills) you parallel Hogback Creek.

At mile 4.5 a short road of 100 yards leads north to a stock trail across Hogback Creek. You can cool your feet or face in the creek, but do not drink the water. The road leaves the immediate creek drainage at 5.3 miles and veers southeast toward a grove of cottonwoods. At the intersection of Hogback Road and Movie Road, mile 5.8, you can either continue downhill on the left fork to Highway 395, or you can turn right (south) on Movie Road, continuing south where you cross Whitney Portal Road at mile 11.5 and ride the remaining 3 miles to Tuttle Creek Campground.

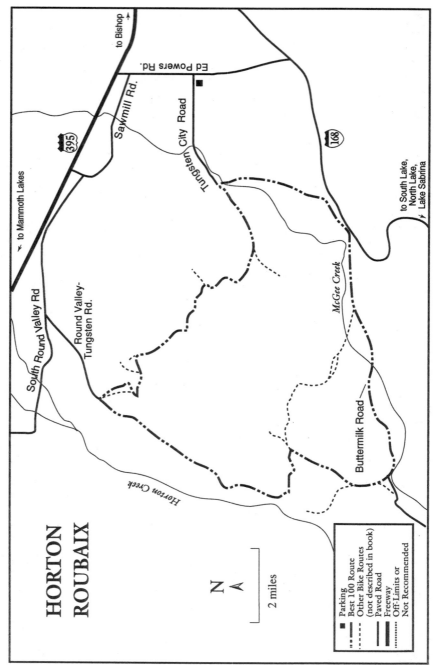

HORTON ROUBAIX

N

2 miles

Parking
Best 100 Route
Other Bike Routes
(not described in book)
Paved Road
Freeway
Off-Limits or
Not Recommended

to Bishop

Ed Powers Rd.

Sawmill Rd.

Tungsten City Road

395

168

to Mammoth Lakes

to South Lake,
North Lake,
Lake Sabrina

South Round Valley Rd

Round Valley-
Tungsten Rd.

McGee Creek

Buttermilk Road

Horton Creek

94 Horton Roubaix

Distance: 19 miles, a good half-day ride with lunch stop
Difficulty: Moderate and technical with strenuous climb for option 2
Elevation: 2,800' gain
Ride Type: Loop on graded dirt road and doubletrack
Season: Spring and fall, also winter when snow level allows
Topo Map: Tungsten Hills

This unusually pleasant and accessible route gives a good physical workout and an excellent variety of terrain and scenic views. You can see wildflowers in abundance in season, view a well-known rock climbing area and mine sites in the Tungsten Hills west of Bishop as you ride just below the High Sierra crest.

Getting There: The route begins at the intersection of Tungsten City Road (graded dirt) and Ed Powers Road. To reach the starting point, go west on West Line Street (Highway 168) 4.5 miles from downtown Bishop. Turn right on Ed Powers Road and go 1.25 miles to Tungsten City Road, which is to your left a quarter mile beyond the four-way stop sign. Caution: Equestrians frequently use the lower part of this route; please give them full right of way and show common courtesy. Park clear of the road.

Cycle west on Tungsten City Road, a well-graded dirt road that heads towards the old mining town site. At mile 1.6, just past the entrance to Deep Canyon (a prominent notch in the hills), you take a left branch downhill and cross McGee Creek. The road now climbs for 2 miles to meet the intersection of Highway 168 and Buttermilk Road (mile 3.6). From this intersection take Buttermilk Road—wide, graded, often "washboardy" and sandy—and head west toward the Sierra crest.

You cross a cattle guard (mile 7.2). Turn right on the doubletrack (ungraded road) heading north. You are now at the high point of the ride (elevation 6,450 feet), and to the right you pass the Peabody Boulders rock climbing area.

Half a mile later you reach a Y intersection (mile 7.7). Take the right branch (the left branch heads towards two tall free-standing boulders). After a mile of gentle terrain you make a hard left and head due west. In 0.5 mile you come to the edge of the dropoff to Horton Creek (elevation 6,120 feet).

The doubletrack now drops steeply down to a water course that parallels, and is east of, Horton Creek. The next section is the Horton Roubaix, named by the locals in honor of France's Paris-Roubaix Race whose route traverses some formidable cobblestone roads. The Horton Roubaix twists around doubletrack of firmly packed cobbles and a few larger rocks and passes thickets of willows on its gentle downhill run.

This fun section ends at mile 10.5 mile, where the track leaves the drainage course and continues down the alluvial fan. In 2 miles you have to make a decision.

Option 1: If you have had

enough climbing or your time and/ or energy are short, continue on this road until it intersects with South Round Valley Road (paved). Turn right. Go to Sawmill Road, turn right and head to Ed Powers Road. Turn right again and proceed to the starting point ahead on your right.

Option 2: To continue on the main Horton Roubaix route, turn right and climb the switchbacks (800 vertical feet) that you see ahead of you. In 1.5 miles (mile 14.0) you

should reach a T intersection in a saddle. Go right, where you reach the high point of this section (elevation 5,600 feet).

At 15.4 miles you reach another T. Go right and head down past the Tungsten Blue Mine, where the road becomes Tungsten City Road. You soon reach the point where—at the start of your trip—you left Tungsten City Road to cross McGee Creek. In another 1.6 miles you return to your original starting point.

95 Buttermilk Country Loop

Distance: 17.4 miles, a good half-day ride or longer with lunch stop
Difficulty: Moderately strenuous because of length and high elevation; nontechnical with rocky spots; can be wet in early summer
Elevation: 5,100' to 8,240' and return
Ride Type: Loop mostly on graded dirt road and doubletrack
Season: Spring through fall when snow level allows
Topo Map: Tungsten Hills

If the Horton Roubaix route whetted your appetite for more of the Eastern Sierra foothills, try this longer loop in Buttermilk country. Come to the Buttermilks on a weekday for stillness and solitude where only the buzzing of bees in sagebrush, the drone of a small airplane or a black fly dive-bombing disturbs the silence. You'll spot jackrabbits, lizards doing push-ups on sun-warmed rocks, and an occasional coyote. The name, Buttermilk, is all that remains of a dairy once located along this route and known in mining days for its fine buttermilk.

Getting There: Start at the intersection of Highway 168 and Buttermilk Road, 4 miles west of the turnoff for Ed Powers Road and 7.2 miles west

of Bishop, as noted in the Horton Roubaix ride. (You could also continue west on Highway 168 to Intake #2's parking lot, where you can leave a vehicle and do the high elevation section of the Buttermilk Loop as a easy out and back.)

From the intersection of Highway 168 and Buttermilk Road, ride west on dirt Buttermilk Road, heading directly towards Mt. Tom (13,652 feet). You pass by Peabody Boulders as the road steepens ("Grandpa and Grandma" are the pair of large boulders to the north). At 3.6 miles you reach a cattle guard and the Horton Roubaix cutoff on your right. About 300 yards ahead (3.9 miles) a short singletrack loop heads left, rejoining the Buttermilk Road in another

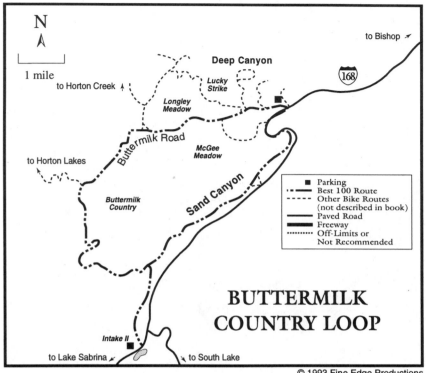

N
∧

1 mile
to Horton Creek ∧

Deep Canyon

Lucky Strike

to Bishop ↗

168

Longley Meadow

Buttermilk Road

McGee Meadow

to Horton Lakes

Buttermilk Country

Sand Canyon

■ Parking
·—·—· Best 100 Route
——— Other Bike Routes (not described in book)
——— Paved Road
━━━ Freeway
·········· Off-Limits or Not Recommended

BUTTERMILK COUNTRY LOOP

Intake II
to Lake Sabrina ↙   ↘ to South Lake

© 1993 Fine Edge Productions

quarter mile. Take this singletrack and listen for a waterfall emanating from the gorge below. A short 50-yard walk takes you to an overlook carved deep in the granite by McGee Creek. By carefully working your way along this gorge you can discover a waterfall where birch, willows and ferns grow along the stream—a nice picnic destination, in itself.

Continue west to rejoin Buttermilk Road, which now becomes narrow and rocky. Jeep trails contour west at 4.0 and 4.7 miles toward the Sierra. The second jeep trail is the approach to Mount Tom. A short road on the left heads to McGee Creek (4.9 miles) at the base of Grouse Mountain. A half mile farther on, there are good primitive campsites near the road.

The first stands of aspen appear at mile 5.7, and the Buttermilk Road levels off from its steep climb and heads south. As you cross the 7,600-foot contour, you can see Table Mountain to the south, Coyote Ridge to the southeast and Grouse Mountain, a large granite outcropping, immediately east. There's a cattle crossing at 6.1 miles and the area is occasionally marshy. To the right of the road, a small trail leads to a spring at mile 6.6.

The road closes in on the ramparts to the Sierra at 6.9 miles, and a trail leads uphill to another spring. You continue to pass springs, marshes and finally pine trees at 7.4 miles. In another tenth of a mile the aspen trees overhang the road and a trail to the right heads up McGee Creek. There are primitive campsites 100 yards before McGee Creek at the 7,898-foot contour (7.5 miles). The route climbs a short ridge to the left before it doubles back and heads west, climbing to the trail junction of USFS 7S01 and 8S17 at mile 8.1, 8,142 feet. Go left at this point, climbing to 8,240 feet, the high point of the Buttermilk Country Loop at 8.4 miles.

The route now heads easterly into aspen and pine trees, passing a jeep road on the right. Within a tenth of a mile you pass Birch Creek culvert.

At this point the road is sometimes bladed and you have a fast downhill. There is a primitive campsite among pines with excellent views to the east at mile 9.0. Continue due east to 10.4 miles, where a road heads sharp right up the ridge, south to Highway 168 (Intake #2). The road is signed: *Notice Locked Gate 0.7 Mile ahead*. Take this road if you want an easy shortcut via Highway 168 back to the starting point.

To complete this loop, turn left and head downhill along a narrow ridge with steep dropoffs, following the Aqueduct pipe. Bishop Creek Canyon and Highway 168 are below you to the south.

You cross over to the left side of the ridge (12.7 miles) where you have an excellent view of the upper end of Owens Valley all the way to Montgomery Pass in Nevada. At a locked gate, a Department of Water and Power (DWP) service road heads west, paralleling the pipeline back up the canyon to Highway 168. You can take this road if you wish to avoid the steep, rocky descent ahead. As you continue east you leave the sandy wash and climb a small ridge to the east (13.9 miles) from where you can see the USFS parking lot below. Be extremely cautious—the next few hundred yards—rocky and rough— are the worst of the entire loop.

The USFS parking lot at 14.5 miles has running water and parking for about 15 cars. At this point, you take Highway 168 to Buttermilk Road to complete your loop. The highway descends steeply; watch for cars and guard against excessive speed. You return to your starting point at Buttermilk Road at mile 17.1 on your left.

96 Coyote High Sierra Traverse

Distance: 21.7 miles
Difficulty: Moderate to difficult due to length and high altitude; some technical sections; route finding skills required
Elevation: Cycling is at an average elevation of 10,000', with some elevations over 11,000 feet; 4,370' gain, 5,000' loss
Ride Type: One way on jeep roads with 5 miles of singletrack; requires car shuttle
Season: June through fall depending on snow conditions
Topo Maps: Tungsten Hills, Mt. Thompson, Coyote Flat

One of the best rides in California, the Coyote High Sierra Traverse has it all: coolness of high elevation, solitude, remoteness, outstanding alpine scenery with meadows, streams and trees, and challenges for the mountain biker. There is a lot of doubletrack, from gentle to steep, with 5 miles of easy to difficult singletrack (mostly downhill) and probably the best views of any ride in the Eastern Sierra.

This ride extends the high altitude portion of the original Sierra 7500 route, which was the most difficult 50-mile mountain bike race course in the country in the mid-1980s. (See *Mountain Biking the High Sierra Guide #1* for additional details on that route.)

Due to its remoteness and elevation, you should be self-sufficient on this route. If you don't mind carrying the necessary equipment, the Coyote High Sierra Traverse makes an excellent overnight trip. The entire route stays within Inyo National Forest, where primitive camping is allowed. The best riding conditions occur just after a summer rain. Pay attention to changes in weather and look out for potential thunderstorms when you cross a high bare ridge late in the ride. Mileages shown are approximate and your figures may vary

from those given. We recommend that you carry the appropriate USGS topo maps.

Getting There: Leave your shuttle vehicle appropriately parked in downtown Big Pine. Then return to Bishop and take West Line Street (Highway 168) west for 13 miles and turn left (south) onto South Lake Road. You can park at a turn-out to the right just beyond (south of) Bishop Creek Lodge. Please do not use the parking area reserved for the lodge or block any of the driveways giving access to the lodge or its cabins. A good place to grab some extra refreshment before you start out, the lodge is open May through September from 8:00 a.m. to 8:00 p.m. (continental breakfast, lunch and dinner offered).

From the lodge if you look across the canyon (east), you can see the first part of the route climbing back to the north on the side of a lateral moraine. Set your odometer to 0.0, hop on your bike, then ride about 500 feet (south) up the paved road to a dirt road on your left (east). Take this road and cross a bridge over Bishop Creek. Beyond the creek, the road becomes a doubletrack, curves north through an aspen grove, and

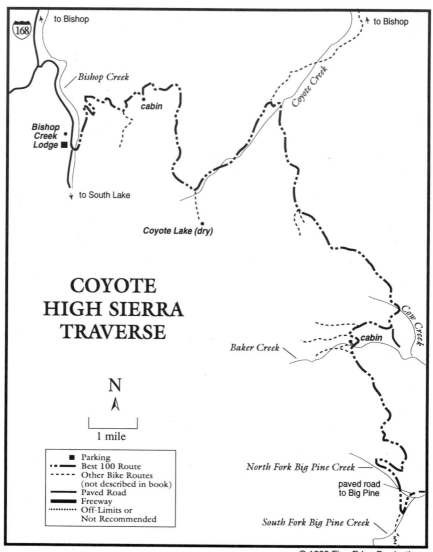

© 1993 Fine Edge Productions

then begins its climb up the lateral moraine. Caution: The soil is loose and sandy, here—the same conditions you find toward the end on the last mile or so of the singletrack into Big Pine Creek.

After ascending the moraine, you round a corner and enter a hang-ing valley at elevation 8,800 feet. Do not take a faint road to the right.

Many switchbacks and sandy spots later, you reach a T intersection at 3.0 miles and 9,850 feet. Head left. (The right branch leads to the Schober Mine and Merrill Prospect.)

A little farther on, you come to

the top of a minor ridge at 10,000 feet. You have now climbed 1,600 feet with another 1,100 feet to go to the top of Coyote Ridge.

A short descent and gentle climb brings you to the remains of an old log cabin at 3.5 miles. From this point on, the road averages a 14 percent grade (!) to the top of 11,070-foot Coyote Ridge at 5.0 miles. The wonderful views of the Sierra Crest to the north are a good excuse to stop along this section as you approach the high point.

Now you begin a 1,500-foot descent in an alpine meadow with a gentle curve to the east. (In a season of good runoff, the meadow has beautiful displays of blue lupine.) Keep in mind that the doubletrack you are on gets little or no maintenance.

At 7.0 miles there is a main intersection at elevation 10,320 feet. Continue straight. The right branch leads to (usually dry) Coyote Lake, a very pleasant camping area.

Another mile brings you to the first crossing of Coyote Creek at elevation 9,950 feet. This is your first chance to replenish water supplies (remember to treat all water).

The road improves as you continue your descent. At 9.2 miles you reach a road junction and decision time. The described route to Big Pine Creek goes right (south) and downhill and heads into Coyote Flat. If—instead of making this turn—you continue straight, you will be on the main jeep road from Bishop to Coyote Flat and—after 5,500 feet of descent—will eventually end up on Reata Road west of Bishop

after some trying sandy stretches. This main route to Bishop is part of the original Sierra 7500 route and is much easier (with the exception of the deep sandy spots), shorter and less technical than continuing south to Big Pine Creek. If you are short of time and supplies, are having trouble breathing, or if the weather is threatening, by all means bail out at this time and take this short way down to Owens Valley.

Continuing south on the Big Pine Creek route you quickly cross Coyote Creek again. After 5.2 more miles of easy riding, you finally reach the southern end of Coyote Flat, a major north-south running plateau. At mile 14.4 you cross Cow Creek. Within a short distance and a cattle guard, you reach a junction and a ridge forming the edge of the Baker Creek drainage.

Take the right branch (west) and head uphill. After climbing to 10,290 feet, you come to another road junction at 15.5 miles and go left (southwest) and downhill. A short distance farther on you reach another junction and go left again (southeast). This leads you to the Baker Creek Cabin at 16.0 miles and Baker Creek at 10,070 feet, the start of the singletrack and the last dependable water until Big Pine Creek.

The next section requires some route finding skills and is more technically demanding. From the cabin, go upstream about 500 feet. Don't take any trail that seems to lead away from the stream on the north side. Cross the stream at this point and you should be just upstream from the swampy meadow area and in the trees. You are looking for a trail that either parallels the creek on the south side, or goes up the hillside to the south. If the trail is paralleling the creek, go left (downstream). If the trail is heading up a hillside to the south, follow it to the south. If you have trouble finding these trails, you probably did not go far enough upstream. (The Coyote Flat 7.5 minute topo map is very useful at this point!)

In 0.3 mile you should reach another trail junction; go left. Shortly afterward you top out on a ridge at 16.4 miles. From here, the singletrack descends 0.6 mile to High Meadow at 10,020 feet. The trail now climbs steeply to a rounded ridge at the edge of Big Pine Canyon. The grand views to the west unfold slowly until you reach some rocks at the southern edge of the ridge at 17.7 miles. You can see several peaks over 14,000 feet high and two of the largest glaciers in the Sierra Nevada. Straight ahead you are looking up the South Fork of Big Pine Creek. To the right is the North Fork of Big Pine Creek into which you descend.

The descent to Grouse Spring is steep and technical. (No skidding, please.) Walk your bike if necessary. There is little, if any, water at Grouse Spring. From there on, the trail is easy to the end of Logging Flat. Then you descend steeply through sand and several switchbacks before contouring around a draw and climbing to a minor ridge.

At this point, the trail drops into Big Pine Canyon to a trail junction at 20.0 miles and 8,600 feet. At this four-way junction, go straight (downhill). Watch for hikers—you are now on a heavily used hiking trail. Within 0.5 mile you reach an abandoned road (washed out in a major flood on the South Fork several years ago). Take this road. A few hundred feet after you cross the north fork of Big Pine Creek, a sign indicates the hiking trail goes left. Continue straight, down the abandoned road.

As you approach the South Fork, watch for a trail that crosses the road at mile 21.3 and is not visible ahead of time. Turn left on this trail. In less than 0.5 mile you reach the trailhead and the paved road to Big Pine. A 9-mile descent of 3,800 feet drops you into town.

The authors are indebted to Pete Lewis, mountain bike framebuilder of Bishop, for his help in describing the Horton Roubaix and Coyote High Sierra Traverse routes. For additional rides in this area, please refer to *Mountain Biking the High Sierra, Guide 1, Owens Valley and Inyo County,* Second Edition, by Don and Réanne Douglass, ISBN 0-938665-01-4 (see p. 304).

CHAPTER 12

Desert Regions

By Delaine Fragnoli

Talk to people who have spent some time in the desert and certain words get repeated—vast, quiet, still, reflective—all qualities sorely lacking in modern life. Perhaps that's why more and more Californians are discovering their desert.

What they are discovering is an intricate environment that is both tenacious and fragile. The California desert, located in the eastern portion of the state, covers a full one quarter of state lands. It contains 1,836 species of plants, 420 birds, 94 mammals, 63 reptiles, 43 fishes and 16 amphibians in 46 distinct ecological communities ranging from riparian marsh to desert forest. Over 100,000 archeological sites, including some of the most concentrated collections of rock art in the world, dot the desert's 90 mountain ranges. As if that weren't enough, the oldest living known organism, a 11,700-year-old creosote ring, lives in the desert. Nowhere else can geology buffs see so clearly the work of wind and water on the land. Yet 38 varieties of plant, animal and insect life are threatened or endangered, including the desert tortoise, California's official state reptile.

As Southern California's population surges past the 16 million mark, more and more people are moving to the desert, and more and more people are seeking recreation and a respite from urban blight in these seemingly empty spaces. Fortunately much of the desert has already been preserved. Its crown jewel, Death Valley, was adopted by the National Park Service in 1933 as a national monument. Three years later, 560,000 acres were protected in Joshua Tree National Monument.

Death Valley and Joshua Tree are among the best areas to explore in the desert. Both feature unique plants and animals as well as mind-boggling geologic formations. They are accessible and have facilities for camping and day use. Many other areas of the desert are remote, accessible only with 4WD vehicles, and lack any facilities. Death Valley and Joshua Tree also have the distinction of being part of a UNESCO (United Nations Educational, Scientific, and Cultural Organization) International Biosphere Reserve as part of the Colorado and Mojave Desert Biosphere Reserve, along with Anza-Borrego State Park and the Santa Rosa Mountains Deep Canyon Research Center.

Despite the influx of visitors to the California desert, a frontier spirit still persists. Curmudgeonly old miners still eke out an existence. Off-road motorcyclists tell stories of finding hidden landing strips, pentagrams and satanic paraphernalia, and men living in caves.

In recent years environmentalists have fought other desert users for control of the desert's remaining areas. It is likely that the California Desert Protection Act will pass in 1993 after nearly a decade of legislative struggle. The act would designate many acres of new wilderness lands (remember, bikes are prohibited in wilderness areas) and would upgrade and enlarge Death Valley and Joshua Tree into national parks. This is unlikely to change mountain biking opportunities in either monument, since biking is already limited to dirt roads.

Those of you interested in exploring the desert more should check the Anza-Borrego Desert State Park section in Chapter 1 and the Mojave Desert rides in Chapter 3 and Chapter 11.

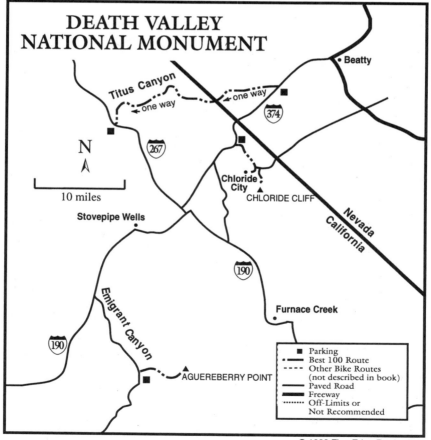

© 1993 Fine Edge Productions

Death Valley National Monument

The ominous-sounding Death Valley is a narrow trench, 4 to 16 miles wide and 120 miles long. The Panamint Range runs along its western flank and the Amargosa Range along the eastern flank. Among the many startling contrasts here is the juxtaposition of low elevations and high elevations. Telescope Peak, at 11,049 feet, towers over the valley, while Badwater marks the lowest spot in the United States at 282 feet below sea level.

The valley was formed millions of years ago when folding and faulting uplifted the surrounding mountains. During the last ice age large lakes intermittently formed in the basin, depositing layers of clay and silt. Their evaporation left salt deposits that are still visible today.

The valley got its name when a group of gold seekers tri:d a shortcut across the desert in 1849. Before long a lack of food and water split the panicked band apart. At least one of the travelers died. This image of death is reinforced by other names in the valley like Devil's Golf Course, Hells Gate and Funeral Mountains.

Other human visitors have had better experiences than the ill-fated gold seekers. Indians occupied the area for some 9,000 years. Borax was a veritable gold mine for prospectors who built roads to transport it, and twenty-mule teams drew loads of the mineral that were as heavy as 36 tons. Abandoned mine sites and several ghost towns can be found in the park today.

Contrary to the image its name paints, the valley contains 900 species of plants and trees, 21 of which are unique to the valley, including the Panamint daisy, the Death Valley sage and the Death Valley sandpaper plant. Staggering geological formations distinguish the park: sand dune formations, sculpted rocks, isolated valleys and volcanic craters.

Dirt roads and more rugged jeep roads crisscross the area. Bicycling is encouraged in the monument, but stay on roads that are open to automobile traffic. Bikes are not allowed on trails or service roads. It's a good idea to check with rangers to find out current road conditions before attempting any rides.

If you don't get enough of a workout exploring the area's dirt roads, you could participate in the Death-Valley-to-Mt.-Whitney road race. The two-day event climbs from Badwater to Mt. Whitney, the highest point in the contiguous U.S. (Technically the race ends at Whitney Portal, a good 6,000 feet short of the peak.) A foot race follows a similar course. Although it too officially ends at the portal, tradition dictates that runners continue up a trail to the summit at 14,494 feet.

Getting There: From Los Angeles, take Interstate 5 or Interstate 210 to Highway 14 (north). Stay on Highway 14 until it joins and becomes northbound Highway 395. (From eastern Los Angeles County, take the 15 or the 215 to Highway 395.) From 395 take Highway 190 to Death Valley. It's about a five-hour drive from Los Angeles.

Stovepipe Wells or Furnace Creek make good bases for exploring the monument. There are hotels and other facilities in both spots, including the luxurious Furnace Creek Inn. A Visitor Center is located in Furnace Creek. Open year round, it can be reached at 619-786-2331. You can pick up a handout there listing suggested mountain bike routes in the monument. Stovepipe Wells has its own ranger station. The ranger station across the state line in Beatty, Nevada is open seven days a week from 8 a.m. to 4 p.m.

There are nine camping areas in the monument as well. Reserve through MISTIX at 1-800-365-2267. You must bring your own firewood. Some campgrounds are closed at various times of the year, usually because of very hot or very cold weather. Fees range from free to $8. You can request a folder, "Camping in Death Valley," from the Visitor Center. Admission to the monument is $5 per car, good for 7 days. The best time to visit is November through April. Winter can be cold, and summer temperatures can reach over 130 degrees. Bring *lots* of water, at least 2 gallons per person per day.

The American Automobile Association (AAA) puts out an excellent map of the area with very good information on the back. It's a good idea to pick up a copy before you go.

97 Titus Canyon

Distance: 26 miles
Difficulty: Strenuous due to length and climbing, mildly technical due to trail surface
Elevation: Begin 3,400', climb to 5,250', descend to 200'
Ride Type: One way on dirt road; requires car shuttle
Season: November through April

This is a one-way road, so you must ride in the direction described (east to west). After crossing desert terrain, the road climbs via steep switchbacks to a crest, then begins a long, gradual descent. Parts of the road are covered with deep gravel—tough and slow going. West of the crest you'll find the rusting remains of Leadfield. For $2 you can pick up a road guide to Titus Canyon at the Visitor Center. The guide describes and explains the geology of the can-yon. Although intended for automobile use, the guide gives mileages and information that are useful to bicyclists as well. Note: Titus Canyon is closed in summer.

Getting There: Begin 7 miles east of the Nevada line on the north side of Highway 374. Leave the pick-up vehicle or have someone pick you up at the canyon's terminus 14.3 miles northwest of the junction of Highways 190 and 374 on Highway 267.

Head up the gradually climbing, well-graded dirt road. I hope you brought a lot of water with you. You don't want to emulate Morris Titus, a young mining engineer who entered the canyon in search of water and never came back. That's the hard way to get a landform named after you!

At 0.9 mile you pass the road to Rhyolite on your right. One of the more successful mining towns in Death Valley, Rhyolite prospered on gold in the early 1900s. At one time nearly 6,000 people lived in the town, but like many mining communities, it eventually went bust, leaving little but concrete foundations and a gloomy cemetery behind.

As you pedal these first few miles you traverse the Amargosa Valley. The Bullfrog Hills are on your right and the Grapevine Mountains are in front of you. At 6.5 miles you pass a dark, rocky hill on your left. Among the youngest volcanic material in the area, this was part of an ancient lava flow. In the next 1.5 miles you pass many other signs of volcanic activity.

In the ensuing miles the climbing gets steeper as you pass more fascinating geologic history. The rocks on your left are older rocks, those on your right younger. About 11 miles out you pass Titanothere Canyon and you summit a couple of miles later. Give your legs a rest, the climbing is over! It's a gradual downhill the rest of the way.

At 15.9 miles you come to the ghost town of Leadfield, one of the shortest-lived towns around—one year during the 1920s. Investors were fooled by an unscrupulous promoter who tricked them into believing the area was rich in lead ore.

As you descend from Leadfield the canyon steepens and narrows. Twisted rock layers of reddish gray dominate. The last 3 miles are a highlight of the trip as the canyon walls soar to over 500 feet above the canyon floor. These narrows are why only one-way traffic is allowed.

In the final section (two-way) you cross a wide alluvial fan. At 26 miles you're at the junction with the paved highway. Hopefully your car or a friend is here to pick you up.

Be sure to ride in the morning when the sun is at your back!

98 Chloride City

Distance: 15 miles
Difficulty: Moderately difficult with some difficult sections, somewhat technical because of trail surface and ruts
Elevation: 2,500' gain/loss
Ride Type: Out and back on rough jeep road
Season: November through April

This rough and rugged jeep road takes you to Chloride City ghost town, a silver mining center in the 1870s and again from 1905 to 1916.

The city's inhabitants are best known for having built a road from Death Valley to Barstow. Little remains at the site today. The trip's real highlight is the panoramic view from Chloride Cliff, just one mile to the southwest.

Getting There: From Stovepipe Wells, head north and turn on Highway 374 toward Beatty, Nevada. Ten miles past the junction, look for a dirt road on your right with a sign that reads: *High clearance 4 x 4 recommended.* Park off to the side of the road. If you are coming from Furnace Creek, go 11.8 miles north on Highway 190 to the cutoff to Beatty, Nevada. When you intersect the 374, go right for 3.4 miles until you see the sign described above.

Saddle up your high clearance mountain bike and head up this narrow two-track. Stay out of the gravel in the middle! You head up a canyon surrounded by lovely red and orange rock. At 1.3 miles you top a small rise and head downhill for 0.5 mile. When you've gone 2.2 miles you come to an intersection, where you make a sharp left to stay on the main road. The downhill ends here and you begin climbing in earnest.

A very rough section greets you at 2.5 miles. Can you clear the ruts and rocks? You pass a sign on your left that reads *Mine Hazard Area.* If you look around, you can make out several mine shafts in the surrounding hills. Next comes a series of short steep uphills. Maintaining traction is your challenge here—keep some weight over that back wheel! Soon the terrain is more undulating but with a general uphill grade.

When the road opens out into a bowl, most of your work is over. At 4.7 miles stay on the main road (don't take the spur on your right). After 5.3 miles the main road continues while a fork branches to the right. Take the right fork toward Chloride City. You can stop and explore the ghost town now or on your way back from Chloride Cliff.

To get to the cliff, go another 1.8 miles to another fork. The right fork dead-ends after 0.2 miles. Follow the left fork 0.3 miles to its dead-end at a scenic overlook at 5,279 feet. Savor the view and be careful on the loose downhills on your way back to your car.

99 Aguereberry Point

Distance: 13 miles
Difficulty: Easy, last 1/4 mile steep; nontechnical
Elevation: Begin 5,000', end 6,433', 1,400' gain/loss
Ride Type: Out and back on graded dirt road
Season: November through April

The approach to Aguereberry Point is pleasant, but it's the view from the top that makes this climb worthwhile. The best time to visit is in late afternoon, when the sunlight colors the Funeral Mountains in soft hues of purple.

Getting There: From Stovepipe Wells head south on Highway 190 for 9.1 miles. Make a left down Emigrant Canyon on Wildrose Road. The junction is clearly signed. Just under 12 miles later, look for a dirt road on your left with Aguereberry Point well marked. Park in the pullout on the right.

Head up the well-graded dirt road. It's washboard in spots, but smooth overall. After 1.5 miles you pass Aguereberry Camp (called Harrisburg on the AAA map, but signed as Aguereberry Camp.) A few ramshackle buildings of relatively recent vintage hunker below a collapsed mine on the hillside. A rusting car sits off to one side, and a sense of unrealized dreams hangs over the place.

Back on the road, at 1.8 miles avoid the spur on the right. It leads to more mine sites. Continue on the main road. The gentle climb grows a tad bit steeper through here. At 3.3 miles things get looser, steeper, a little rougher. Four miles of riding puts you in a lovely little canyon. The road winds through here and temperatures are cooler. Half a mile later the road opens up again and flattens out. Ignore the spur on your right.

After 5.8 miles the road grows steeper again, and at 6.2 miles you hit a flat spot with a port-a-potty. There's a great view here, but don't stop pedaling yet. Make a left and climb a steep quarter mile to Aguereberry Point, named for a Basque shepherd turned prospector. Presumably he, too, enjoyed the view here, 6,433 feet above the valley floor. The Funeral Mountains are in front of you.

Put on a windbreaker before you head down. It can get windy and chilly up here in the late afternoons.

Joshua Tree National Monument

Two large deserts, the Colorado Desert and the Mojave Desert, meet in Joshua Tree National Monument, where they offer a vivid illustration of the differences between the low and high desert.

The Colorado Desert, at elevations under 3,000 feet, occupies the eastern half of the monument. The area is dominated by abundant creosote with small stands of spidery ocotillo and jumping cholla cactus (yes, it does jump when in bloom). The western half of the monument, the Mojave Desert, is higher and slightly cooler and wetter. This is where you find extensive stands of the monument's namesake. In addition, five oases, graced with stately palms, draw abundant wildlife to their naturally occurring surface water. In spring visitors throughout the area are treated to a brilliant wildflower show.

Joshua Tree also contains very interesting geologic displays—rugged mountains of twisted rock and exposed granite monoliths show the tremendous earth forces that shaped the land. In the summer of 1992, a 7.5 earthquake dislodged boulders and sent rocks tumbling throughout the area.

Early morning and evening are the best times to see wildlife, which normally wait out the daytime heat. Coyotes, lizards, jackrabbits, rats, owls and bobcats all inhabit the desert. Keep an eye out for golden eagles and roadrunners as well. Less pleasant creatures—stinkbugs, tarantulas and sidewinders (a kind of rattlesnake)—keep you from getting too careless.

Although the most common human visitor to Joshua Tree these days is of the rock climbing genus, the earliest inhabitant—indeed, one of the earliest inhabitants of the whole Southwest—was Pinto Man, who hunted and gathered here during wetter times. Later, other Native Americans traveled through, following the harvests of pinyon nuts, mesquite beans, acorns and cactus fruit, leaving behind rock paintings and pottery ollas. Some of the rock paintings can still be seen today.

During the 1800s, explorers, cattlemen and miners changed the face of the land, leaving behind Lost Horse and Desert Queen mines among others, and the Desert Queen Ranch. The area is still full of old mine sites. Stay clear of abandoned mine shafts—don't let your curiosity get the best of you. Some of the shafts are hundreds of yards deep. The cattlemen left tanks, small dams constructed to catch rain water.

Today a half million acres constitute the monument, 467,000 of which are wilderness (bikes prohibited). In the remaining areas bikes are limited to paved roads, dirt roads and 4WD roads. All trails, service roads and any roads closed to vehicles are closed to bikes. Off-road bike travel is prohibited—probably a good thing since cactus is not friendly to tires or human flesh.

Getting There: Joshua Tree National Monument is 140 miles east of Los Angeles, about a two-and-a-half-hour drive. From the west, take Interstate 10 to Highway 62 (29 Palms Highway) to the park's north entrances, one in the town of Joshua Tree, the other in Twentynine Palms. The south entrance is 25 miles east of Indio and can be reached from the east or west by Interstate 10. The north entrances give you access to the western part of the park, while the south entrance accesses the eastern half.

There is a campground, visitor center and picnic area at the south entrance. Mountain biking possibilities here are limited to three dirt roads—Pinkham Canyon Road, Black Eagle Road and Old Dale Road (which turns into Gold Crown Road). These are best done as out-and-back rides. Fashioning a loop would require long rides with much pavement. Paved roads in the Monument are narrow and offer no shoulder—not the most pleasant riding environment.

I recommend the western half of the park. There is an information station

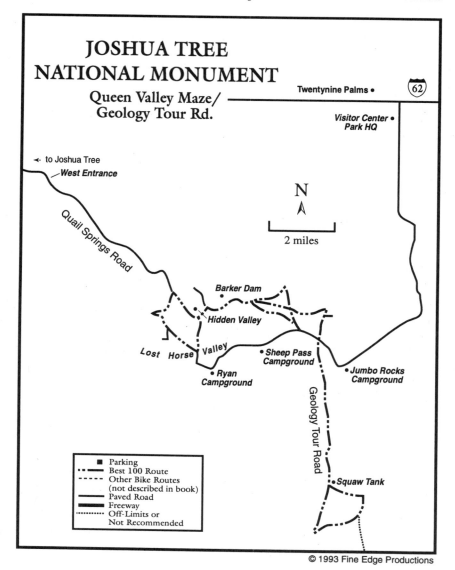

JOSHUA TREE
NATIONAL MONUMENT
Queen Valley Maze/
Geology Tour Rd.

Twentynine Palms •

62

Visitor Center •
Park HQ

← to Joshua Tree
West Entrance

N

2 miles

Quail Springs Road

Barker Dam

Hidden Valley

Lost Horse Valley

• Sheep Pass
Campground

• Ryan
Campground

• Jumbo Rocks
Campground

Geology Tour Road

■ Parking
Best 100 Route
Other Bike Routes
(not described in book)
Paved Road
Freeway
Off-Limits or
Not Recommended

• Squaw Tank

© 1993 Fine Edge Productions

at the west entrance in the town of Joshua Tree, but the main entrance in Twentynine Palms has the Oasis Visitor Center—a good place for maps and brochures. The $5 per vehicle entry fee is good for seven days.

Once inside the Monument, head for Hidden Valley Campground, Ryan Campground, Sheep Pass Campground or Jumbo Rocks Campground. These are the most centrally located and provide access to the best riding in the area. They are on a first come, first served basis. Fees vary from free to $10 per night, with group sites also available by reservation. Most of the campgrounds have toilets, fire rings and picnic tables, but no showers or water. Bring all the water you will need, and do not underestimate—this is the desert! Rangers recommend at least one gallon per person per day, two gallons per person per day if you're involved in strenuous exercise. Some water is available at Oasis Visitor Center, Indian Cove Ranger Station, Black Rock Canyon and Cottonwood Campgrounds. Also bring firewood and kindling—all of the park's vegetation is protected. Services are available at Joshua Tree or Twentynine Palms. There are several day-use picnic areas, too.

Spring and fall are the best times to visit. Winter can be cold and windy. I was hailed and snowed on one weekend in February. Summer is scorching. Avoid canyons and washes during rainstorms, since flash floods do occur.

100 Queen Valley Maze

Distance: 12 miles
Elevation: Route is virtually flat
Difficulty: Easy, nontechnical
Ride Type: Loop on dirt road and pavement with recommended short hikes
Season: Spring and fall best

A 13.4-mile network of roads crisscrosses this valley of boulder piles and Joshua trees. Several bike racks have been placed in this area so you can lock your bike and go hiking. What I recommend is a biking/hiking tour that takes you to the area's best sights.

Beginning at Hidden Valley campground, take the dirt road that heads east, following signs to Barker Dam. Continue straight and stay on the main road. At 1.5 miles take the spur on your left and go a quarter mile to the parking area and trailhead.

Lock up your bikes (there's a rack) and hike the 1.1-mile loop trail to Barker Dam. It was built to collect water for the cattle of early ranchers. On the way back to the parking lot, the trail takes you past Native American petroglyphs. These authentic carvings were unfortunately painted over by a film crew in an attempt to make them more visible. Do not touch or disturb any carvings or artifacts in the monument!

Backtrack to the main dirt road and make a left, away from the direction you originally came. At a four-way intersection at just under 3.0 mile you can take your pick of the two open routes. Both eventually lead to paved Quail Springs Road. The right fork is the most direct route. This is typical desert riding—hard pack alternating with washboard sections and sand traps.

When you intersect the paved road at 5.3 miles, turn right. You are now heading west on bumpy pavement that's mostly downhill.

Stop at Sheep Pass Campground if you like and lock up your bikes. From here you can hike up to Ryan Mountain. The 1.5-mile trail is moderately strenuous as it climbs to 5,461 feet. The trail offers several lookout points with fine views of Queen, Lost Horse, Hidden and Pleasant valleys.

Back on the paved road, you pass Ryan campground, also on your left, at 9.5 miles. Stay on the main road. Do not take the turnoff to Keys View. Continue back to Hidden Valley campground. If you have an aversion to pavement, you can return to Hidden Valley on the same dirt road you took out.

Note: You can start this loop from any of the three campgrounds named in the description.

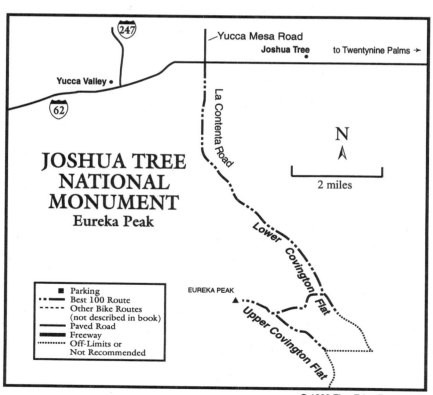

101 Geology Tour Road

Distance: 20.8 miles
Difficulty: Easy to moderate, mildly technical
Elevation: Approximately 1,000' loss/gain
Ride Type: Pavement and dirt road loop
Season: Spring and fall best

Starting at Jumbo Rocks, either the campground or the picnic area, head west on the paved road. After two miles of pedaling, turn south (left) onto a dirt road. This is the 4WD Geology Tour Road. Pick up a road guide at the turnoff. The road's two highlights are the prehistoric Native American rock carvings and the panoramic view at the end.

Traveling through a fascinating landscape, you head into a bumpy, sandy, mostly downhill section. After 5.4 miles you hit Squaw Tank. From here you can take a 6-mile circular route that explores Pleasant Valley. The route is equally nice in either direction. Back at Squaw Tank after completing the loop, follow your tread marks back to Jumbo Rocks.

102 Eureka Peak

Distance: 7.6 miles, 14.1 if you ride to the backcountry board
Difficulty: Moderate, mildly technical
Elevation: High point 5,516'
Ride Type: Out and back on dirt roads
Season: Spring and fall best

The climb to Eureka Peak (5,516 feet) takes you past some of the lushest vegetation in the monument and to a great view of Palm Springs and the Morongo Basin.

Getting There: From Highway 62, 2.8 miles west of the junction with Highway 247, head south on paved La Contenta Road. After it crosses Yucca Trail/Alta Loma Drive at 3.9 miles, the road turns to dirt. It can get sandy, so call for road conditions, especially after a rain. At 5.8 miles go left at the sign to Covington Flats. Two miles later you pass into the Joshua Tree National Monument.

At 9 miles go right at the fork, and at 12 miles go left at a fork toward the picnic area. Park here. The picnic area is undeveloped—there's a picnic table and a port-a-potty, but no water.

Begin the ride by backtracking to the fork and going left. The road climbs gradually through sand, washboard and rock. At 2.1 miles you come to a T. Go right. You get a brief downhill respite here before climbing again. You're close to the end when the road gently switchbacks before coming up on a ridge. Fom here you have great views in both directions. To your right you can make out Yucca Valley. At 3.8 miles you reach a parking area with a vista. Take the time to hike up the short trail to the actual peak—it's worth it for the panoramic views.

This area features the largest Joshua trees in the monument as well as junipers and piñon pines. No one knows how the Joshua tree got its name. Some say it was named by Mormons who thought the giant yucca looked like it was raising its branches in prayer. You may want to pray or meditate yourself as you take in the surrounding desert.

On the way back, if you want to add mileage you can go straight at the T intersection and continue to Upper Covington Flats and over to the backcountry board, where there's some good hiking. Going there and back would add 6.5 miles. Otherwise, you can just head back the same way you came.

APPENDIX

ABOUT THE AUTHORS

Don Douglass was the first land access director and board of trustees member for National Offroad Bicycling Association (NORBA). He was the founder and first president of International Mountain Bicycling Association (IMBA) and has been inducted into the Mountain Biking Hall of Fame. He has written extensively on the need for environmentally sound and responsible riding habits.

Réanne Douglass, freelance writer and editor, has published articles on a number of topics and is currently writing her first book. She led the first women's cycling team across Terra del Fuego. She and her husband Don pioneered many cycling routes in the Eastern Sierra.

Delaine Fragnoli, currently Associate Editor of *Mountain Biking Magazine,* has taught English at Cal Poly, Pomona. She is a past editor of *Southwest Cycling* and frequently rides with the Pasadena Mountain Bike Club and the WOMBATS in the San Gabriel Mountains and greater San Diego.

Jim Hasenauer, a founding member and the current president of IMBA, has written and lectured widely on land access matters. Also a founding member and director of CORBA (Concerned Off-Road Bicyclists Association), he sits on a number of trail advisory groups. He is a tenured professor of Communications at Cal State, Northridge, and an active member of the Sierra Club.

Mark Langton, editor of *Mountain Biking Magazine,* has been a long-time advocate of sound cycling principles and open trails. His writings document much of mountain biking's present and past history. He is a founding member of CORBA and has been nominated to the Mountain Biking Hall of Fame.

Paul Maag has been a spokesman for the biking community in the Coachella Valley for several years. He has served on numerous task force committees with the BLM and USFS regarding access concerns in the Santa Rosa Mountains. Paul has published a guide book in partnership with the BLM, with profits going to land access.

Mickey McTigue has been a backcountry cyclist since 1958. Active in trail building and maintenance, he leads cycling expeditions in Los Padres National Forest.

Robert Rasmussen, Orange Country businessman and avid mountain biker, researched the trails of the Cleveland National Forest and presently assists the Orange County Trails Coalition.

Robert Shipley, a new convert to mountain biking, has cycled extensively for 33 years (including in China). He owned and operated a well-known bicycle shop near UC Riverside for a number of years. Currently he consults with the USFS and other agencies on bicycle access and safety matters.

Allen Thibault, commercial artist and environmentally aware cyclist, has been exploring ways to present computer-generated cycling maps.

Mike Troy is a cofounder of the Grapevine Mountain Bicycling Association, and he regularly performs trail building and maintenance in the Angeles National Forest.

Kevin Woten pioneered many popular routes in the Saugus District of the Los Padres National Forest. He was also a cofounder of the Grapevine Mountain Bicycle Association and is a member of IMBA's south region Board of Directors.

RECOMMENDED READING

Cycling

Ballantine, Richard, *Richard's Bike Book*, Random House, 1982.

Cuthbertson, Tom, *The Bike Bag Book*, Ten Speed Press, 1981.

Hefferon, Lauren, *Cycle Food: A Guide to Satisfying Your Inner Tube*, Ten Speed Press, 1983.

Kelly, Charles, *Richard's Mountain Bike Book*, Random House, 1988.

Schubert, John, *Richard's Cycling for Fitness*, Random House, 1988.

Sloane, Eugene A., *The Complete Book of Bicycling*, Simon and Schuster, 1988.

————, *Sloane's Complete Book of All-Terrain Bicycles*, Simon and Schuster, 1991.

————, *Sloane's New Bicycle Maintenance Manual*, Simon and Schuster, 1991.

Van der Plas, Rob, *The Mountain Bike Book*, Bicycle Books, 1988.

Backcountry Travel and First Aid

American Red Cross, *Standard First Aid and Personal Safety*, Doubleday, 1979.

Cobb, David, *Guide to U.S. Map Resources*, American Library Association, 1986.

Darvill, Fred T., *Mountaineering Medicine*, Wilderness Press, 1983.

Dodd, K., *Guide to Obtaining USGS Information*, U.S. Geological Survey Circular 900, 1986.

Fleming, June, *Staying Found*, Vintage Books, 1982.

Graydon, Don, ed., *Mountaineering, The Freedom of the Hills*, 5th edition, The Mountaineers, 1992.

Lentz, M., S. Macdonald, and J. Carline, *Mountaineering First Aid*, The Mountaineers, 1990.

McKinney, John, *Day Hikers Guide To Southern California*, Olympus Press, 1981.

Rand McNally, *Rand McNally RV Park and Campground Directory: U.S., Canada, and Mexico*, Rand McNally, 1988.

Natural History

Bailey, H. P., *The Climate of Southern California*, University of California Press, 1966.

Hall, Clarence A., Jr., ed., *Natural History of the White-Inyo Range, Eastern California*, University of California Press, 1991.

Hill, Mary, *Geology of the Sierra Nevada*, University of California Press, 1975.

Hill, Russell B., *California Mountain Ranges*, Falcon Press, 1986.

Jaeger, Edmond C. and Arthur C. Smith, *Introduction to the Natural History of Southern California*, University of California Press, 1971.

Larson, Peggy, *A Sierra Club Naturalist's Guide: The Deserts of the Southwest*, Sierra Club Books, 1977.

Little, Elbert L., *Audubon Society Field Guide of North American Trees*, Knopf, 1987.

MacMahon, James A., *Deserts—Audubon Society Nature Guide*, Knopf, 1985.

McConnaughey, Bayard H. and Evelyn, *Audubon Society Nature Guide of the Pacific Coast*, Knopf, 1986.

Peterson, Roger Tory, *A Field Guide to Western Birds*, Houghton Mifflin, 1961.

Shelton, John S., *Geology Illustrated*, W. H. Freeman and Co., 1966.

Smith, Genny Schumacher, ed., *Deepest Valley*, Wilderness Press, 1969.

Whitney, Stephen, *Western Forests*, Knopf, 1985.

History

Santa Barbara Museum of Natural History, *California's Chumash Indians*, EZ Nature Books.

ROUTE INDEX

TOPO MAPS & GUIDE BOOKS FROM FINE EDGE PRODUCTIONS

ALL THE
APPROVED
PLACES TO
EXPLORE BY
MOUNTAIN
BIKE!

WRITTEN
BY
LOCAL
EXPERTS

MOUNTAIN BIKING & RECREATION TOPO MAPS

Six Color, Double-Sided, Includes Trail Profiles & Route Descriptions

		Retail
Eastern High Sierra-Mammoth, June, Mono	ISBN 0-938665-21-9	$9.95
Santa Monica Mountains	ISBN 0-938665-23-5	$8.95
Santa Ana Mountains, Cleveland N.F.	ISBN 0-938665-25-1	$8.95
San Gabriel Mountains –West	ISBN 0-938665-13-8	$8.95
North Lake Tahoe Basin	ISBN 1-879866-06-4	$8.95
South Lake Tahoe Basin	ISBN 1-879866-07-2	$8.95

GUIDE BOOKS

Mountain Biking the High Sierra

Guide 1, Owens Valley and Inyo County, 2nd Ed. by Douglass	ISBN 0-938665-01-4	$8.95
Guide 2, Mammoth Lakes and Mono County, 3rd Ed. by Douglass	ISBN 0-938665-15-4	$8.95
Guide 3A, Lake Tahoe South, 3rd Ed. by Bonser	ISBN 0-938665-27-8	$8.95
Guide 3B, Lake Tahoe North, 2nd Ed. by Bonser	ISBN 0-938665-07-3	$8.95
Guide 13, Reno/Carson Valley by Miskimins	ISBN 0-938665-22-7	$10.95

Mountain Biking the Coast Range

Guide 4, Ventura County and the Sespe, 3rd Ed.,by McTigue	ISBN 0-938665-18-9	$8.95
Guide 5, Santa Barbara County, 4th Ed. by McTigue & Douglass	ISBN 0-938665-25-1	$8.95
Guide 7, Santa Monica Mountains, 2nd Ed. by Hasenauer & Langton	ISBN 0-938665-10-3	$8.95
Guide 8, Saugus Dist., Angeles N.F. with Mt. Pinos by Troy & Woten	ISBN 0-938665-09-X	$8.95
Guide 9, San Gabriel Mountains, Angeles N.F. by Troy	ISBN 0-938665-11-1	$8.95
Guide 10, San Bernardino Mountains by Shipley & Thibault	ISBN 0-938665-16-2	$10.95
Guide 11, Orange County and Cleveland N.F. by Rasmussen	ISBN 0-938665-17-0	$8.95
Guide 12, Riverside Co. & Coachella Valley by Maag & Shipley	ISBN 0-938665-24-3	$8.95

OTHER BOOKS & MAPS AVAILABLE

Mountain Biking Southern California's Best 100 Trails, Ed. by Douglass & Fragnoli, Foreword by Cindy Whitehead; features classic routes by 12 authors; 66 maps, 300 pages	ISBN 0-938665-20-0	$14.95
Favorite Pedal Tours of Northern California, by Bloom; features classic road and fat tire routes	ISBN 0-938665-12-X	$12.95
Marin-Sonoma Counties Map, California	ISBN 1-879866-01-3	$7.95
Excelsior Dist. Tahoe N.F., Hwy 80 Map	ISBN 1-879866-02-1	$6.95
Crystal Basin, Eldorado N.F., Hwy 50 Map	ISBN 1-879866-03-X	$6.95
Moab, Utah, Slick Rock		$5.95
Ski Touring the Eastern High Sierra by Douglass & Lombardo	ISBN 0-938665-08-1	$8.95
Exploring California's Channel Islands, an Artist's View by Gates	ISBN 0-938665-00-6	$6.95
CAPE HORN, One Man's Dream, One Woman's Nightmare by Hemingway-Douglass, hardbound.	ISBN 0-938665-19-7	$24.95

To order any of these items, see your local dealer or order direct from Fine Edge Productions. Please include $2.00 for shipping with check or money order. California residents add 7.25% state sales tax. 20% discount on orders of 5 or more items.

Fine Edge Productions, Route 2, Box 303, Bishop, California 93514.
(619)387-2412 / FAX (619)387-2286

FINE EDGE
Productions
BISHOP, CALIFORNIA